Sirocco

to Cilla
thank you so much
for liking my Book.
Best wishes
[signature]

Sirocco

A FRENCH GIRL COMES OF AGE IN WAR-TORN ALGERIA

—⁓—

DANIELLE A. DAHL

cp
coffeetownpress
Seattle, WA

coffeetownpress

Coffeetown Press
PO Box 70515
Seattle, WA 98127

For more information go to: www.coffeetownpress.com
www.dadahl.com

Cover design by Sabrina Sun

Sirocco
Copyright © 2014 by Danielle A. Dahl

ISBN: 978-1-60381-194-1 (Trade Paper)
ISBN: 978-1-60381-195-8 (eBook)

Library of Congress Control Number: 2013952688

Printed in the United States of America

To my brothers and sisters

"*Et qui donc a jamais guéri de son enfance?*"

"And who has ever recovered from his childhood?"

Lucie Delarue-Madrus
("*L'Odeur de mon pays …*" Poem 1902)

Acknowledgments

SIROCCO WOULDN'T HAVE BEEN successfully completed without the unrelenting dedication of my long-time critique partners, Donna Campbell, Howard Lewis, Linda Lovely, and Jean Robbins, who virtually looked over my shoulder, whispering on-target dos and don'ts as Nanna's story came to life one word at a time.

Heartfelt thanks to:

Mary Buckham, whose keen evaluation encouraged me to cut out some twenty-five thousand words, resulting in a tighter story line.

The Readers' Feast Bookclub, my Beta readers, whose acute observations and encouraging comments kept me on the right track.

My friends: Ernestine Norungolo, Annette Woodward, Ute Brady, Susie Thompson, Mary Ann Rice, my Clemson Ladies bowling league, the Greenville chapter of Sisters In Crime. My family. My husband and step family, and cousin Drew.

Thank you all for your moral support, endless interest, and faith in *Sirocco's* success.

Amanda Wells, my agent, whose enthusiasm for *Sirocco* swiftly called Nanna's story to the attention of Coffeetown Press.

Catherine Treadgold, publisher at Coffeetown Press, Jennifer McCord, Associate Publisher, and Emily Hollingsworth, Assistant Editor, who cared and tirelessly buffed Nanna's story to a shine.

A special debt of gratitude to C.D.H.A, the *Centre De Documentation Historique Sur L'Algérie*, and its magazine, *Mémoire Vive*, for graciously authorizing the use of their documentation on historical facts, personal testimonies, and pictorial archives.

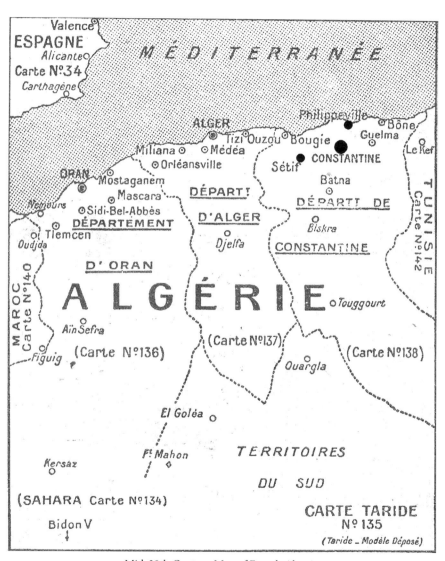

Mid-20th Century Map of French Algeria

Family Tree

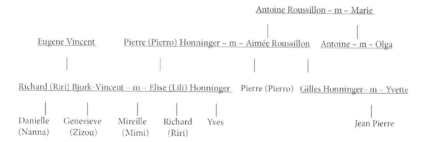

Antoine Roussillon – m – Marie

Eugene Vincent   Pierre (Pierro) Honninger – m – Aimée Roussillon   Antoine – m – Olga

Richard (Riri) Bjork-Vincent – m – Elise (Lili) Honninger   Pierre (Pierro)   Gilles Honninger– m – Yvette

Danielle   Genevieve   Mireille   Richard   Yves   Jean Pierre
(Nanna)   (Zizou)   (Mimi)   (Riri)

Contents

Prologue

Constantine, Algeria, October 1954

A TREMOR SHOOK THE SOARING rock and its crowning city. A shudder as familiar to Constantine and its dwellers as the searing Sirocco wind that, in season, blew howling sand from the Sahara desert, hundreds of miles south.

Then, as abruptly as it started, the quake rumbled away and the city settled in its limestone bed as if nothing had happened. Fooling no one.

Everyone knew—the Berber boy herding his goats in the searing North African sun, the Muezzin in the Kasbah, calling the day's prayers, the Synagogue's Cantor striking his mournful chants and, certainly, ten-year-old Nanna riding in the back seat of the family car—everyone knew that "*événements*" had been set in motion.

Events that would revive Constantine's eons-old tradition of seesawing between peace and war, abundance and devastation.

Numidians. Carthaginians. Romans. Vandals. Arab and Berber dynasties. All had ruled her. But she endured and, one hundred and sixteen years after the French wrestled her from the Turks, Constantine still commanded the vast western plain, the chasm of the Rhumel River, and the four eastern bridges that anchored her to the land across the gorges.

THE CHARCOAL-GRAY CITROEN CROSSED the Sidi Rached Bridge, driving Nanna and her family from their home in Sidi Mabrouk into the city.

"Son of a bitch." Nanna's frustrated father slowed the car to match the pace of a caravan of donkeys carrying bundles of hides to leather artisans in the Kasbah's souks. These Algerian beasts, the size of large dogs, plodded under the relentless sun. They dotted their passage with pungent dung—heedless of the insistent buzzing of flies and blasts of klaxons from the vehicles behind.

The blaring horns and raucous braying of a reluctant ass filled the shimmering air, spilled into the gorges below, and bounced in rich echoes against their opposite walls, dislodging flocks of crows from the crags and grottos pocking the gray cliffs. The black birds swooped in muddled formations up and down the chasm—churning omens of doom that raised prickles of dread on Nanna's forearms.

Ever since Algeria had become the French province Nanna's French forefathers had helped settle, propelling it into the twentieth century, restiveness on the part of some native Muslims seeking independence from France had become a ripening abscess. In fact, on the very day the French toasted the end of World War II on Constantine's café terraces and danced in her streets, Muslims massacred European settlers in Sétif, fifty miles east of the rock and its city. As expected, the French army quelled the rebellion, but the unrest continued to flare on and off.

Now, on the eve of All Saints Day, 1954, the abscess was ready to burst.

Chapter One

Sidi Mabrouk

Suburb of Constantine, Algeria, October 30, 1954

Papa spread his firearms across the kitchen table. First the shotgun, then the pistol, then the revolver. Maman said he started the routine of checking his weapons before taking road trips nine years ago on Armistice Day. I was a year old and mankind was celebrating the end of World War II.

On this eve of our yearly All Saints Day trip to the home of my great-grandparents, Pépé and Mémé Roussillon, Maman put baby Yves and three-year-old Riri to bed. "Say good night, girls," she called from the bedroom.

Mireille approached Papa and, stretching as far as her six-year-old body allowed, kissed him on one cheek then the other. "Good night, Pa, good night, Pa," then tugged Zizou's sleeve. "You're coming?"

Zizou, two years my junior, shoved an elbow in my side. "Coming, Nanna?"

"*Aïe!*" I yelped, massaging my ribs. "What did you do that for?"

She arched her brows. "Are you coming to bed or not?"

Planning to sneak in a few precious moments alone with Pa, I sighed, "In a minute."

Ma walked into the kitchen with the baby's empty bottle. "It's time for the news. Turn on the radio, Nanna."

I knew she wanted to hear that the roads would be open and safe from *fellagha's* attacks. That we wouldn't have to cancel our *Toussaint's* trip to her grandparents' at the last minute because of Arab rebel ambushes, like last year.

While Ma washed Yves' bottle, the news bulletin concluded with no special alert. "Does this mean we're going to Saint Arnaud, Pa?" I asked.

He peered into the breach of his shotgun. "We'll see," he muttered, dashing my excitement.

Ma dried her hands on her apron. "I'll finish packing, so we'll be ready."

Snapping the gun barrel shut, Papa polished off his fingerprints with a chamois cloth, set the gun aside and picked up his revolver.

Nose twitching at the sharp tang of gun oil, I hunched over the table, elbows propped on the flowered oilcloth, hands cupping my face. "Can't we go, anyway, Pa? I really want to see Pépé and Mémé Roussillon."

"Are you deaf?" he spat. "I said, 'We'll see.'"

I swallowed my hurt feelings and watched his long, tan elegant fingers load his weapons. One purposeful round at a time.

Finally, desperate to make him commit to the trip, I prodded, "Aren't you looking forward to seeing Pépé and Mémé, Pa?" I crossed my arms on the table, leaned toward him, and begged, "*Allez*, Pa. Say *oui*."

Only the riveting gleam of bluish gunmetal answered with the hypnotic effect of a gold ring swinging at the end of a string—conveying a vision of my great-grandparents' farmhouse.

During each visit there, I had fallen more in love with the walled-in compound. I could never have enough of exploring the farm's wonders. The brilliant orange of loquats and vibrant purple of grapes popping up against the brownish gray of the garden's adobe walls. The bumble bees humming in the shade of the mulberry tree, its sharp, winy smell competing with that of the tart, ripening figs.

But the most thrilling time of each day at the farm was waking up to the sore-throated call of the rooster as I stretched lazily under the shimmering white cotton bedspread. I'd breathe in its subtle lavender scent and listen to the arm of the water pump thunking against the pump's bronze body, wishing I'd wake up here forever ….

"Go to bed, Nanna, you're falling asleep," Maman broke in. "I'll wake you if Papa decides to go."

I pushed away from the table and kissed my pa and ma *bonne nuit*—to me, a never-ending night I spent tossing and turning, worrying we might not go to Saint Arnaud, after all.

THE GLARE OF OUR bedroom light jolted me out of another restless doze. "Get ready, girls, we leave in one hour," Maman announced.

I jumped out of bed like a coiled spring, whipped into action by the smell of brewing coffee streaming from the kitchen. I pulled the blanket off my sister. "Get up Zizou. Let's make the bed."

She sat up, glowering. "What's wrong with you? Why're you so cheery this morning?"

"We're going to Pépé and Mémé's," I beamed. "Get up. Quick."

An hour later, we loaded the car in the warming November dawn and started on the road to Saint Arnaud.

Saint Arnaud

November 1, 1954

Riri's constant squirming on Zizou's lap and the tight mountain road twists and turns didn't result in the usual nausea or spoil my happiness. Only Papa's cigarette smoke made breathing difficult. I cracked open my window. The forced air thrummed in my ears and made my short hair flutter against my cheeks.

Squeezed between Mireille and the car door, I stretched my limbs as best I could. "Papa, how much longer?"

"Two hours," he exhaled between two puffs.

Two hours! The little adobe shacks and tethered donkeys we just passed on the right had seemed much closer to Saint Arnaud, two years ago.

Wedged between Zizou and me, Mireille squirmed. "I need to go *pipi*, Papa."

"I'm not stopping in the fucking middle of nowhere," Pa growled. "You should've gone before we left."

I felt sorry for Mimi, but the thought of our car pausing on this lonely mountain road worried me. First, I envisioned the troops of frenzied baboons that, at times, roamed the landscape, assaulting travelers, and a sudden pain squeezed my throat as if it was in the grip of fangs. Then the feel of the long, sharp canines morphed into the familiar, indefinable sense of dread fanned by the news of sporadic *fellagha* attacks against cars and isolated farms. Attacks that kept the bloody memory of the Armistice Day Massacre alive, further feeding my fears with rumors of slashed throats, disemboweled bodies, raped women, and babies splattered against walls.

I'd had trouble visualizing the human carnage until, three years earlier, when I was seven, our Arab neighbors across the street slaughtered sheep for their festival of Eid.

* * *

It was the summer of 1951. My fingers gripped our yard's fence, and my forehead was pressed against the cold wire. I stared as the men forced the bleating animal down onto its side, tied its legs together and, pulling its head backward, slashed its neck with a flick of the wrist.

The spurting blood was nothing new to me; I was used to Pépé Honninger, Ma's Pa, killing and trussing chickens and rabbits. Here, however, the sheep thrashed forever and bleated like a baby in agonizing pain.

Repulsed by the sight of blood soaking the poor beast's wool and the sound of its weakening cries, I pushed away from the fence and ran to the backyard, my hands clasped over my ears. In the end, the bleating, thrashing, and spurting blood had given horrifying substance to my mental pictures of slashed throats and gore.

I now linked the sheep's slaughter to that of butchered humans and understood Papa's need to protect his family. Why he never set off on a road trip without his weapons.

* * *

THE FANGS OF THE imaginary baboon had loosened their hold on my throat. Now I quelled my dread of a possible fellagha attack by reassuring myself that Pa was the best shot ever. I was safe with him. I took a relaxing breath and let the rushing wind bring memories of the summer winds that fanned Mémé's fig trees.

I couldn't wait to see her and Pépé Roussillon again. I never tired of playing and replaying their story in my mind.

* * *

ONE HUNDRED AND SIXTEEN years ago, along with hundreds of other families, Pépé and Mémé's parents emigrated from France to the brand-new French province of Algeria. Living in abject poverty, they settled the land with backbreaking work. Multitudes died from malnutrition and fever contracted from the swamps they drained and, in due course, transformed into gardens of Eden.

When Pépé and Mémé married, he practiced his trade as a saddler and she worked their tiny farm, raising poultry, a cow, a horse, a goat, a couple of pigs, and thirteen children.

Now in their late eighties, they lived in their own dwelling, on one edge of the yard across from their son Tonton Antoine, his wife, Tata Olga, and their four sons.

The air carried through my window made me drowsy. I closed my eyes and smiled at the images of my great-grandparents playing against my lids.

MÉMÉ WAS A WHITE pebble at the side of a spring, Pépé, the forest's mightiest oak.

She wore gray housecoats reaching down to black ankle-shoes, and bore a hump—wide and proud—on her left shoulder.

Pépé and Mémé Roussillon.

His smile glowed amid grizzled cheeks like embers under ash.

She smelled of violets and warm peach jam; he, of leather and saddler's wax.

She embraced with fierce strength and her clear blue eyes pierced your thoughts.

He clasped you to his solid belly and patted your back so hard it nearly stilled your heart.

I leaned against my seat to ease the tightness in my chest. *For how many more Toussaints will my great-grandparents be alive? For how many more trips will I be able to feel their hugs?*

La Toussaint Rouge

I AWOKE TO THE SOUND of tires crunching over the farm's graveled yard. But instead of the usual festive welcome, the entire family greeted us as if we had come back from the grave. Tata Olga even wiped a tear off her face with the corner of her apron.

Had someone died?

Maman took Tata Olga's hand. "What's wrong?"

Tata said, "We'll talk later," and guided us through her front door.

After we settled in at the long kitchen table, Mémé Roussillon and Tata Olga served homemade lemonade to Maman and us children, and *Pastis* to the men.

Thin-lipped, Mémé suddenly slammed a glass in front of Papa. "Why did you come?"

We all stared at her, wide-eyed.

Always prickly when dealing with Mémé, Papa uncoiled like a released spring. "Get your things, children, we're leaving."

Tonton Antoine put a calming hand on Papa's arm, inviting him to return to his seat. "Wait, Richard, what Mémé means is why would you travel on that road after what happened last night?"

"What happened last night?"

"Don't you know? *Le Front de Libération Nationale's* guerillas attacked government and military installations, police stations, and public utilities across the country."

I knew that the *Front de Libération Nationale* was a group of Muslims who wanted to free Algeria from French control, but never felt they were a direct menace to me and my family. Now, the sudden and widespread FLN attacks on the French Government caused my forearms to bristle with apprehension.

Before Papa could reply to Tonton Antoine, a neighbor rushed through the open door. "Excuse me, Antoine, for crashing in on you like this, but I saw your family from Constantine is here, and I wondered if you knew what happened."

Tonton Antoine said, "Yes, we know what happened last night."

"No, not last night. Today."

"What happened?"

"The FLN ambushed the car of pro-French Government Muslim officials outside Philippeville. They shot the occupants, including two school teachers newly arrived from France. One of them, a woman, is barely alive."

Tonton Antoine half turned on his bench seat and turned on the radio, catching a voice in mid sentence. "... outrage has already been dubbed '*La Toussaint Rouge*.'"

The Red All Saints Day—*like La Saint Bartelemy de 1572 en France?* I remembered a painting I had seen of *La Toussaint Rouge*. Angry Catholics carrying torches and weapons, forcing open the doors of Protestant dwellings. Dragging sleepy men, women, and children onto the cobbled streets and slaughtering them. Faces flickered under the dancing flames of torches while they died; mouths open in soundless pleas for mercy ....

The somber radio voice droned on. "In a broadcast from Cairo, the FLN called on Algerian Muslims to unite in a national fight for 'the restoration of the Algerian state, sovereign, democratic, and social, within the framework of the principles of Islam.' It is the opinion, in some circles, that the assassinations of pro-French Muslim dignitaries and innocent young French teachers might be the spark that will set off an all-out conflict."

Tonton Antoine turned off the radio. In the dumbfounded hush, sparks crackled as a burning log shifted inside the cast-iron cook stove.

I didn't understand why and how *Les Événements* had taken such a serious turn, but the grim expression steeling the adults' faces turned my guts into rubber pipes.

We barely touched the evening meal and, after conferring over coffee, the men determined that we would return home if no more attacks took place before morning.

I went to bed rebelling against the FLN, my parents, Tonton and Tata, even Pépé and Mémé who had all decided we must go home. It wasn't fair. Now I'd have to wait one more year before waking up to the rusty call of the rooster. One more year before stretching lazily under the gleaming white bedspread and listening to the rhythmic thunk of the water pump. It wasn't fair.

EARLY THE NEXT DAY, when the stars still stitched the velvet sky and the rooster had yet to smooth its feathers, we got ready to leave. The men loaded the car, little Yves slept in Maman's arms, and Mémé embraced each of us, time and again. "Be careful on the road, now, d'accord? Call Madame Sanchez at the post office, here, and let us know you have arrived, d'accord?" She stuffed a piece of paper in Maman's pocket. "Here is the post office number, d'accord?"

While Mémé patted our cheeks in the dark yard, the yellow rectangle of light spilling from the doorway cast anguished shadows across her chiseled face. She looked so old and fragile, my heart ached at the thought I might never be able to hug her again and I was no longer mad at her.

After scores of hugs, kisses, and tears, foodstuffs were jammed into the car—a ham, compliments of a late resident hog, a plucked duck, fresh eggs and vegetables. The very best was the checkered cloth tied around a bunch of Mémé's cookies, confectioned from the cream she skimmed off the top of boiled fresh milk.

THIRTY MINUTES LATER, WE were approaching Saint Arnaud's boundary when Papa said, "Pay close attention to what I am going to say." He threw his cigarette out the window. "If we are ambushed, you must scrunch down in the car. I'll slow down as if to stop, then accelerate and try to force the car through. Once we have passed through and they are no longer in sight, I'll stop the car and Nanna and Zizou will run in opposite directions."

I exchanged a quick frown with Zizou before catching Papa's stern glance in the rearview mirror. Each one of his words struck my chest like hurled rocks. "You will hide quickly, flat on your stomach. Your mother and I will drive on to draw anyone who pursues us away from you. You will not scream. You will not cry. You will not move. If they find one of you, you must say your parents drove on, leaving you behind to hide. No matter what the other sees or hears, she must not leave her hideout. If she does, instead of one, they'll kill both of you—"

Mireille's gasp caused our father to pause before he carried on. "Stay hidden throughout the night and do not show yourselves, even to each other, until you see a military vehicle on the road. Do you understand?"

Zizou and I shared anxious glances. She batted her eyelashes. "*Oui, Papa,*" we said in concert.

I caressed Riri's blond curls as he slept in my arms. "What about Riri, Yves, and Mireille, Papa?"

"They'll remain in the car with us."

Maman's smile was pinched as she turned around. "Do exactly as Papa says and you will be all right." Then she leaned over baby Yves sleeping on her lap and pulled two handguns from the glove compartment, placed one under her thigh and the other on the seat between herself and Papa.

For miles, we saw little traffic. But for the grating shift of gears up and down the mountain road, an ominous silence had settled among us, giving free rein to my anxiety. In the gray predawn light, the scenery was a blur of shadows briefly aroused by our car's headlights—shadows, I feared, of armed men waiting in ambush. I pressed sleeping Riri tighter against my thumping heart.

After what seemed like forever, the sunglow cleared the crest of the Aurès Mountains and the rugged terrain about us revealed familiar shapes. Solid, hard rocks, oleander bushes, and clumps of prickly pears—not the crouching terrorists they first appeared to be. I relaxed against my seat with a sigh of relief and gazed at the moving landscape. Here and there, the smoke of early cooking fires rose in light gray ribbons against the dark brown of the land,

and the acrid smell of burning cow dung rode the air. Saliva filled my mouth as I imagined the *kessra*, the unleavened Arab flat breads, blistering on the *cannouns* grids, reminding me I was hungry.

Riri stirred and shoved his thumb into his mouth then resettled in my arms with avid sucking sounds. My sisters and baby brother slept while Pa drove and Ma kept watch. Feeling safer now, I settled in my seat and gazed at the mountaintops with an almost religious reverence. Yellows, oranges, and golds streaked the sky above their towering crags in a show so majestic I felt tinier than the tiniest grain of desert sand. Tears of awe filled my eyes.

As the sun rose in blinding glory, we cleared a sharp bend and spotted, far ahead, parked trucks and a barricade across the road. My bowels turned to mush and, for a second, I thought I would wet myself. I squeezed Riri's small body closer to mine. One hand on the wheel, Papa picked up the gun at his side and put it on his lap. "Get down."

Fully awake now, the four of us huddled on the car floor. Stuck underneath me, little Riri squirmed, trying to push me off him, whimpering. I felt the car stop. Papa said to Maman, "Can you tell who they are?"

I turned my head sideways and saw Maman lean forward in her seat and squint. "I can't tell, *chéri.*"

Papa put the car in reverse. Maman said, "Wait, Riri. Look, a Jeep is coming our way. It's the military. *Oui,* it's the military, *chéri.*"

Papa stopped the car. "Get back into your seats."

I returned to my place at the window, behind Papa, and smacked a merry kiss on Riri's round cheeks. The Jeep drew up beside us while soldiers pointed a mounted machine gun in our direction.

One soldier jumped out and approached the car with caution. He saluted Papa and asked for identification. Noticing the guns on our parents' laps, he put his hand to the holster at his hip. "What are these weapons doing here, sir?"

Papa smirked. "What do you think officer? Would you believe: to defend my family?"

The officer bent on his knees and studied each of us. "You won't need these weapons while we are around, sir. Put them away. We are forming a convoy to escort travelers along the road to Constantine."

He pointed at the roadside behind a truck full of soldiers. "Pull over there on the shoulder until more cars arrive. Please, remain in your vehicle."

By the time a long line of cars interspersed with military trucks and Jeeps took the road, Maman had untied Mémé's cookie checkered cloth and Riri was laughing. But, even as I bit into the sweet treat, I couldn't repress a vague, creepy feeling that our lives had changed forever.

Chapter Two

Home, Sweet Home

Sidi Mabrouk, November 2, 1954

BACK AT THE HOUSE that evening, we enjoyed a late bowl of onion soup with bread and butter and the warm feeling of being home safe. Zizou wiped a breadcrumb off her lip. "Are we going to school the day after tomorrow, Pa?"

I cocked my head. *Why not?*

Papa's soupspoon hovered above his bowl. "Is the day after tomorrow a school day?"

"*Oui.*"

"*Alors*, why ask a stupid question?"

"Because of what's been happening, with people killed and things."

"If you break your arm, are you still going to school?"

A cynical smile tugged the corner of my mouth. Sure she would. Pa would make us go to school even if we had *one* arm and *two* broken legs.

"I think so," Zizou said. "My friend Viviane broke her leg and she went to school."

"*Et alors?*"

Zizou sighed heavily. "I guess we'll go to school the day after tomorrow."

Mireille asked, "Me too, Papa?"

"Why not you?"

"Because I am little and I have *un souffle au coeur*?"

Zizou and I rolled our eyes at each other. Mireille often used her heart murmur to get away with things.

Zizou cut in, "Do you think you are special because he was going to let you stay in the car? Save the poor little girl with a *souffle au coeur* and dump us at the side of the road?"

Maman was horrified, "*Ma Zize!*"

Papa's face turned ashen, his spoon splashed into his soup, and his breathless voice rattled, "Get out of my sight, little bitch."

Zizou stood, nudging her chair with the back of her knees, turned to leave the table, and cast an imperious look at our father. "You *did* want to dump us."

Papa sprang up, sending his chair crashing to the floor.

Maman screamed, "Riri, *NON.*"

But he had already picked up the wine bottle from the table and thrown it at Zizou, as flawlessly as an Olympic athlete throws a javelin.

Zizou dove forward. The bottle missed her head by a hair, hit the wall flat on its side, and shattered on the tile floor as she skittered away.

Ooh là là!

In the midst of the appalled silence, I was stunned by my sister's behavior, feeling first shock, then admiration, and finally envy deep in my guts. Why couldn't I stand up to Pa as she just did? Why couldn't I have her backbone?

Saalima

TWO DAYS LATER, MY sisters and I lugged our heavy satchels up the long road to school. During class breaks, the schoolyard usually echoed with the squeals of the youngest girls, while the oldest strolled in groups of twos or threes, whispering secrets. The third set, of mixed ages, played handball, hopscotch or dodge'm games. This was my group.

I was very good at dodge'm, but even better at *la bataille de coq*—cockfight. In this game, a small girl, the *coq*, climbed on the shoulders of a big girl, the horse. The goal of each two-person team was to force the *coqs* of the other teams to fall down until only one remained mounted.

The horse initiated the skillful attacks or evasions. As tactician, she chose her teammate.

Saalima always chose me from the girls willing to be *coqs* and, each time she did, a great pride expanded my chest as warm breath fills a balloon.

Saalima, an Arab girl, was older than me. She was tall, slim, and strong-boned, and the colorful robes descending to her ankles never seemed to impede her long stride. At *bataille*, she took off her shoes, exposing callused feet, flicked back her long braids, and squatted. I climbed astride her shoulders and she rose, holding my ankles. Her clothing smelled of cooking fires, rancid butter, and the deep red henna that, on special occasions, dyed her hair, the palms of her hands, and soles of her feet. When the battles began, I rode on her shoulders, breathing deeply of her, knowing no fear.

That school day following *la Toussaint Rouge*, the European girls gathered

House in Sidi Mabrouk. The balcony on the right is Nana's room.

in small, low-voiced groups. Saalima and the other Arab girls sat on the ground, at the far end of the schoolyard.

I went to her. "Saalima, you want to play *à la bataille de coq?*"

She shook her head with a sad smile.

Unsure of what to do next, I fingered one of her braids. "Maybe tomorrow, Saalima?"

She looked up at the sky. "Maybe tomorrow."

I left her group and scanned the yard for my sisters. They were doing their own things, so I retrieved the book I had started and found my own corner. But as my eyes skidded over the words, a nameless sorrow flooded my chest—a sense that my friendship with Saalima was unraveling.

A few weeks later, instead of her usual dress, Saalima came to school wearing the garb of the Muslim woman, meaning she had come of age. The black *chador* cloaked her body and white *hayek* hid her face. Only her eyes remained—black and polished like basalt pebbles drowning in pools of unshed tears.

While she stripped off her coverings, I asked, "Saalima, are you going to stop coming to school?"

She carefully folded her things. "At the end of the school year."

"Will you get married, then?"

"Soon after."

I beamed at her. "Is your fiancé very handsome?"

"I don't know. I'll meet him on my wedding day."

"How old is he?"

"Sixty-five."

I was embarrassed to ask, but I did, "How many wives does he have?"

Her features hardened, slowly, as water turns to ice. "I'll be wife number three."

"And children, how many children do they have?"

The school bell almost drowned out her answer. "Ten."

We broke away in opposite directions to join our classmates lining up in rows of two before the classroom's doors.

For a while, the *batailles de coqs* went on, but Saalima's heart was no longer in it. To my growing distress, she and I played less and less often and then, we stopped.

On the last day of school, Saalima shrouded herself in her *chador* and, without saying good-bye, passed the schoolyard's gate and, black chimera, vanished into the crowd.

Months later, my heart beat harder as I recognized her long, familiar stride across the street. I walked toward her and saw her big belly. "Saalima?"

Above the *hayek*, her eyes softened then shifted away as the old man who was with her shoved her forward.

I felt both anger and sorrow as I watched them walk away, knowing I would never see her again. *Oh, Saalima. If this happened to me, I'd throw myself from the Sidi Rached Bridge.*

At home, Pépé Honninger searched my face and asked, "Did something happen at school?"

"*Non*, Pépé. Nothing."

His arched eyebrows probed. So I told him. "It's my friend Saalima." My eyes welled with involuntary tears. "She's only three years older than me and they made her marry a sixty-five-year-old man and she's going to have a baby soon and I don't think he's nice to her."

Pépé rolled his shoulders, stretched his neck in a familiar tic and said,

"This is their custom, *ma petite*. Nothing you can do about it." He turned his back and walked to his bedroom, returning with a chocolate bar, which he handed me without a word. He was like that. Just when I thought he was hard and unfeeling, he'd do something nice.

The first time I remember meeting Pépé Honninger, my ma's papa, he bought me a *zlabeiya*, a deep-orange honey sweet, from the Arab baker next door. Shortly after that, I was sent to live with him in the country outside Constantine. There I learned, reluctantly, to let this stranger into my life.

The Tin Can

Sidi Mabrouk, Summer, 1948

I WAS FOUR YEARS OLD. Zizou and Mireille had fallen sick, so I was sent to live with Pépé Honninger and his son, Tonton Gilles, at their house in Sidi Mabrouk.

At first, I felt lost and missed my family dreadfully, but soon, the house's many rooms and unfamiliar furniture turned into mysteries I had to explore.

One day, I made up my mind to find out what lay behind the closed door of the room next to the kitchen. I waited for Pépé to go to work in his garden. Using both hands, I twisted the brass doorknob and pushed. In the house's dark silence, the door squeaked like a trapped mouse, making me jump with fright and causing me to utter a squeal of my own. After my heart stopped banging, I pushed the door an inch farther, then, with great care, peeked around the doorjamb. Large shapes loomed in the near darkness. My heart started bumping again until I recognized the shape of furniture. I sneaked into the room and closed the door.

French doors to the balcony were pushed open against the walls, and subdued sunlight filtered through the angled slats of the closed shutters. I walked over to them and rose on tiptoe to peer through the open space between two slats. Beyond the balcony and stairs' wrought-iron banisters, I could see Pépé Honninger in the front yard, one floor below, where he kneeled, staking giant Snap Dragons. His battered straw hat looked white under the burning sun, and the kerchief around his neck dripped with water. "To keep me cool," he explained.

I unfastened the shutters as silently as I could and inched them open to let more light into the room.

It was a large room with a high ceiling. I oohed and aahed with delight at the giant poppies spread over the cream wallpaper. Their orange red petals bounced glimmers of light against the mahogany furniture, coloring my hand as I reached for them. Then a small piece of furniture sitting before the French door caught my attention. I couldn't resist the tempting long, narrow doors on each side and opened them, uncovering two vertical sets of drawers. I knew Pépé would be mad at me. "I don't like snoopy kids," he had warned. But I couldn't help myself. I pulled open a drawer to have a peek. Just a tiny little peek.

Oh là là! Was I glad I had.

A wealth of ribbons, pieces of fabric, and bobbins of many colors spilled out, revealing an emerald tin box with pictures of cigars on top. I sat on the floor with the box on my lap and, with a tongue-pulling effort, popped the lid open. A lavish assortment of buttons burst out and clattered across the room. In a panic, hoping Pépé had not heard, I scurried on hands and knees along the tile floor—a floor cold as my frightened heart. The buttons hid amid the golds, maroons, and greens of the Italian tiles. The geometric patterns concealed them well, but, in time, I managed to stuff the runaways back inside their box. With a sigh of relief, I stuffed fabrics and bobbins back into the drawer but couldn't bear the thought of letting go of the box and its contents. It was the most beautiful thing I had ever seen in my whole life. I had to keep it. Besides, when I explained to Pépé about "finders, keepers," I was sure he would understand. So I stuck the box under my arm.

At dinnertime, Pépé tipped his chin at the green box sitting next to my plate. "Where did you get this?"

I pointed to the wall separating the kitchen from the other room. "*Là,* Pépé."

"Who gave you permission to take it?"

I shrugged. "Nobody."

"Then put it back where it belongs."

Tonton Gilles frowned. "*Allons,* Papa, let her have it. This box has been in my mother's sewing machine for ever." He winked at me. "You'll take good care of it, *oui?*"

I opened my eyes wide to show my good faith and nodded so hard, I thought my head would roll off my shoulders.

Pépé stared at me for a while then gave a dry smile. "*D'accord,*" he said, stretching his neck to the side. "But don't lose anything."

I shook my head with a vigor I dearly hoped showed my good will.

Later, after Pépé had gone to bed, I asked, "Tonton, *pourquoi* was Pépé *en colère?*"

"He was upset because no one has touched my mother's things since she died."

"If she was your mother, that means she was Pépé's wife?"

"*Oui.* That makes her your grandmother."

Nanna with Tonton Gilles, Route du Cimetière.

"So, she was my Mémé Honninger?"

"She was."

"When did she die?"

"Oh, a very, very long time ago. Your Ma was eleven years old, your Tonton Pierro was nine, and I was six."

"And what was her name?"

"What do you mean?"

"Well, like you are Tonton, but your name is Gilles. What was her name?"

"Aimée."

"Oh. That's my middle name!" I felt as if Tonton had given me a rare present.

After that, I held onto my tin box the way a puppy holds onto its rag doll and sleeps with it.

I'd sit on the front steps and take out the buttons. Arrange them by size and color in one line or several, a circle, semi-circle or any other pattern. I liked some buttons more than others. I especially liked the ones that glittered with jet-black or diamond-like stones—but, as I was not used to having things of my own, I cherished them all.

Then, later that summer, Malika came along.

Malika

MALIKA WAS THE YOUNG Arab girl who cared for me during the day. She was tall and very thin. A red kerchief, tied at the nape of her neck and sewn with beads and pieces of mirror, partially hid her blond hair. A narrow blue rag, wrapped around the length of her single braid, ran down her back like the tail of a giant mouse.

She wore beads of vivid red and blue around her ankles, shimmering yellow and purple around her wrists. Heavy silver earrings stretched the holes in her earlobes, and the thin colored *babouches* on her hennaed feet gave her the look of the fragile princess in my picture book of *One Thousand and One Nights*.

In the morning, when Malika knocked at the door, I'd give Pépé and Tonton a hurried kiss before running out to look into Malika's face—a blend of shiny day and starry night.

Her smile was radiant as the desert sun, her right eye blue as a spring sky and her left, white and glossy as a full summer moon.

"Malika, why is your eye white?"

"I was born like this."

"Can it see?"

"No, but the other can see for both."

"I like it a lot."

A small cloth bag hung from her neck, smelling like a blend of menthol and mothballs. She called it, *"Kafur."*

"Pépé, what is *kafur?*"

"It means 'camphor.' From the camphor tree."

"What does it do?"

"It fights infection and helps with breathing problems. It also keeps insects away."

One morning, Malika arrived with a little pouch she had sewn at home and filled with camphor crystals. She pinned it to my dress.

"What is that for, Malika?"

"This will clean the air you breathe."

She showed me how to string garlic cloves into a necklace and hang it around my neck.

"To fight the Evil Eye," she said.

Along with her *kafur*, Malika wore a flawless piece of glass, in the shape of half an oversized pigeon egg. I called it, *"L'Oeil de Malika."*

"Malika's Eye" reflected the world around us, bending it in curves, and when I touched it, the tips of my fingers grew much bigger than the rest of my hand.

She showed me how to make dolls out of flat pieces of wood swathed in rags with pencil dots for eyes and a mouth. I learned to play jacks with small stones from the yard.

We collected the pits of apricots and let them dry in the sun. Then Malika lined them up in little mounds—three pits at the bottom and one on top—against a step riser, and we threw pits at the mounds to topple them.

We looked for special stones and leaves for my green box and observed lizards, scarabs, and cicadas.

Malika combed my hair and adorned it with flowers. She hugged and kissed me, always with that shiny smile on her pretty face.

But then, one day, she simply stopped coming.

Each morning after that, I leaned over the second-floor landing and stared down the road.

I asked, "Malika doesn't like me anymore, Pépé?"

He said, "Yes, she likes you."

"*Alors,* why doesn't she come to see me?"

"When I hired her, her parents did not tell me she was *poitrinaire*."

"Oh." I vaguely knew that tuberculosis was bad, but had no idea what it meant.

"So, you don't like her, Pépé?"

"Yes, I like her. She took good care of you, but she is sick and could infect—make you sick—too. I told her parents she could not come back."

Despite his words, every morning I sat at the top of the stairs, waiting. Until, one day, she came slowly up the road.

"Malika!"

From afar, she put a finger to her lips to keep me silent.

I ran down and met her at the wrought-iron gate with the letterbox. She slipped her lean arm between the railings and opened her hand. Nestled in the center of her hennaed palm lay *L'Oeil de Malika*. She took hold of my hand and placed the warm glass into it. Without a word, she stroked my cheek, flashed her glorious smile, and walked out of my life.

After that, I took to peering into a mirror, holding Malika's Eye in front of my eye and pretending to be her.

And, at the end of the summer, when my parents and two sisters moved into Pépé's house, I hid my box with Malika's Eye under a stack of linen at the bottom of the china cabinet, hoping it would be safe.

Chapter Three

⁓

DURING THE NEXT EIGHT years, life consisted of dreary things like school, catechism, and Sunday church, counterbalanced by the pleasures of Christmas, Easter and summer holidays—that is, until the dreadful events of *La Toussaint Rouge* threw a stone into the quiet pond of our lives.

After the All Saints Day Massacre, the *Fellagha*—one of the meanings in Arabic was *highwaymen*—cut off roads, gunned down vehicles, slaughtered passengers on the spot, or abducted them to inflict slower, more painful deaths. These attacks effectively curtailed road travel, forcing people to organize caravans of civilian cars and trucks interspersed with army vehicles carrying armed soldiers. In this carefree fashion, business took place in relative security across the country and families escaped to Philippeville or Bône on one-day trips to the seaside for a few hours of relief from the broil of summer.

FOR THESE EXCURSIONS, FAMILIES met before dawn on the fringe of town. An air of carnival prevailed as people hailed each other through lowered car windows. MPs organized the line of civilian cars. They dropped into place between military vehicles like Scrabble tiles in their board slots until ready to set off into daybreak. The ignition keys turned, and the engines coughed in sequence up the line. Then, to the cheer of impatient children, the column advanced slowly, like an earthworm stretching from head to tail in a caustic fog of exhaust fumes.

By sunrise, we were winding down a road towered on the right by the sheer cliff of the plateau where Constantine sat like the Queen of Sheeba. Far below on our left, La Vallée du Hamma spread wide and lush toward the distant spurs of La Petite Kabylie's mountains.

On its way down to the valley, La Route de la Corniche snaked through a series of short tunnels blasted through the rocky hillside. The road wove in and out of these tunnels, causing the panorama below to vanish and pop up like countdown numbers at the end of a cinema newsreel.

On the Road

August, 1956

A T THE AGE OF twelve, I was still thrilled by the unfurling panorama. Filled with awe. This is how it must feel to be a hawk—to fly so close to the cliff that your wing grazes the rock and so high that your gaze stretches forever. A tilt of the tail and you soar with the winds, lose yourself in the blinding sky, or free fall to the valley, where a boundless tapestry of vegetable gardens and orchards shoots up to greet you: "As-Salaam Alei-Kum to the garden of Eden." To which you respond with a triumphant shriek, "That peace be with you also."

For hours, we climbed then descended then climbed again through passes across this mountainous, sun-baked land. Blowing in through lowered windows, dry air charged with dust culled from the roadside, and fumes from the military truck ahead burned my eyes and turned my tongue into sandpaper.

"Maman, *j'ai soif*," Mireille whined.

Zizou and I snickered. Nobody was getting a drink of water, which might trigger the need to go *pipi*. Once a convoy started, it did not stop. Not for *pipi* stops. Not even when someone suffered from motion sickness—they had to vomit out the car windows, leaving an array of breakfasts on their car doors for everyone to see.

I was thirsty too and queasy, but it would be a while before we arrived at Philippeville.

For something to do, I stuck my head out the window and looked up. I could never have my fill of the fathomless cobalt blue above or forget the burnt sienna of the rugged Atlas slopes and their maquis of thorny acacia shrubs, rosemary, lavender, and white, pink, and purple oleanders. A spray of dirt and stones darting down the slope drew my attention to an escarpment, where I saw a glint of sun on metal at the edge of the rock. My insides clinched.

I yelled, "*Attention*, Papa, *fellagha!*" Just then, a staccato of machine guns fired at the outcrop from the military trucks, drowning out my scream.

"Down!" Papa shouted. My siblings and I crashed pell-mell over our seat, and the car picked up speed as the convoy moved to clear the area. I closed my eyes tight, trying to shut off the outside world. In spite of the heat and the press of bodies, a thin layer of ice sheathed my skin. I tasted bile.

Five-year-old Riri clung to my neck. I opened my eyes. His were blue pools of fear. I turned to my side and held him snugly against me. "Listen," I whispered. The clack, clack, clack of helicopter propellers grew louder as it reached the heights above us. I sat up and pointed at the dust storm raised by the low-flying aircrafts. "See? They're going after the *fellagha*. It's over." I raised my voice over the rotors' racket. "It's over. Right, Papa?"

"Looks like it, but stay down."

I sat up and hung out the window, waving at what looked like toy soldiers in the helicopter's open side. "Sit down," Papa bellowed.

Keyed up, I looked up and down-wind of the convoy and cheered. "Nobody was hit, Pa."

"Sit down, Nanna," Maman, Zizou, and Mireille chorused.

Nerves still quivering, I dropped back on my seat and drew Riri into my lap. Beyond the car, the rocky slopes had yielded to citrus orchards. Oranges, grapefruits, and lemons peeked through waxy leaves dulled with dust blown in with the last Sirocco wind. The air thickened with the cloying scent of oil as we approached an olive grove. Zizou made a face. "What's that smell?"

Riri and Mireille sniffed the air.

"It's the smell of raw olive oil," Maman said.

The family anointed itself with the scent of oil as if to purge the lingering taint of our earlier fear. I too embraced the cleansing distraction, pointing at the gnarled trees bearing egg-shaped fruit cloaked in silver leaves. "See the olives in the trees?" I asked Riri. He nodded. "They pick them and squish them until the oil comes out; then they put the oil in bottles and we cook and make salads with it," I explained.

Meanwhile, Zizou and Mireille wrinkled their noses as we passed tiny villages, small farms, and single-family *gourbis*. The scent of oil blended with the sharp smell of manure, goats' milk, and parched dirt. The earthy mélange thrilled me, giving me renewed strength.

Children's songs spilled again out of car windows as if the failed ambush never happened. Riri's head lolled in the hollow of my shoulder as he fell asleep.

A few kilometers later, the convoy passed an Arab family. They walked by the roadside, led by a donkey carrying a set of *panniers* across its back and his master astride its rump. The man's burnoose screened his face while his white, cropped cotton pants exposed lean, sun-baked calves that bounced in tempo with the donkey's gait.

Following single file, a teenage boy kicked an old tin can ahead of him. In his wake, a younger girl carried a baby strapped to her back, and an even younger one walked backward, pulling at the rope of a reluctant goat. Closing the procession like an inverted black exclamation mark, a chador-clad woman cradled a toddler in her arms while balancing a large cloth bundle atop her head.

With a tap of his stick and kick of his heels, the man pointed his mount out of the convoy's path. His family stopped and half-turned to watch us stream by. My eyes briefly met those of the girl, who was about my age, carrying the baby.

How does she feel about us as we spew road dust and engine smoke into her face? Does she wish she were sitting in this car? Is she content with her life or is she resigned to her Maktoob—her destiny?

The cars following us quickly hid her from sight. I sighed, grateful to be cradling my little brother in comfort rather than trodding barefoot in the heat, a baby strapped to my back.

As we lumbered on, the parched landscape gave way to fields of maturing wheat. They rippled in the mountain breeze like the nap of golden cloths under a stroking hand, and among the swaying ears, poppies trembled like drops of blood on pricked fingers.

"Look here. Look there!" I pointed, savoring each detail of the passing scene: the shriek of a hawk gliding over the maquis, the bleating of a goat tethered to a prickly fig. My heightened senses could even spot the ever-present rasp of cicadas, muted within the convoy mayhem of whining engines, straining gears, and laughter and songs streaming out of car windows.

Then, drained by such stimulation, I sat back and observed the occasional military watchtower perched over the buttes. I was grateful the French army tracked our convoy's progress from high above the road and, like friendly Djiins leaping out of smokeless fires, materialized to assist our convoy in time of need.

The failed ambush alarm fading with each turn of the wheels, I once again focused on the looming humiliation that awaited me once we'd reach Jeanne D'Arc beach, when I put on my bathing suit.

The Bathing Suit

ON THE OCCASION OF my twelfth birthday, two months earlier, Ma decided that it was time to replace my bottom-only swimsuit with one that covered my torso. Way ahead of her, I had been ogling the glorious two-piece suit sold *aux Magasins du Globe* in town. The bottom was a conservative up-to-the-waist number. The top looked like a bra with skinny straps. Nothing like the itsy-bitsy-yellow-bikinis girls wore in the American movies, but it was a two-piece, and the colors—olive green with orange splashes—made my heart thrum in my throat.

Maman was all for buying it but had reservations. "Let's ask your father first," she offered.

"NO!" he said.

"But, Papa, that's the kind the other girls wear at the beach."

"I will not have my daughter look like a slut."

And that was that.

The next morning, Maman buried her head inside the old steamer trunk in the attic then straightened up and shook out what appeared to be a dark blue wool sweater. Shoving it into my hands, she said, "Here it is, *ma fille.*"

I held the sweater at eye level. *Smells like mothballs. Doesn't* have sleeves. "What is it?"

"My swimming suit when I was about your age. My mother knitted it for me. It is yours now."

A swimsuit made of wool? Dark wool? For the beach? In the North African heat? I'll die of shame. "Ma, it's full of holes!"

She grabbed the suit and examined it. "Moth holes. Not so many that they can't be repaired."

Yeah, enough of the suit left to make it usable. Just my luck.

She patted my cheek. "Your aunt Yvette showed you how to darn. You can do it."

Of course, we had no dark blue wool or even cotton that approached that color. Crestfallen, I used a black sewing thread that formed little puckers where the hole used to be and changed the elastics on the leg openings. Then I sulked.

It wasn't fair. Why did I have to wear this …. this …. thing. I had no *nénés* to cover up, only two miserable little bumps that stared at me from the mirror like long-dead bird's eyes. Even younger girls' were bigger than mine. At the school gym, they paraded their pretty pink, blue, or white lace bras. *Moi*, I'd prefer satin—pink—no ribbons.

Too small to hold a bra, my *nénés* pushed up against my tops in two little peaks I knew everybody stared at—so embarrassing. So humiliating. "Why wasn't I born a boy?" I moaned, not for the first time.

I stretched the suit against the light to catch missed holes and, with a sigh of resignation, pulled it on to have a look at myself in Pépé's armoire mirror. The itchy wool covered my body up to the neck—front and back—my long legs and arms protruding. All skin and bones.

Zizou appeared in the mirror behind me. "Let me have a look." She inclined her head sideways and batted her eyelashes. "Turn around."

I slowly spun, holding my arms away from my body, and paused facing her, awaiting her verdict.

"Nice sweater," she chuckled.

* * *

ONCE AT JEANNE D'ARC, I adjusted my rough suit with a scowl and ran with Zizou to join a game of volleyball in progress. While we played, two young French soldiers sat on the beach not too far from our tents and watched the game.

When the ball dashed my way, I jumped to hit it back; it grazed my fingertips and bounced in the direction of the soldiers. I chased after it. As I picked the ball up, one of the young men said to the other, "Give her a couple of years and she'll be a looker."

I straightened up, holding the ball against my chest, and looked around to have a peek at *la belle du jour,* but no one was there but me. I strolled back to the volleyball game in a daze. Could they possibly have been speaking about me? A future looker? In this … suit? *Naw, not me.* I sighed with regret and sent the ball to the players behind the net.

The game over, I dropped beside Zizou on the band of cool, wet sand. She had not yet graduated from bottom-only swimsuits and studied mine and the way I scratched here and there. "You look like the monk in a horsehair shirt we saw in the movie at the parish cinema last Sunday. What horrible sins have you committed, Nanna?"

"What d'you mean?" I side-glanced at the lounging soldiers and blushed.

Zizou chuckled, for she knew I had all the confidence of an over-cooked noodle. "I mean that ever since you went after the ball, those guys over there," she pointed her chin at them, "have been watching you." She batted her lashes, vamp-like, and said, "Could it be that they like your winter swimsuit?"

I felt hot, itchy, and bitchy. "Next summer, this suit will be too small for me." I pointedly stared at her chest. "Looks like you will need it then. Might be a tad big, but you'll grow into it."

Her grin vanished and she lifted protective hands to her nipples. Then she recovered and blustered, "Not me. Not this suit. No way."

She must have been clairvoyant, for the strangest thing happened sometime during the following fall, winter or perhaps, spring. When it came time to prepare for the beach again, the dark blue wool suit had new holes as big as my fist. Couldn't have been moths. Must have been a lone rat that had bypassed the rattraps, poison, and other rat-nefarious ruses our grandfather was so good at setting.

Must have been the most famished, intelligent, and lucky rat in all of Sidi Mabrouk.

Later on that summer, while Maman and I made pizzas for the next day at the beach, she sighed, "Tomorrow is the anniversary of your uncle Pierro's death."

I knew the story of Tonton Pierro's death quite well.

When their mother died, Maman was eleven, Tonton Pierro, nine, and Tonton Gilles, six. So Ma became a mother to her brothers.

∗ ∗ ∗

In 1945, before going home for the summer, Pierro and four friends had spent the day at the beach to celebrate passing their exams at their engineering school in Algiers. While in the water, one of the young men was caught in a riptide. A second swam to his rescue, but the current took him. Each of the remaining boys went in to rescue the others until all five had drowned.

Pierro was my uncle and my godfather. He was sixteen when he died and I was one year old. I cannot remember him, but Maman gave me the poems he wrote for me. I know he was a painter like Mémé Honninger and he loved to read. Like me.

∗ ∗ ∗

The smell of garlic cloves Maman minced brought me back to our pizza making. I arranged slices of tomato on top of the Gruyère cheese lining the dough. "Ma, tell me again how I met Papa after Tonton Pierro died."

She spread the garlic on top of the tomatoes. "Pépé, you, and I took the train from Constantine to Algiers to claim your uncle Pierro's body. I carried you down the hotel's staircase to join Pépé Honninger in the lobby …."

The Day I Met Papa

Hôtel d'Alger in Algiers, Summer, 1945

I knew this story well also. Maman was minding her steps while descending the stairs of the Hôtel d'Alger in Algiers when an emaciated, unshaven, and ill-looking soldier, wearing a tattered military coat too large for him, barred her way. "Lili? What are you doing here?" he asked in a raspy voice.

Maman backed up two steps to get away from the filthy stranger. He put a hand on her arm to steady her. She looked around for help. "Don't touch us."

"Lili, it's me, Riri, your husband."

She searched the stranger's eyes. They were the same green she remembered from not quite two years past, but now they looked older than those of a man of twenty-one years, tired, and glossed over with fever.

While my father was at the war, Maman had pointed at his photo. "Papa," she said enough times that eventually, when asked, "Where is Papa?" I pointed at the picture on the wall. This picture was a large framed affair showing *my* papa as a child-thespian, costumed for the leading role in Charles Perrault's fairytale, *Le Chat Botté*. He wore a rapier, thigh-high turned-down boot-tops, and bouffant pants, a wide-sleeved shirt, and embroidered bolero. He had long black whiskers and pointed cat ears. So, when this bad-smelling, scratchy-faced stranger took me from my mother's arms, saying, "Papa .... Papa .... *Dis bonjour à* Papa," and kissed me, I shrieked, and squirmed, and turned away.

The stranger slapped my face and shoved me into my mother's arms. With a mean expression, he asked, "What are you doing here?" A man whose very young and beautiful wife has been husbandless for two years could come to no worse conclusion. He had seen it happen to other soldiers. "Have you been whoring in this hotel while I risked my life?"

"She came here to collect her brother's body and does not need any more grief. Not even from you." Pépé Honninger had come in search of his daughter and heard his son-in-law's accusation. Pépé took me from Ma's arms and wiped the tears off my face. "And what are *you* doing here?" he asked Papa.

"Just off the boat from France, waiting for my military discharge before going home."

"Then I suggest you clean yourself up and get a new attitude before I throw you down the stairs on your ass," growled Pépé.

This was Maman's account of how my father and I first met. An episode I couldn't recall, but which might account for the mixed feelings of awe and fear my pa inspired in me through the years.

Papa playing Le Chat Botté.

Nanna.

Chapter Four

AFTER PAPA CAME HOME from the war, the world settled like sand after a Sirocco storm. My family moved into a home, close to the cemetery where Papa worked. Even seven years after the move, at the age of twelve, I could still picture it as if it were projected on a movie screen.

The house stood at the bottom of *la Route du Cimetière*. The road ran downhill to the outskirts of Constantine. It leveled out by our house and converged with another sloping road into the wide circular cemetery plaza, as if into a giant eddy. From there, the two roads merged into one, channeled by the walls of the Christian and Muslim cemeteries, then dissolved into the countryside.

A curved stone bench lined each side of the twin portals of the walled Christian cemetery, where both Arabs and Europeans sat to wait for the electric tram back to the city.

Past the portals, the cemetery's main avenue darted downslope, just as a swift arrow mimics the earth's curvature.

On each side of the avenue, a row of cypresses, dark and streamlined, pointed to the sky like Roman legion lances. At their feet along the roadside, narrow troughs replenished a string of small in-ground tanks with running water used to fill pots of cut flowers and clean monuments.

On its way down, the avenue bisected perpendicular roads, themselves intersected by paths, thus creating quadrilateral plots that emulated city blocks. However, while cities fragment their neighborhoods into rich versus poor, this city of the dead did not discriminate—haves and have-nots lay side-by-side.

A Day with Pépé Vincent

European Cemetery in Constantine, June, 1950

EARLY IN THE MORNING of my sixth birthday, Papa had left me with my grandfather, Pépé Vincent, at the cemetery. There, father and son practiced their craft, building a metropolis where plain stone graves rubbed shoulders with granite or marble tombs, elegant crypts, ornate chapels, and flamboyant mausoleums.

I loved to peer into the tanks' water, at the rippling, upside-down world, tinged green by the slime-covered tank walls. I'd stare at my reflection, suspended between the seemingly bottomless water and the fathomless sky behind me, and observe what looked like my first grade teacher's pictures of farm animals and people floating mid-air in hues of greens and smothered blues.

"I warned you to stay away from those tanks." Pépé's rebuke broke the spell.

"I'm careful, Pépé. See?" I held on to the tubular fence surrounding the water and gave him my most beguiling smile.

The stern expression shadowing his usually kind face told me that, at the moment, my charm was not working on him.

Abashed, I sat on the low wall of a nearby mausoleum—knocking the heels of my swinging feet against the gleaming, beige granite—and watched him work.

Pépé sat on a low wooden stool, knees apart, chiseling a family name on a slab of gray-veined marble. The hammer in his right hand clinked-clinked, clinked-clinked in a familiar cadence against the flat head of the burin's dark steel, causing sparkling chips of marble to arch about him like falling stars.

Amid the soothing quiet of the tombs, the clear metal sounds harmonized with the chirping of sauntering sparrows and cries of diving swallows. These emerged from the tall, dark green cypresses, as if from church spires and—curved carbon blades—dive-bombed toward the ground until, almost on the verge of crashing, they arced back up to the sky with jubilant shrieks.

With no set direction, a Tiger butterfly fluttered from one flowered grave to another.

"Please, Pépé, can I go and catch the butterfly?"

"You may." He closed his eyes and blew mica dust off his work. "But stay where I can see you."

"*Oui*, Pépé."

While I slithered down my perch, the butterfly had veered and flickered across the avenue. I followed and stalked it to a single bloom. But, no sooner had my hand's shadow darkened its brilliant wings, it took off and disappeared into the folds of a pointed-tipped cypress—a slow metronome swaying in the breeze.

At times, instead of real flowers decorating the graves, wreaths and bouquets of tiny glass beads shimmered in colors of rainbows. I spent many hours stringing these beads into rings, necklaces, bracelets, and earrings, but Pépé said I should not do this.

"Why not, Pépé? They are so pretty."

"One does not steal from the dead."

"But Pépé, if they are dead, they don't need it."

"It is not they who need it; it is the others, the people who are alive who do."

"How's that, Pépé?"

"Well, it's like this. Being dead means you are not alive anymore. But the family and friends of a dead person can keep this person alive in their thoughts and hearts. And as long as they do so, the dead person is dead in body, but not in spirit."

"But what about the bead flowers, Pépé?"

"Well, one of the many ways to keep the spirit of the dead alive and help their families and friends miss them less is to bring flowers, fresh or beaded, to their dead. If someone steals the flowers, it's as if they stole the love of the living for the dead and that makes them dead forever and the living very sad.

I looked at him. "But Pépé, a lot of graves don't have flowers. Does that mean their spirits are dead?"

"*Non.* There are reasons why some people cannot come to the cemetery— they live far away or are too busy, but their dead still live in their hearts. That is why we celebrate *la Toussaint.* Once a year, on All Saints Day, people do not work and come to the cemetery to bring chrysanthemums and visit with their dear departed. That makes these people feel good—"

"Oh, you mean, it feels like when I come to see you, even though you are not dead, Pépé?"

He grabbed and squeezed me hard against his chest. "And like when I go to see *you.*"

His clothes smelled of cement dust, cigarette smoke, and bay rum. I hugged him back and peered into his craggy face. Right above the wing of his left nostril, there was this familiar little dot, blue like a tattoo. "But, it is all right to play with the bead flowers that fell on the ground, the ones that are not on a grave?"

After a second's hesitation, he said, "These, you may play with."

He tapped me on the derriere. "Let me do some work now and remember, don't go far."

I skipped away. "*Non*, Pépé. I won't."

I moseyed from graves that barely rose above ground, to sober tombs, to imposing chapels, and towering mausoleums. I peeked through condensation holes and slits at the back of monuments. The dank, musty darkness inside barely revealed the faint glint of coffins perched on trestles.

I cupped my hands around my mouth and, as one drops stones to test a hollow's depth, blew into the holes, "Who, who."

"Whoo, whoo," came back the echo, an old dog's breath.

At the side of a grave with a leaning cross and moss-covered stone, I found scattered lengths of tiny beads still strung on their metal thread. I gathered them and sat on the grave's hot stone. I twisted two strips together, shaped them into a circle I slipped around my wrist, "*Là*," I sighed and, contented, surveyed my surroundings.

Under the relentless sun, the blinding whiteness of life-size statues reflected into the buffed planes of marble and granite monuments—standing angels with open palms and serene smiles consoled the grief-stricken with promises of redemption. Cherubs proffered stone garlands of everlasting roses, and genuflecting monks, faces in hands under cowls, shared in the distress of the bereaved.

On headstones, words of love, grief, or hope carved in gold letters testified as to who lay there—a little boy, a grandmother, a friend, a soldier, members of generations of the same family.

Freshly cut flowers, scented messages from this world to the next, trembled in the breeze until, in time, as happens with all living things, they withered and died. They left long stems and leaves decaying in stagnant water. The odor reminded me of the times at school when we spat on our own arms, rubbed the spittle hard into the skin, and gave each other the smell test. "Yeak, you smell like a dead corpse."

A woman sobbed. I followed the sound to a white tomb where a pretty lady knelt. Underneath the black lace veil her pale face shined like a moonbeam. She reached out with trembling fingers to the picture of a girl's face. It was trapped within the glazed depths of a sepia photograph set under glass, on the page of an open book carved in marble. The girl's mischievous eyes belied the serious set of her mouth. The incised gilded message on the book read,

> To my Emilie,
> Gem of my life.
> Your sweet, smiling eyes
> Will forever

Shine in my heart.
Your Mummy
Always.

Nanna, age 6, at the cemetery.

Behind the convex oval glass, the girl in sepia met my eyes. Her lips, blurred by the sky's reflection, at this moment seemed to smile.

I waited behind a nearby cross until the sad lady wiped her eyes and walked away, round-shouldered, as if bearing a boulder.

I climbed and stood on tiptoe atop the marble bench at the side of the tomb, stretched until I could just stroke Emilie's cheeks. It felt as if I caressed my own image—the same fringed, bobbed, sandy hair, clear, smiling eyes, and solemn mouth. It felt as if I were back at the water tank, peering down at my reflection as it meshed with the upside-down sky, and I smiled back.

"Nanna, Where are you?"

I hastily slid the bead bracelet off my wrist, hooked it around the marble book's corner, and jumped off the bench.

"Here Pépé, I am here."

He came and took my hand. "Your Maman is bringing lunch. Let's go and wash our hands."

Ma arrived with a basket of food, four-year-old Zizou holding on to her skirt. Mireille, still learning to walk, hung on to the basket. My heart overflowing with a love bigger than the sky, I watched Papa stroll down the road, hands shoved in his pockets and whistling to himself.

I remembered loving this place so much then and Pépé, and Pa and Ma, and my little sisters, I could hardly breathe as I sat down for my birthday picnic party among the graves.

Little did I know that, five years later, the year I turned eleven, my tranquil city of the dead and others like it would be the resting place for victims of unspeakable deaths like the ones in El-Halia.

Chapter Five

Sidi Mabrouk, August, 1955

TONTON GILLES, HIS WIFE, Yvette, and a couple of my parents' friends had dinner at our house. The adults' sober conversation covered recent events in Philippeville and the nearby villages of El-Halia and Filfila. Their covert words and the careful looks they cast toward my brothers, sisters, and me alerted us that something worse than usual had happened. A somber Monsieur Martinez retrieved square, glossy black-and-white photos from his coat pocket. "It would not be a good idea for the children to see these," he hinted.

Leaning against my arm, Zizou whispered, "It's like in the movies; each time they are going to kiss, the actors pull a curtain or close a door in our faces so we can't see anything."

Maman said, "*Ma grande*, please, take the little ones to play in the garden." She always called me "my grown-up girl" when there was a chore to be done. But, being eleven and the eldest, I guess I was considered more mature than my siblings. I picked up Yves and grudgingly nudged Mireille and Riri out the front door.

"You too, Zizou," Papa said.

At dinnertime, Maman called us back inside to join the grown-ups at the table. Over deviled eggs, pork roast, potato Elise, and Yvette's yummy peach tart, the conversation—to Zizou's consternation and mine—turned to mundane matters. After coffee and *Eau de Poire* for the adults, our guests were ready to leave. Papa sent me to fetch their purses and jackets.

The last in the pile on my parents' bed was Monsieur Martinez's jacket. I picked it up by a sleeve and a jagged-edged photo slipped out, landing face down at my feet. I draped the coat on my left arm and picked up the picture. A penciled note read, "*Les Blanches Colombes du FLN.*" I turned the photo over to have a look at "The White Doves of the FLN."

Five small children—out of what seemed a long line of bodies—lay side by side on the open ground. Ribbons, like tattered butterflies, were plastered in the clotted, curly hair of one little girl. The pillows under their heads suggested they might be asleep, but twisted limbs, heads at odd angles and rumpled clothing said otherwise.

I realized with a chill of horror that, had the pictures been in color rather than black and white, the smudges coating bodies and clothing would have been blood-red rather than mud-black.

I had barely taken in the gaping throats and mangled bodies when Zizou entered the room. "Mr. Martinez is waiting for his jacket." She looked from my face to my hand. "What's that?"

I whipped the picture behind my back. "*Rien.*"

She circled me. "It's not nothing. Show me."

I shoved the photo into the jacket pocket and pushed past my nine-year-old sister. "Here is your jacket, Mr. Martinez."

Once everyone was gone, the dishes washed and dried and we lay in bed, Zizou snuggled up to me and whispered, "What was in the photo?"

"Nothing. Just dirty pictures."

"Like the ones they sell in the streets?"

"*Oui.*"

She turned over and went to sleep while, in the darkness, I stared at images of little Yves, Riri, and Mireille's faces floating mid-air. *Will they also be* Blanches Colombes *one day? And Zizou, and Papa, and Maman, and Pépé, and Tonton, and Yvette, and everyone I know. Will they all die like this—ducks flapping upon the parched earth, heads chopped off with axes or blunt knives, blood drying in puddles to feed swarms of flies?*

Will there be anyone left to bury us all?

The next day, I learned there would always be someone around to bury the dead. The front page of *Le Magrebien* showed a pressing crowd of men and women in their Sunday clothes, framing a line of flower-smothered coffins cropped by the picture frame. The headline read, "Unbearable, Barbaric Atrocities. What was the culpability of the El-Halia's children?"

While I skimmed down the page, the veins in my temples throbbed like a pigeon's throat pinched between finger and thumb. My God! The sixty coffins captured in the newsprint contained thirty-four El-Halia victims; fourteen from Philippeville—whole families wiped out—and twelve soldiers who had fought the assailants in the streets.

I realized I had blanked out when I felt Zizou pull my arm. "Are you all right, Nanna?" She tried to grab the newspaper out of my hands, but I shoved her and her shoulder hit the wall. "Leave me alone."

Though a thousand prickles stung the lining of my eyelids, I reread the article's closing paragraph. The same French government officials who had refused to let the El-Halia mine workers arm themselves drove from Constantine to Philippeville to assist at the burials. But they did not stay long. They wisely fled for their own safety when the mourners turned violent against them.

I wiped off tears of rage. "I wish they had beaten up *les salauds*." Reading over my shoulder, Zizou echoed, "These sons of bitches."

In a sidebar, *Le Magrebien* reported that the military secret services had known about an imminent attack on Philippeville and nearby villages but failed to share the information with the civilian population. My rage against the irreversible loss and our leaders' irresponsibility knew no bounds. "*Salauds, les salauds!*" I hit the wall with my fist. "*SALAUDS*. I hope the same horror happens to them."

El-Halia

A FEW DAYS LATER, I knocked on the bathroom door. "Zizou are you finished? You've been there for hours. I can't wait anymore."

I heard the toilet flush, a rustle, and Zizou opened the door. The front of her dress looked padded from underneath. "What were you doing?"

She crossed her arms across her belly. "*Rien.*"

"What do you mean 'nothing'? What did you do?"

She looked around and, pulling me by the arm, stepped into the bathroom and locked the door behind us.

"What's going on, Zizou?"

She put a finger to her puckered lips and blew a sour breath. "Shush." Then she bent down and, raising the hem of her dress all the way to her waist, revealed what looked like a small newspaper tucked between her stomach and underwear.

"What's this?"

She tugged the paper out and smoothed it against her chest. It was *la Gazette du Littoral.*

"Where did you get this?"

"My friend, Viviane, found it on top of a newspaper pile. She let me have it." Zizou thrust the paper forward as if challenging me to read it. "Here."

Under the headline banner, "I was in El-Halia," the *Gazette* ran the photograph of two women who looked like life-size rag dolls thrown helter-skelter. They lay in a small, spartan bedroom in pools of what must be blood. The woman on the floor had lost a shoe, and the other lay on her stomach atop a simple metal bed set in the corner of two spattered walls. Under the picture, the caption read, "Two Victims of El-Halia." Beneath, a subtitle read, "A young El-Halia woman's tale of horrors."

Zizou squeezed my arm. "Read."

I read.

> My name is Marie-Jeanne Pusceddu, I am a Pied-Noir, born in Philippeville in 1938 from French parents of Italian descent.
>
> My parents were blue-collar workers, all my family, brothers, uncles, cousins, worked at the El-Halia mine, near Philippeville.
>
> This small village of El-Halia was only a village of mineworkers, artisans who worked hard at the iron mine.
>
> There were also Arab workers with whom we shared, during our respective holidays, our pastries and friendship. They had their customs, different from ours. We respected each other. We were happy.
>
> Les Événementsd'Algerie started in 1954. But, for us, life was the same. We were not wary of our Arab friends.
>
> I was married the 13th of August, 1955. We had a beautiful party and all our friends were here, notably C---, the Arab taxi cab driver whom we knew well. With my husband we went to our honeymoon.
>
> On the 19th of August 1955, with my husband André Brandy (Engineer of mines at the Bureau de la Recherche Minière d'Algérie,) we took C---'s taxi to go back to El-Halia.
>
> On the way, C--- told us: "Tomorrow, there will be a big celebration with lots of meat."
>
> I told him, "What celebration? There is no celebration." I thought he was kidding—"

"*Mon Dieu*," I whispered, guessing what would come next.

Zizou urged, "Go on. Read."

I read on, a knot in my throat.

> The next day, August 20th, all the men were at work at the mine, but for my husband. It was noon, we were at the table, when suddenly, we were surprised by strident screams, the ululations of Moorish women, and gunshots.
>
> At the same time, my sister-in-law, Rose, holding her last born, Bernadette (three months old,) in her arms, arrived, panic-stricken,

followed by her children, Genevieve 8, Jean-Paul 5, Nicole 14, Anne-Marie, 4. Her eldest Roger, 17 years old was at the mine with his father.

With my mother, my brother Roland 8, Suzanne my sister 10, my other sister Olga 14, and my husband, we understood something very grave was happening. The screams were horrible. They screamed: "We want the men." I say to my husband: "Quick, hide in the laundry room!"

We locked ourselves in the house, but the fellaghas barged in by breaking the door down with an axe. To our great amazement, it was C---, the taxi driver, the "friend" who had been a guest at our wedding. I still see him as if it were yesterday. He ran after us to the dining room, then the kitchen; we were trapped. C---, with his hunting gun, threatened us—

"I knew that was going to happen," I cried out. I closed my burning eyelids. Zizou nudged me and I picked up the story's thread, hoping against hope that I was wrong. That C--- would spare them.

He immediately shot my poor mother, right in the chest. She was trying to protect my little brother Roland. She died on the spot with Roland in her arms, he also was severely injured. My sister-in-law Rose was killed by a shot in the back. She held her baby against the wall, my younger sister Olga threw herself, hysterical, upon the gun, he shot her point blank, badly. He taunted us with his gun. Bravely and panic stricken, I told him: "Go on! Shoot! I am the only one left—"

I was so charged with anger that I hit the wall with my hand. "That's my girl. Good for you." And screamed, "Tell him off. Tell le salaud off. Show him what you are made of—"

Zizou put a finger to her lips. "Shush. Pépé's going to hear you."

I bit my lip and returned to Marie-Jeanne's story.

He shot me, a bullet hit me at hip level, I did not even realize it and he left—

The scene unrolled inside my head like a silent movie. Even my sobs were soundless. I sat on the tile floor, back pressed against the wall, to ensure I'd face any danger that might come at me. Zizou sat close and cupped her hand over my shoulder. "Nanna, you don't have to read on. Let go."

"Non. I want to know." Filled with bottomless pity for the victims and rage and hatred for the murdering animals, I read on.

I took the children, hid them under the bed with me, but I was in great pain and wanted to know if my husband was still alive. I went to the laundry room and hid with him behind the aviary. The fellaghas, C---'s sons came back. Hearing noise, they walked in our direction, but one of them said in Arabic: "It's nothing, it's the birds." And we remained, frightened, lost, not moving until five in the afternoon. The screams, the strident ululations, the smoke …. What a nightmare!

A private airplane flew above the village and sounded the alarm.

The army arrived at seventeen hundred hours. And then, we entered the house to discover the horror. My little brother Roland was still breathing; he was in a coma for five days and recovered. Unhappily, my sister Olga had been raped and murdered. My sister Suzanne, had a head wound, which still shows.

Then the army gathered us.

Ma famille Azei, all slaughtered with knives, my mother's sister, her husband, her two daughters, one paralyzed, one of the daughters who was on holiday with her baby was, also, murdered with knives (It was the fiancée of her brother, who was hidden who saw it all and told us.) The baby had been shattered against the wall—

I grabbed Zizou's hand and pressed it hard to my lips to stifle a moan. She leaned against my arm. "Come, Nanna, let's forget it," she whispered, wiping tears off her face.

"*Non!*" I said, hitting the floor with my fist.

Then my cousin was killed with pitchforks at the mine restaurant, my mother's brother, Pierrot Scarfoto, was also massacred with knives as he tried to save his children. His private parts stuffed in his mouth. The same happened to my nephew Roger, who was 17.

My father, deaf at birth, wounded with knives, took refuge in an abandoned gallery. He did not hear the army, he was found fifteen days later dead from his wounds. He must have been in agony. My young brother Julien was slaughtered as well.

Thirteen members of my family were thus tortured, massacred by the FLN.

My whole body quivered, and I skipped the reporter's closing paragraph to read a short article farther down the page.

It relayed an interview with Doctor Baldino, a pediatrician enlisted to help at the understaffed Philippeville hospital:

The first wounded was a Muslim pastry cook working at a European shop. A fellow Muslim had come into the pastry shop shooting him several times in the chest ....

The interview stated that two hundred victims had been severely wounded. Some by high-caliber homemade bullets stuffed with hair and rusted metal that inflicted injuries practically impossible to repair. Others, pregnant women for instance, were eviscerated—mutilated by sharp instruments such as daggers, cutlasses, and axes. Doctor Baldino compared the slaughter to "the traditional ritual sacrifice of the sheep."

The image of Abraham preparing to sacrifice his son flashed through my mind, and I bitterly reflected that, this time, God had not intervened. He didn't substitute His El-Halia children with sacrificial lambs. *WHERE WAS HE?*

I scrambled to the toilet bowl and threw up.

"I vomited, too," Zizou said, handing me a piece of toilet paper.

"I know. I smelled it on your breath," I said, and stuffed half of the *Gazette* into Zizou's hands. "We need to get rid of this." I tore my half into small pieces. "We cannot let Mimi and Riri see it. If Papa knew we'd read it, he would kill us."

We pulled the chain repeatedly to flush the pieces a few at a time until Pépé Honninger called through the door, "What's going on in there?"

Zizou shook her hand up and down, meaning, "What do we do now?" but said, "It's the water tank, Pépé, it keeps on flushing." She stifled a nervous snicker, pinching me in her excitement. "My behind is getting all wet."

"All right. I'll see what's wrong when you get out.

AFTER READING THE *GAZETTE*, Zizou and I wondered about the Arabs who lived at the edge of our daily lives. "I bet you, this one could cut our heads off," she'd whisper about a whiskered man walking down the street or a beardless youngster glancing at us. She slashed the tip of her thumb across her throat. "Just like that."

I could not bring myself to agree with her, "He does have small eyes, but we have known him all our lives."

"It won't make a difference," she said. "Remember, the victims of El-Halia and Philippeville? They trusted their Arab friends and neighbors too."

Chapter Six

Bedtime Story

THAT NIGHT, PAPA CAME back late from *La Guinguette*. Frustrated with his missing dinnertime again, Maman hadn't stayed up to serve him. I sat in bed, reading, listening for his tread on the stairs. When it came, I jumped out of bed and ran to open the door for him.

I kissed his cheek. "*Bonsoir* Papa."

"Is your mother up?"

"She went to bed, Pa."

He marched down the corridor and checked on her. "Lili, are you asleep?"

She did not answer. Her eyes were closed, but I knew she was faking. Pleased to be alone with him, I trailed my father to the kitchen and heated up his dinner. I pounced on these evenings when it was just him and me, like a cat on a mouse. On these evenings, when he had only me to speak to, I felt important. Special.

I served Pa's food, placed the comic book he had been reading next to his plate, poured wine into his glass, and sat, arms folded on top of the table, studying his face. "It's not too hot, Pa?" He threw a tantrum when the food was too hot.

He shook his head. "I can live with it."

I already knew that—I had tested it with my little finger.

To stop him from becoming absorbed in his magazine, I jumped in with the questions that had been on my mind. "Papa, why did the *fellagha* kill all these poor people in Philippeville?"

Papa swallowed his mouthful of food and took a sip of wine. "I really don't want to talk about this. Besides, you're too young to understand."

"I'm eleven, Pa," I reminded him, trying to hide my hurt feelings. "I can understand if you explain it to me."

He sighed and pushed his plate and comic book aside.

"Very simple: realizing that most Arabs don't support its cause, the FLN slaughtered innocent Europeans. This forced the French government to strike back at the FLN, inevitably killing innocent Arabs in what is known as 'collateral damage.'"

Though knowing better, I interrupted him. "But, Papa, we don't want to kill the good Arabs. Do we?"

"Of course not. But if the terrorists hide among the general Arab population, how can we tell who's who?"

"But can't the good Arabs tell us who the bad Arabs are? Then they won't be punished for something they didn't do."

"It's not that simple. Let's say I am a terrorist, and me and my acolytes come to your neighborhood or village and tell the community leader, 'You will feed us. You will hide us. You will give us your money and, if one of you reports us, we will come back, torture and kill all of you—your children and wives first.'" Papa paused and raised his eyebrows. "What would you do?"

My finger traced a yellow flower on the shiny oilcloth. "It would be hard, but I'm pretty sure I would not tell on them."

"*Et voilà*," Papa said, with a flourish of his hand.

"But, how can the FLN let their own people pay for their crimes?"

"Ah. *That* is the question. Terrorists don't have 'their own people.' Terrorists have a cause. They sacrifice everything, everyone—even their own lives, in the service of that cause. This is why they are called 'extremists.' They'll do whatever's necessary for their principles to succeed."

He pulled a cigarette from the pack in his breast pocket, lit it, and took a long drag as he waved the match in the air.

Knowing better than to rush him, I held my breath while he dropped the smoking match in the ashtray and picked up the thread of his monologue. "This is the beauty of the theory, you see …." As an afterthought, he asked, "Do you know who Carlos Marighella is?"

Eyes wide, I shook my head and shrugged.

"He's a Brazillian guerilla leader who advocates terrorism in order to get the support of the masses."

"How's that, Pa?"

"Simple. Imagine you're the government of a given country, any country, and guerillas perform deliberate acts of sabotage that kill innocent people. What would you do?

I raised my shoulders and opened my hands wide. "Obviously, I'd send troupes to catch the terrorists and make them pay for their crimes."

"At any cost?"

"*Et bien, oui.* I think."

"But the guerillas hide among the general population or use them as shields. What then?"

I exhaled deeply, trying to find my way. "If …. If I don't go after the bad guys, they're going to keep on killing people, so … maybe I … I'd go after the terrorists, even …."

Papa peered at me through slit lids. "Even if it means hurting innocent people?"

I nodded with reluctance, my heart pounding as if I were one of the ones I had just condemned to die. Then I took a deep breath and absolved myself. "I'd die inside, but I think this is what I'd have to do."

"Yep," Pa said. "And that's exactly what Marighella's counting on: the government retaliates, causing collateral damage, which in turn moves the general population to forget the terrorists were really the ones who started the bloodshed in which they were the victims and they side with the terrorists."

Feeling lost in a maze, I asked, "So, Papa, what's the solution? What's going to happen now?"

He crushed his cigarette in the ashtray. "Let me tell you what's going to happen—and mark my words …."

I could tell, now, that I had his unreserved attention. I almost purred with satisfaction. Warming up to his subject, Pa flicked one finger at a time, counting.

"One. After the French retaliations against the Philippeville massacre, most of the moderate Muslims will side with the FLN.

"Two. The Governor General of Algeria, Jacques Soustelle—who until now was urging the integration of the Muslim community within French Algeria—will start promoting repression against supporters of independence.

"Three. In Metropolitan France, this bloodshed against the Arab population will sicken our countrymen, who will turn against the government policies of *Algérie Française*, therefore against us, *les Pieds-Noirs.*" Pa lit a new cigarette, sucked on it, and exhaled gray smoke then continued, "And, remember this: *les Pieds-Noirs* will ultimately end up being the scapegoats for the French government's bungling."

My father had always been right in his predictions and tonight he scared me. My face usually betrayed my inner feelings, but I wanted Papa to go on with his prophecies, so I kept a poker face as he spoke his mind.

He flipped another finger. "Four. The United Nations—including the United States as well as the Communists around the globe and the Muslim countries—will dub us the villains." He flicked a hand in a closing gesture and picked up his fork, for once not caring that his food was cold.

I waited until he finished his dinner before daring another question. "But Papa, who is going to be on our side?"

He raised his arm in a powerless gesture and left the table. "You mean, 'Who's going to be against us?' The answer is, everyone." In an afterthought, he turned and added, "Unless a couple of the generals like Salan and Massu decide enough is enough and side with us, but that's another matter."

Not wanting to try his patience further, I kissed him. "*Bonne nuit*, Papa," and began to stack dishes in the sink.

"*Bonne nuit, ma fille*," he said. I loved it when he called me his girl.

As he started toward his bedroom, I pushed my luck and asked, "Papa, why do the *Patos* call us *Pieds-Noirs*?"

He stopped in the kitchen doorway. "Because name-calling is human nature. It's what people do to groups who are different from them." He took his pack of *Gauloises* out of his breast pocket and stared at it. "We call the French born in Metropole, '*Patos*' and they call Europeans born in Algeria, '*Pieds-Noirs*.'"

"Yes, but what does that mean, Pa?"

He pulled a cigarette halfway out then pushed it back in and returned the pack to his shirt. "*Patos* means ducks. By extension it means clumsy oaf, gauche; it refers to the way clog-wearing peasants walk—like ducks. And, as the majority of Metropolitan French live outside big cities, they are lumped together as peasants—therefore, *Patos*.

"And the *Pieds-Noirs*, Pa?"

The most probable explanation for '*Pied-Noir*' is that the Napoleonic armies who conquered Algeria wore black ankle boots while the inhabitants of Algeria went barefoot or wore *babouches*. In that they are a culture that expresses itself through imagery, the Arabs equated the color of the boots to the people who wore them, ergo, 'Black Feet.'"

I sighed with relief. "So '*Pied-Noir*' isn't an insult?"

"Not unless it is used in the connotation of 'dirty or unwashed feet,' which is, most likely, what the *Patos* mean."

"So, they are insulting us?"

"No. They are unifying us."

"How's that, Pa?"

"When you reduce different categories of people—like the French, Italians, Germans, Spaniards, Jews, and many others who have settled here—to a single group by calling them pejorative names, they'll close rank and fight back as one, no matter what their ethnic and religious differences." Papa turned on his heels. "Let me go to bed now, Nanna," he said, and left the kitchen and a daughter pleased by his special attention and armed with loads of information to process.

LIKE MOST CHILDREN, I gleaned my information about *Les Événements* by asking questions from adults, eavesdropping on their conversations, or paying attention to radio and newspaper reports of random shootings of Europeans by the FLN. Of grenades thrown in restaurants, movie theaters, cafés, and buses with no mind paid to collateral damage to their fellow Arabs.

"*Le Téléphone Arabe*," or word-of-mouth, was another channel the *Pieds-Noirs* and Arab population used to spread news of butchered farmers and their families, their cattle slaughtered, their farms, crops and schools burned, their vines and fruit trees chopped down.

Eyes wide, partly from fear, partly from fascination with the ghoulish, we children relayed among ourselves whispered tidbits about the *fellagha* cutting off tongues, ears, heads, and visiting unspeakable horrors upon Muslim officials working for the French, upon their families, and upon those who sided with the French, like the Harkis—the Arab soldiers serving in the French army.

Zizou whispered in my ear, "Nanna, do you think they cut the throats of the soldiers they catch before they cut off their balls and stuff them in their mouths or," she made a face, "do they cut their throats after?"

"I don't know," I said, trying to quell the horrid images and, at the same time, sound learned and wise to my younger sister. "I hope they cut their throats first, but it would be meaner to cut them after."

Zizou gulped. "And when they take unborn babies out of their mothers' stomachs, do you think the babies feel anything?"

"I don't think so, but it has to be really horrible for their mothers."

It felt as if each tale of needless violence decreased my ability to feel other people's pain. I feared that my heart was drying up a little bit at a time. "You know," I said, "I read that, a long time ago, some Indian tribes in America did things like this. They'd make a hole in a prisoner's belly, pull a piece of their guts out, tie the end to a tree and force the prisoner to run around the tree until all his guts were wrapped around it."

Zizou's eyes dilated. "You mean like Maman unravels an old sweater and makes a ball out of it?"

"Just like it."

WHILE OUR HISTORY WAS being written in blood, we went about our business, believing it possible that we and our families might not see the end of each day. Then came a time when violence, mourning, and uncertainty became ordinary fare. Nevertheless, our lives went on like carts lumbering on square wheels.

Chapter Seven

Djebel Ouach

April, 1956

ONE OF THESE BUMPY, square-wheeled rides led us along to Easter celebrations. Following the yearly tradition, and in spite of the war, Europeans who lived in or nearby Constantine continued to spend Easter Monday at Djebel Ouach—a breezy plateau crowned with stands of oaks, pines, and eucalypti that hugged five artificial lakes supplying water to the plains region.

Extended families, neighbors, and friends gathered in small groups seated on blankets spread over patchy grass. After the midday meal, the picnickers doused the coals, wrapped up the leftover food, exchanged news, played cards or *Boules,* fished, or took a nap. The best time was after siesta, at about four, when people danced to the music of accordions, drums, and trumpets. Pépé Honninger pulled out castanets from his pocket and accompanied the band with a gusto he'd never show otherwise. My enthusiasm was such that I'd grab Zizou's or Mimi's hands and we'd shuffle or hop as we mimicked the dancing adults.

At the close of one of these Easter lunches, Pépé Honninger grabbed his fishing pole, lures and worms and Maman clapped her hands. "It is time for a nap, *les enfants.*"

Under Papa's rule, we took our siestas when he took his. Being almost twelve and the oldest, I had to set the example. So I lay flat on my back, arms along my body, and breathed slowly, willing my lids to become heavy with sleep. However, the air vibrated with repressed energy.

Flying insects wove darts of light as they flitted from sun to shade. I inhaled the bitter tang of crushed weeds, the sharp essence of pines, and the eucalypti's delicate fragrance. I had slipped into a cozy half doze—low-droned bits of conversations dissolving into the breeze off the lakes—when a bug landed on my cheek. I slapped it, sat up, and no longer willing to remain still, slipped on my sandals, taking care not to wake my father. I adjusted my shorts and sleeveless top and strolled toward the trees. Tall grasses of pale gold tickled my legs. Small animals scurried away. Buzzing insects dashed from dots of sun to spots of shade, looking like fireflies. Grasshoppers hopped, revealing dark red wings, and cicadas played like violins nursing a cold. A thrilling sense of freedom put a spring in my step, taking me farther into the trees.

A gnarled pine tree rose in my way, its trunk blanketed in dark-brown moss with long thin stems crowned with tiny pods. In one spot, the bark oozed sap that congealed into beads of translucent amber. I pinched a blob between index and thumb and brought it to my nose. It was sticky and smelled of the gumdrops Pépé Honninger gave us for our sore throats. I put my tongue to it and tasted turpentine.

While I wiped my fingers on a tuft of grass at the foot of the tree, my eyes followed the moss-covered trunk to its bristled crown. *What fun it would be to look down at people from high up.*

The trunk's slight incline made it easy to scale, and soon I clung to it several feet above the ground. The moss felt soft against my skin.

We had just studied moss at school, and I wondered what type it was.

Strange. Shouldn't it be growing on the north side of the tree, like lichen? Why was it growing all around?

Another thought followed. Isn't this place too dry for moss to be growing?

Curious, I hugged the trunk with both my legs and left hand and, with my other hand, plucked a tuft of moss by the pods. The pinched stems stirred. I took a closer look. *They look like legs!*

LEGS?

My heart thumped once. I stopped breathing. This wasn't moss I was hugging. These were hundreds, no, THOUSANDS, no, MILLIONS of spiders with long legs and tiny bodies.

I yelped, let go of the tree, and fell to the ground. Scuttling to my feet, I sprinted to the picnic area. While I raced, *BILLIONS* of spiders scurried over my feet, my legs, my hands, and my lower arms. The faster I ran, the more spiders covered my skin.

At the camp, I flung myself onto the blanket, shrieking, rocking back and forth to shake them off. Papa uncoiled like a snake from his blanket. He bore down on me and brought me to my feet. "What's wrong with you?" He turned to Maman. "Is she hysterical or what?"

I squealed. Batted at his hands and the spiders. He shook me. "Get hold of yourself."

Djebel Ouach. Nanna is the little girl with short hair. Maman on her right. Pépé Honninger in front with bottle of champagne. Debbah with hat, third from left.

Maman threw a mug-full of water at my face.

Suddenly, the spiders were gone and everyone at Djebel Ouach stared.

Maman came close and brushed wet hair from my face. "What happened, *ma fille?*"

"Didn't you see the spiders?"

"What spiders?"

"The spiders that were ALL over me?"

"I did not see any spiders."

"*Oui, oui,* they were HERE and HERE and HERE, they were ALL OVER me." With each word, I hit a part of my body—hard.

"I am sorry, *ma fille,* there were no spiders."

"Yes there were, and I'll show you where I got them."

I grabbed her hand and pulled hard. Zizou and Mireille hung close. Papa and the onlookers followed. Far behind, trying to keep up, Yves hung on to a grinning Riri.

At the foot of the tree, I pointed at the trunk. Triumphant. "Here they are."

Papa and two other men picked curiously at the "moss," agreeing that these were indeed spiders. "However," they wondered, "what made her believe she was crawling with them?"

Papa slipped into the role of "*Inspecteur* Vincent," as he called himself whenever he was in an inquiring mood. He ordered me to reenact my story from the time I reached the foot of the tree.

I clutched Maman's arm. "*NON.* I don't want to go up that tree again."

"All right. Let's say, you are climbing the tree, what happens?" Papa asked.

"My legs and my arms are around the tree, and I see that the moss on the trunk is not moss but TRILLIONS of spiders."

Zizou chuckled. Mireille swatted at invisible spiders crawling up her arms. The boys were still trying to catch up with us. Ma took my hand. Papa's mouth twitched at one corner. "Let's not lay it on too thick now, shall we? What do you do then?"

"I fall down and then I get up real quick and I run real fast and then spiders run ALL OVER me."

"*Alors,* do it," Pa said.

I watched him, puzzled. He stood tall, feet apart, cigarette loosely dangling from his lips, one eye half-closed against the rising thread of blue smoke, hands on hips. "Get," he barked.

I sprinted toward the campsite. Waist-high grasses lashed at my skin. I screeched, then stopped. The thin golden stalks bore crowns of maturing hairy seeds that tickled as I waded through them. Mortified, I walked back and confessed, "I thought the weeds were spiders."

Papa walked away, shaking his head, scowling, one hand in his pants pocket, the other, holding the cigarette, flung into the air as if to say, "My poor girl, you are such an asshole. What am I to do with you?"

The onlookers followed, talking and laughing. I tagged along, the boys, finally caught up, by my side.

Back at the picnic ground, humiliated and exhausted, I dropped down on our blanket, my brothers on each side of me.

"Spider," Riri warned, as he cast a dry leaf at my face and laughed.

I scooted backward with a whimper.

Papa picked up his *boules* for a game of *pétanque* and walked away. "When will you learn to get your head out of your ass and start living among us?" he snarled over his shoulder.

I sat on the blanket, shivering in the warm air, as the first beats of an accordion and the clacking of Pépé's castanets announced dancing time.

A Dream

THAT VERY NIGHT, AFTER I finally managed to fall asleep, I woke up in the center of a greenhouse. The glass-paneled ceiling and walls muffled outdoor sounds. A heavy coat of grime and dust filtered the bright daylight.

I brushed aside the drapes of thick muslin surrounding me. Their ripples revealed more folds. I spun slowly, looking for an exit. But there was none.

TRAPPED!

I held my breath and charged through the hanging layers. Arms extended. Head low. Eyes slitted. The drapes tore in swatches of tacky dust and stuck to my head. My arms. My clothes. I plucked them off my face. They clung to my fingers. I moaned. *What's this stuff?*

Like a caged bird, my heart banged against my ribs. I screeched, "Wake up, Nanna!" But this was not a dream. I thrashed and spun in a mindless whirl. The webs pinned my arms against my sides. Swathed me in a cocoon. Eyes sealed open. I moaned. Panted for air. A lump of dusty muslin plugged my mouth ....

"Hush, *ma fille*, hush. It's only a nightmare."

I gulped a lungful of air and opened my eyes. Saw Ma bending over me, holding my bloodied hands. "You scratched your ears." She dabbed ether on the lobes of my newly pierced ears. "They look all right. We can leave the earrings in." She bathed my face and hands with cold towels, gave me water mixed with sugar and Aspirin, and then stayed with me until I fell asleep.

The next morning, she asked, "Do your earlobes hurt, *ma fille*? Do you need to take your earrings off?"

I shook my head. The small gold earrings had been Mémé Honninger's then Maman's, given to them at their *Communion Solennelle*. Now they were mine for my own First Communion. The prettiest things I'd ever owned. "They sting a little, Ma, but I'll keep them on."

Communion Solennelle

By First Communion day, my earlobes had healed, and while I admired the reflection of the earrings sparkling on each side of my face, I glared at the dress waiting for me on a hanger.

For years and years, I had marveled at the girl communicants in their bride-like fluffy white gowns and veils, dreaming of when it would be my turn to look like the doll on top of a wedding cake. I had it all planned. My gloved hands would smooth back the veil—floating in the spring breeze like a wisp of cloud and held into place by a crown of pristine flowers. The dainty white suede shoes would crunch over the graveled church square while bells called for the two rows of boys and girls to pass the church portals. Each of us would hold a tall candle adorned with a white bow, while the choir sang hymns and the smell of incense heralded our walk down the aisle.

I cast a resentful eye at the habit I was to wear. The dream of many years shredded faster than a wisp of cloud in a storm. The only feature this dress held in common with that of my dreams was the color. *Adieu*, fluff, *adieu*, veil—only a nun-like white tunic, complete with wide pleats from shoulders to hem, long, wide sleeves, and a rope tied at the waist. *Yuck.*

Most horrid of all was the skullcap that made my head look like a snow-capped Kilimanjaro.

There was a reason for this new austerity: at the ten o'clock Sunday mass, Le Père Attar had announced that, from then on, the *Communion Solennelle* would return to the true significance of the ceremony—"the renewal of the baptismal profession of faith, instead of an occasion to coddle girls' vanity and stretch their parents' wallets." He believed the alb, cross, and candle, symbolizing the virginal aspects of Baptism, were de rigueur.

"But, Papa, not everybody is obliged to wear the alb."

"Get out of here; I don't have time for your crap."

"*Si*, Papa. *Le Père* said it was up to each family to decide how much money they wanted to spend on their daughter's communion. He said that, for this year only, people can choose if they want to dress the new way OR the old way and that the church is going to rent out the albs at a low price and he hopes that everyone will make the right choice."

Papa frowned. "Does he think I cannot afford to buy a dress for *ma fille*?"

I looked at him with brows arched, arms half stretched in front of me, palms open heavenward, shoulders raised—hoping to convey with my body language, "What can I say?"

Papa's eyes flashed green and mean. "I'll talk to Attar."

YES! Sparks would fly and Papa was going to win this one for me.

Everyone knew that Papa and *le Père* could not be in shouting distance of each other without getting into a semantic crusade. They both clearly enjoyed their clashes over widely conflicting interpretations of the Bible, but their antagonism was robust.

Waiting for the inevitable result of the collision between Papa and Père Attar, I prepared for the choices I would soon be facing.

Did I want a satin or lace dress? With a lace dress, obviously a lace veil would not do. *Hm, I am not sure—I'll ask Yvette.*

Tonton Gilles' wife was a dressmaker and had offered to make my Communion dress and veil.

Perhaps I could have Maman convince Papa to let me wear shoes with a small heel, instead of my usual flats. Of course, my being not yet twelve, the heels would have to be really tiny-little-bitty to get a nod from Papa. I crossed my fingers.

We'd also have to get a pair of these dainty, embroidered, flimsy gloves with

Nanna's First Communion, age 12, in back garden, 1954.

ribbons at the wrist—my Sunday mass mesh cotton ones would definitely not do.

I rolled my eyes upward for inspiration. Did I want a flower crown to hold the veil in place, instead of pearl hatpins? If so, should the flowers be fresh or silk? Nah, silk flowers were more glamorous.

For several wrenching days, I waited in silence for Papa's verdict.

"For once," he said, "I agree with Attar. Families who have a problem making ends meet should not feel they have to keep up with the Durands.

Those of us who don't fit this profile should set the example. And I shall."

"That means I'll wear the alb?"

"*Oui.*"

Apparently, le Père Attar—*tricky soul*—had convinced Papa that, as a comfortable member of the parish—*Liar!*—it was his duty to spare the pride of the less affluent and set an example by having me wear the alb.

And that was that.

One for le Père Attar, ZERO for Pa, and the Alb for me.

Chapter Eight

Mireille and the Swing

ONE SUMMER DAY FOLLOWING my communion, Maman joined Papa at his cemetery office to help with the accounting books. Riri and Yves went fishing at *la Rivière des Chiens* with Pépé Honninger. That left Zizou, Mireille and *moi* to wash the lunch dishes and gather the laundry from the line in the backyard.

Zizou and I left Mireille to finish drying the dishes and ran out the front door. We galloped down the stairs, skipped around the corner of the house, and rushed up the three steps leading to the backyard. The laundry shack stood close to the fence separating our property from that of our Arab neighbor. Next to it was the enclosed woodshed and next to that, the farmyard.

The laundry shack's wash waters, suds and all, drained into a dense cluster of tall bamboo, wet haven to a colony of frogs that fed off mosquito larvae among the mud puddles. All would have been well if frogs had been the head-honchos on the food chain. Alas, Mother Nature designed snakes that found a heavenly food supply amid the copse teeming with batrachians.

Careful not to encroach on the reptiles' territory, Zizou and I ended our race at the top of the three steps, beneath the grapevine arbor. In its dappled shade, bumblebees hummed among the grapes. Sparrows chirped in the mulberry tree. Sheltered from the broiling sun, they gorged on the grainy fruits swollen with sticky juice the color of Cabernet.

Next to the steps, the empty wicker basket waited for the collection of dry laundry. It was a spacious, oblong basket with a handle at each end. In the relative coolness of the arbor's shade, the woven reeds had achieved that burnished honey color bestowed by time.

Beneath splashes of sun dancing through the stirring grape leaves, the amber reeds appeared to throb—in the same languid way butterflies shift their wings as they flirt with flowers.

It seemed to say, "Doesn't it feel cool and peaceful, here?"

Inebriated by the magic of the moment, Zizou exclaimed, "Letttt's build a ssswing."

She meant a swing like the one we sometimes hung from the bower at the front of the house. The rope was somewhere, probably in a corner of the woodshed. We would tie it to the pipe of the arbor and use a small wooden plank to keep the looped rope open and serve as a seat.

"Do you know where the plank is?" I asked.

"The last time—hmm." Zizou twisted her mouth to one side of her face and the tip of her nose to the other side. "The last time we used it was …." Her eyes rolled upward, searching. "It was …. when we found the turtle. Remember?"

I remembered. We had used the board as part of an enclosure we built to hold the turtle, at the foot of the laurel tree. I giggled. "It dug a tunnel underneath and disappeared."

I marched to the laurel tree and brought the plank back. Then I bent down beneath the arbor, hands wrapped around my ankles. Zizou climbed on top of my back, rope in hand.

On tiptoe, she reached up, tied each end of the rope to a pipe, and stepped down. I balanced the plank horizontally on the resulting loop, and Zizou centered the basket perpendicular to the plank. "*Et voilà*," she said.

Satisfied, we sat on the steps with a sigh. I leaned back on my elbows, looking up at the swarms of insects. Some dashed from hanging grapes to mulberries rotting on the ground; others fluttered in a drunken whirl.

After a moment of silent swatting, I said, "*Vas-y*, Zizou, get in the basket."

"*Non, non, non.*" she replied. "You have the right of pri-mo-geni-ture. You go first."

Such a big word from someone who did not read much made me snort. "*Yaa*, Zizou. Where did you learn that word?"

She peered at me with contempt. "In history class. Last week. Go."

No way am I going. "Well, why build a swing if nobody swings in it?"

The wheels of our combined minds ground hard. One could smell the smolder of evil at work. We grinned as we both said, "Mireille!"

Sensing Satan had elected to dwell among us, a duck in the poultry yard quacked and pecked at another's head. The old rooster flapped its iridescent red and purple wings, blood-gorged cockscomb wagging as it chased the white pullet that had not yet laid her first egg.

Meanwhile, unlike Jason of the Golden Fleece who avoided falling prey to the Sirens, Mireille answered our honeyed calls. "What?"

"Mimi, look at what we made for you."

Our eight-year-old sister circled the swing and appraised the balanced basket and board with a frown. "This looks a little wobbly to me."

Possibly recalling another of her school classes, Zizou explained, "Oh, but you have to understand that it is all a matter of balance and weight. You stay balanced in the middle of the basket and your weight keeps the basket on the board."

Brilliant. I added, "Besides, when the swing begins to sway, it will be as if everything is glued together. It's like when you spin a bucket full of water around and around, the water stays in the bucket. Pure physics."

Mireille shook her head with a little moue of disgust. "Well then, why don't YOU do it?"

The age-old explanation came in unison. "Because."

"Because what?"

In the hush, we could hear the rustle of a snake searching for frogs among the bamboo.

"Because … I get seasick."

"That's when you ride in the car. What about you, Zizou? You never get seasick."

Coming up dry, Zizou cajoled, "Come on, you are not a sissy, are you?"

Mireille picked up a mulberry from the ground, took a few steps, and dropped it through the chicken wire for the hens to fight over.

Piqued by Mireille's carefree manner, Zizou tried a new tack. "If you don't do it, you'll be sorry."

Mireille turned around, raising a defiant chin. "Sorry how?"

Obviously without a clue of how, Zizou said, "You'll see."

Mireille picked up another mulberry.

I waved a hand and blew, "*Pfftt*, never mind." Turning around, I started down the steps and said, "Come on, Zizou."

Mireille cried out "All right, I'll do it." Then she quickly countered, "I'll do it, but I want some *Caca de Pigeon.*"

Now, *Caca de Pigeon,* or pigeon's poo, is a paste-like candy made, mostly, of ground nuts and honey. Its unscientific name—if one knows about pigeons and stuff—is descriptive of its consistency and the variegated colors of light green swirled with sick brown and some hot pink in-between.

We were crazy about the *Caca* and never seemed to have enough private funds to satisfy our craving for it.

Zizou singsonged, "All right, but it will have to be a little bit of *Caca.*"

"No, I want a big bit."

I was not only older, but also more rational. "Listen, Mimi, all we have is one five-franc coin, so make up your mind."

Pocket money was rare. Mireille must have decided that five francs worth of *Caca* was better than no *Caca* at all.

She agreed to climb into the basket and we told her to sit in the full center "at all times. Do not move by even *un millimètre*," we warned.

She nodded and grasped the ropes. Zizou gave a guarded push. The swing moved gingerly forward, came back, and twisted slightly on itself as it bypassed its plumb line. The second, third, and forth push were bolder. The swing settled in a smooth pendulum mode. As the pushing became bolder, the swing went higher.

At the apogee of the eighth thrust, Mireille moved her torso forward. The board seesawed. The basket pitched. Mireille took off. Zizou and I screamed, "Mimi!" as she landed head first in the middle of the steps.

In the ensuing consternation, bees buzzed, birds chirped. Atop the woodshed, pigeons cooed. Within the little mud-shack school nearby, Arab boys droned verses of the Qur'an. Down the street, a sonorous donkey brayed.

Meanwhile, sprawled in the middle of the steps, Mireille bawled.

We sprinted to her side and while we helped her up, Zizou yelled, "Why did you move?"

I asked, "Are you okay, Mimi?"

"*Oui.* But my head hurts."

Her forehead was developing a terrific off-center welt, just below the hairline.

What to do? I recalled, from reading our old wives' remedy book, that pressure applied to a burgeoning swell prevented blood from accumulating and that a coin would do the job.

"Zizou, get the five-franc coin."

She ran to the house.

"And bring my blue scarf too."

Back in no time, Zizou held the large coin over the growing lump while I secured it with tight loops of my scarf. Mireille squirmed.

After a final knot, I asked, "Do you feel better now, Mimi?"

She hesitated, then she whined, "*Non,* it hurts. Oh, it hurts!"

"Let's be patient, just wait."

"Oh, *non, non, non,* it hurts too much."

"Now, stop that."

"Take it off. TAKE IT OFF."

I could tell that, for once, she was not faking and quickly unwound the scarf. The coin did not fall—the flesh had puckered, holding it like a beveled cabochon.

My gnawing sense of guilt morphed into cold, analytical curiosity. The kind that urges you to pull the wings off a grasshopper, blow on the silk of milkweeds, or pour water down an ant hole—just to see what happens next.

In this instance, we set out to separate our sister from her currency. Zizou held Mireille's head. I inserted a cautious fingernail behind the edge of the coin and flicked it. It came loose with a sigh and fell to the ground, twirled on its rim, and came to rest at our feet, tails up.

Mireille moaned and covered her wound with a cupped palm. Zizou brushed it aside to have a look. One glance and Zizou and I fell into a laughing fit, eyes watering, bellies aching.

Mireille whined, "You always make fun of me."

We helped her to the house and cooed. "Là, là, ma petite chérie."

Wary about what so much tenderness on our part meant, she shrugged us away. However, once she looked into the mirror we held for her, she giggled along with us. The coin had left a perfect intaglio. A faultless negative replica of the chiseled face of Marianne, symbol of the French Republic.

Soon after, we all went across the street to Saiid's grocery store and bought five francs worth of *Caca de Pigeon*. Back at the house, Zizou and I sat on the front door stoop next to Mireille and, elbows on knees and cheeks in hands, watched her eat her *Caca*.

Even though the candy had been carved from a mound used as a landing pad by myriads of flies, Zizou and I still hoped to get a taste.

Alas, not even a speck fell from Mireille's lips.

So Zizou and I returned to the backyard, collected the laundry from the line, and brought it home in the basket. While we folded the bed sheets, Zizou batted her eyelashes. "Mimi, what will you tell Papa?"

Eyes downcast, Mireille licked her fingers.

I pressed, "What are you going to tell him about the swing?"

Both the sweet taste of *Caca* and that of our barely-disguised shameless begging seemed revenge enough. "I will tell him I ran and fell down the stairs."

The sigh of relief had not yet expired upon our lips that she added, "*If …* you do my chores for ten days."

DURING THE NEXT FEW days, Papa gave the impression he had swallowed Mireille's accidental fall version, but he couldn't control the dubious spark in his eyes as he watched the three of us on the sly. Then one afternoon, home early from work, he exploded. "What's going on here?"

"What d'you mean, Pa?" Mireille asked, poker-faced.

"When did you start doing each other's chores?"

The three of us exchanged swift glances. Zizou's hazelnut irises lit up like embers behind the woodstove's mica window in winter, and her long, curly black lashes fluttered. "Well, Papa, as Mireille has *un souffle au coeur*—you know—Nanna and I decided it would be lovely to give her a hand."

Chapter Nine

———

PAPA MEASURED EACH OF us with narrowed eyes and, obviously unhappy with Zizou's explanation, marched to his bedroom, shaking his head. The three of us watched him reach for his wallet on top of the chest of drawers and come back to the kitchen, where Maman prepared the evening meal. He announced, "Lili, I'm going to *La Guinguette*."

"How long will you be, *chéri*?"

"I don't know. I'll be back when I'm back."

We trailed him out the door and watched as he lit a cigarette, pulled on it, sauntered down the stairs, and walked across the front yard, into the street, all the way up to *La Guinguette*.

We returned to the kitchen. Maman stood at the sink, her back to us, a dishtowel straddling her shoulder. "Ma, do you want us to do something?"

Still facing the sink, she brought the corner of the towel to her eyes and said in a squeaky voice, "You could peel the potatoes I set on the table."

We peeled for a while, eyes willfully lowered to the task, avoiding Maman's tears of hurt feelings, breaking the silence only when we were through. "Can we play hopscotch until we eat, Ma?"

She dropped an extra log into the cook stove, her face reflecting the coals' red glow. "Go ahead. I'll let you know when it is time to eat."

Time to eat was a widely flexible concept at our house. It meant "wait for Papa to come home from work or back from La Guinguette." This anti-schedule applied, mostly, to every evening and Sunday lunches.

Weekly lunches were more predictable. Either Papa was out of town for work, or he needed to get back to work right away after eating, except in the full of summer. Then everyone had to take a siesta to avoid the blaze of early afternoon sun.

In the evening, while waiting for dinner, Mireille, Zizou, and I drew chalk lines on the corridor's tile floor and played hopscotch under the spare light hanging from the ceiling.

We took turns hopping on one leg, pushing ahead an old shoe-polish can filled with sand—from Earth to Heaven and back to Earth again.

"Ma, when do we eat?"

"As soon as Papa comes home."

We hop-scotched. Pépé mended one thing or another in his workshop downstairs. The boys played Lego or Cowboys and Indians. Maman kept the food warm and knitted—the nervous click, click of her needles, static to the music, news, or games on the kitchen radio.

"Ma, can we eat?"

"Can you wait a little longer, *ma fille?*"

Mimi held her stomach with a tragic look. "Not too much longer, Ma."

After the nine o'clock news, Maman wrapped her knitting in a towel. "*Allez, les filles,* it's time to set the table. Riri, tell Pépé we are eating."

When Pépé joined us at the kitchen table, the soup steamed in our bowls. I hated soup. Soup in winter. Soup in summer. Every single night, dinner started with soup. No respite. I hated soup.

I think Pépé must have felt as I did about Ma's soups because he often splashed red wine in his. Judging by the resulting color, we could not imagine how he could eat such revolting stuff.

One evening, he noticed each of us staring as he poured wine into his bowl. "Don't sneer at what you don't know." He rolled his shoulder. "Bring your spoons over."

He filled each of our spoons with soup and rotated his shoulder again, asking, "What do you think?"

Standing behind him, Zizou rolled her eyes.

Mireille said, "I like it, Pépé. Can I have more?"

Riri made gagging faces.

Yves said, "Yak. It tastes just like it looks."

Pépé half-turned to him, his eyes magnified by the thick lenses of his glasses. "What does it look like?"

"Vomit."

I lied, "Well, it's not too bad."

Pépé moved his lips in a silent monologue then scanned our faces. "At least now you have an opinion based on personal experience. It's called empirical evidence."

La Soupe au Chien

REMEMBERING PÉPÉ'S "EMPIRICAL EVIDENCE," I was glad to return to tonight's fare, even though it was what, behind our hands, we called, "*La soupe au chien.*"

This "Soup for the dog" consisted of stale leftover bread soaked in a large pot of boiling water in which Maman combined salt, olive oil, and garlic cloves.

"Garlic has medicinal properties. It is good for you," she said.

The resulting mush was her brainchild and intended, originally, to provide sustenance for Bellone, the wild and crazy German shepherd bitch tied up in our backyard.

It had not taken a great leap of imagination for Maman to conclude, later, that if *la soupe* was good enough for *le chien,* it had to be good enough for *les canards.* We children thought this hurdle entertaining until she decided that if *la soupe* was good enough for the ducks, it had to be good enough for *les enfants.* Meaning us.

After serving us this concoction for a while and seeing that our palates were a tad more discerning than the yard's tenants, she adjusted her recipe, adding TWO bouillon cubes and, for good measure, ONE more garlic clove.

It was fair to say that, in rare moments of munificence, Maman replaced the good old bread with a handful of angel hair pasta. This she crushed between her hands with an enthusiasm that made us shudder, for we knew the end result would be overcooked and slapped on our plates like globs of glue.

With no right of appeal, we ingested the solid soup with theatrical distaste and mused about the yet unnamed Sunday when we would have one of the ducks for dinner, a hint to which Maman would reply, "They have to be fattened first."

Glancing around the table and seeing how skinny we were, we sighed, thinking that these ducks would not see a pot just yet.

The Poultry Yard

BUT THERE WAS MORE to our farmyard than just quacking, waddling, slimy-water wading ducks. Lots more, if one counts run-of-the-mill nothing-to-the-eye bland chickens or, in contrast, the rooster—ah, the rooster! What a magnificent full-of-himself strutting-hennizer, aging Don Juan-in-plumage. Always running after one hen or another, pecking heads, if nothing else—a real Guy.

The dainty little guinea hens, graceful white dots adorning black robes, paraded long, denuded necks encircled with a ring of delicate duvet—the pullet version of Toulouse Lautrec's "Woman with a Black Feather Boa."

The pigeons held a much more exalted position within the yard's population, as evidenced by the placement of their dovecote, high above the rabbit hutches. Every morning, Pépé pushed open a trapdoor in the enclosure's chicken wire roof and freed them to feed among the neighboring fields. "Free ranging gives them a richer taste," he said, rolling his shoulders.

"But, Pépé, why do they come back to our yard every night, when it's like going to jail?"

He stretched his neck one way, then the other. "Because, when they hear my little bell, they know they'll have my special *pâté* to eat."

Then, there were the rabbits, harbored in spacious cement compartments lined up along the back wall, like low-budget row houses. A wood-framed picture window of chicken wire held secure each one-room cubicle. Off-the-floor wooden slats isolated the residents from the cold cement and provided spaces between slats for the droppings to fall beneath.

Each rabbit had its personal booth, that is, until the does were in season, at which time, Pépé unlatched the doors to the hutches and, grabbing the bucks by the scruff of their necks, removed them from their bachelor pads and paired them with the does.

In charge of cleaning the rabbit hutches, filling their water bowls, and feeding them, Zizou was fiercely dedicated to her furry *lapins*. Personally, I found them kind of stupid—crouching inside their hutch, long ears immobile, and vacuous eyes staring. Even cows looked at passing trains with more interest and warmth.

The rabbits' only moving parts were their twitching noses and mouths that constantly munched, whether eating or not. Pépé said they needed to grind their teeth nonstop to keep the incisors from growing out of their mouths. They did this teeth-grinding thing even in the throes of passion.

During mating season, when Pépé joined the does and bucks in unholy matrimony, Zizou and I watched, mesmerized, as a male straddled a female's back. He squeezed her sides with his forelegs, bit the skin at the back of her neck to steady himself, and pumped quickly four or five times before falling flat on his side as suddenly as if shot dead.

Meanwhile the doe munched on air, nose twitching, eyes staring at nothing. We always waited for the buck's abrupt fall, finding it as funny as one of the jerking silent movie characters at the Sunday parish cinema.

The products of such hasty encounters were, of course, *des petits lapins*. Hideous as skinless rats at birth, the little rabbits became cuddly and precious in the fullness of their baby coats, soft as mimosa blooms.

Then we'd sit at the back of the house on Pépé's workshop stoop where Zizou, with proprietary magnanimity, allowed me to hold them, tenderly passing them from her lap onto mine. She named each according to its markings and coloring and followed its daily maturing till adulthood and doomsday, when Pépé selected a rabbit as the main ingredient for his *Lapin Chasseur* dish.

"Not this one Pépé, please, Pépé, not this one," Zizou pleaded, and down the line of eligible *lapins* they went. Running out of patience, Pépé gathered a pair of long ears at random and before he had time to whack the beast on the back of its neck with the side of his free hand, Zizou was running away, sobbing. She never ate a meat dish whose name started with the letter "L." However, she had no such scruples with any of the other letters of the alphabet, including the letter "O" for *oie*.

Ah, the goose! Long-necked and virginal-white as a swan—and just as mean—waddling, and slimy-water loving as a duck. Definitely the by-product of some unsupervised tea for two, between an eye-roving quack and a love-starved Lady swan, under the curved nave of Noah's Ark—anything can happen in times of turmoil. Have I mentioned "Fattening?" Don't worry, girl, you'll be centerpiece at Christmas dinner.

Chapter Ten

The Day before Christmas at Yvette's

Constantine, December 24, 1957

WHILE THE GOOSE WAS being dressed at my home in Sidi Mabrouk, I spent the day before Christmas at the apartment of Tonton Gilles and Tata Yvette in Constantine.

Tata Yvette sat by her sewing machine, putting the last touches on the pink silk rose that would be the lampshade's crowning glory.

With her help, I had stretched white organza with pink dots on an octagonal wire frame and lined it with blue silk as a Christmas present for Maman's parlor lamp. Uncle Gilles, Aunt Yvette, their one-year-old baby, Jean Pierre, and I would soon drive from their apartment in town to my house, ten kilometers away.

Dimmed by snow clouds, the mid-afternoon shed a cold light through the voile curtains of the sewing room. The radio played quiet Christmas music. From the kitchen came the rattle of bottles of champagne Tonton Gilles lined up in cardboard boxes. Jean Pierre napped in his room.

Yvette put a finishing knot on the rose while I held the shade above her lamp to see how it would look lit from the inside. Delighted with its prettiness, I fished for compliments like a nine-year-old instead of a mature girl of thirteen. "Yvette, don't you think it looks pretty?"

"Of course. It is beautiful. You did a wonderful job."

"Do you think Maman will like it?"

She brought the rose to her lips and cut the thread with her teeth, "*Ma fille*, with your mother, one never knows."

"*Oui*, but don't you think this is the most beautiful thing she has ever had in the house? Don't you think she will be VERY happy?"

She handed me the rose. "I should hope so."

Keeping the shade at arm's length, I held the stem between forefinger and thumb, positioning the rose here and there against it, tilting my head from side to side, lips pouting, eyes appraising. Finally satisfied, I asked, "Yvette, how do you like this?"

"Try a little lower."

I moved the rose.

"*Très bien, ma fille.*"

I sat down, placed the shade on top of my knees, and began to attach the silky bloom. Yvette gathered the evening dress the Mayor's wife would pick up in half an hour. She arranged it delicately over her lap for last-minute touches and hummed softly along with the Christmas carols.

In this peaceful moment, I looked up from my work and observed her. The heels of her red-slippered feet rested on the highest rung of her chair, keeping her lap and the dress close to her hands. She had slender, tapered fingers crowned with long, almond-shaped nails. They glistened in shades of muted pinks as her right hand held the dress and the left pushed the needle through the fabric with swift, concise, and oh-such-neat stitches.

The lamp at her side shed a golden aura around her pert, attentive face, highlighting the auburn curls recently freed from the rollers that lay in a heap on a nearby chair. The flowered blue and cream robe she wore gaped slightly at the top, exposing a white touch of lacy slip. Her serene features and no-nonsense affection warmed me to my toes. I wanted to hold onto the moment, but Tonton Gilles came into the room rubbing his hands together as if washing them.

With a broad smile that stretched his trim moustache, he chanted, "How are we doing, my little chickadees?"

Yvette kept her eyes on her moving needle. "We are almost done. Have you finished packing the car?"

"Yes, the presents, the stuffed dates, the *oreillettes*, and Jean Pierre's bed and bag have been there for a while. I just put the champagne in the trunk. When do you think you'll be ready to go?"

Yvette got up, held the long dress by its shoulders, shook it, examined it closely, and put it on a hanger she hooked to the top of the half-open closet door. "As soon as Madame Fayet picks up her dress."

Tonton approached her, planted a big smacking full-mouthed kiss on her lips and, with a loving slap on her derrière, left the room, singing, "Are we going to have a smashing Christmas or what?" Then he returned, his laughing brown eyes sending coded signals to his wife. "Do you want to take a shower with me, Vivette?"

She gave a faint smile. "I already had my bath. All I need to do is get Jean-

Pierre ready and get dressed. Please, let him sleep until I can take care of him."

Always the tease, Tonton wiggled the stump of his right index finger under my nose and left, dancing a cha cha cha on his way to the bathroom.

Yvette glanced at the big clock ticking on the wall. "Gilles is really looking forward to spending Christmas with his sister. Let's hope your father will behave, for once," she said, and rose to her feet to get ready.

She was nearing the door of the sewing room when a tremendous explosion shook the building and echoed outside like a runaway roll of thunder. Fine dust came down from the ceiling. We searched each other's eyes, holding our breaths. I thought, *Too powerful for a grenade. It has to be a bomb—God knows how many people are hurt.*

Yvette cried, "Jean Pierre!" We both flew to his bedroom.

Her face pale and hard as an ivory cameo, Yvette banged the door open. The baby was standing in his bed, squealing like a stuck piglet. He cried so hard he could not breathe and his face had turned purple. Tonton Gilles ran in, razor in hand, face covered with shaving soap. Yvette picked up the child and examined him quickly then smacked him on the back until he took a breath. I sprinted to the kitchen and ran back with a glass of sloshing water. Yvette fed it to the baby. Water dribbled along his chin and coursed down her hand to the floor. This time, she did not mind the spill on her polished wood. Tonton, who until then had stood still, took his son in his arms, cooed and tickled him and rubbed his soapy face to his, until the child laughed. Suddenly, Tonton boomed, "Son of a bitch. *Le champagne.*"

His expression of horror, along with the soap on his face looked so clownish that Yvette and I burst out laughing, which did not please him at all. "Do you realize how much I paid for that champagne? Let's hope it was not blown to smithereens."

Yvette took the baby from him. "Where did you leave the car?"

"*Merde.* It sounded like the explosion took place in *la rue* Saint Jean. That's where I parked the car. We'll be darn lucky if we even *have* a car." He wiped his face, slipped on his boots and coat, and went out the front door without his hat on.

Meanwhile, as an accompaniment to the hard "Painpom, painpom" of police car and ambulance sirens, came, filtering through the dining room door, the faint clinking of tiny ice cubes against the walls of crystal glasses. I thought of Yvette's beloved crystal and fine china, and glanced at her. Impervious to everything but her child, she rocked the sighing baby whose cheek rested on her shoulder, eyes feverish, a frown puckering his forehead.

I approached the dining room door, turned the knob slowly, and gave a timid push with the tip of my fingers. Nothing came crashing down from the ceiling. I pushed more firmly with the palm of my hand. The door's bottom gritted against the wooden floor like fingernails against blackboard. I stepped into the room. Cold air blustered through the now paneless French window and broken glass crunched under my feet. Pinned to the floor at the hemline by a heap of shattered glass, the sheer, embroidered, hole-peppered curtain billowed like the wind-filled sail of a racing Clipper ship.

The smell of looming snow, mixed with that of dust from shaken buildings, permeated the air. In the street below, the scraping of running boots underscored anxious voices. Through the curtain, first snow flakes, and fading daylight, I could make out the buildings across the street—shutters destroyed, windows shattered.

I pivoted slowly on one foot to assess the damage. There were a few scratches on the highly polished rosewood tabletop and a myriad of tiny pieces of glass embedded in the floor and the wall opposite the window. To my relief, Yvette's wedding china, crystal, and her collection of precious objects stood untouched behind the china cabinet's beveled glass. The voile curtain had been sturdy enough to contain most of the blown glass and long enough to ensnare it at its bottom.

In the warm glow of the streetlights that had just flicked on, the litter of shattered glass at the foot of the curtain looked more like an open trunk full of scintillating diamonds caught inside a heavy spider web in Ali Baba's cavern than the fallout of a terrorist blast. And the shard-poked wall transformed the darkening room into an enchanted field of fresh snow, shimmering under the glow of an oil lamp.

However, enchanting or not, this mess needed to be picked up. I was at the hallway closet, collecting a broom, bucket, and dustpan, when the front door opened and Tonton Gilles came in. He stamped his feet on the entrance mat, looked up at Yvette and asked, "How's Jean Pierre?"

"He's eating a cookie. Was anyone hurt?"

"The bakery Bartin is leveled. A bomb was concealed outside the store. Lucky it malfunctioned and blew up after closing time. The Bartins were still in the backroom, cleaning up. They're hurt, but were able to walk to the ambulance."

Yvette helped Gilles remove his coat. "They are fortunate. Today, of all days. I'll go and see them the day after Christmas. By the way, how is your champagne?"

"All right. The car is fine and not one bottle blew its cork."

As if to celebrate the welcome news, the doorbell chimed.

Yvette hung Tonton's coat in the closet. "It must be Madame Fayet, coming for her dress." I grabbed my broom, dustpan and bucket and marched to the dining room. From there, I heard Yvette's and Madame Fayet's muttered comments as the client tried on the dress.

Must be talking about the blast.

"*Oui*," Madame Fayet said later, as she walked to the front door, "it looks like we'll have a white Christmas after all."

"I hope the snow will not stop us from reaching Sidi Mabrouk. Have a *Joyeux Noël*, Madame Fayet."

"You too, Madame Honninger. *Joyeux Noël*, and thanks again for the last-minute work on my dress."

"But it was my pleasure, *madame*."

Yvette closed the door and joined me. "*Non, non, non*. We are not cleaning now."

"But Yvette—"

"*Non*. Let's close the shutters. There will be plenty of time to clean up when I return. Besides, you have to get ready. We'll leave in twenty minutes." She clapped her hands. "*Fissa, fissa*," the Arab way of saying, "*chop, chop*."

Twenty-five minutes later, we were on our way. By the time we crossed the Sidi Rached Bridge, the snow was already accumulating. In the car lights, enormous snowflakes assaulted the windshield like a storm of converging meteorites while, beyond the side windows, they danced like graceful feathers floating in the lee of a rambunctious pillow fight.

Fifteen minutes later, we seemed to be plowing through the inside of a gigantic down comforter—warm harbinger of the wonderful family gathering in waiting. And the hypnotic whirl of snow beyond the car windows stirred visions of my twelfth Christmas, the previous year.

Chapter Eleven

Christmas Magic

Sidi Mabrouk, December 24, 1956

THE WEEK BEFORE MY twelfth Christmas, Debbah, Papa's Arab righthand man, Debbah's cousin, Ahmed, and two other workers from the cemetery's workshop carried the Christmas tree from the truck bed up the stairs and into the dining room. That tree was the tallest Christmas tree ever and Pa had to top it to make room for the star.

While the workers returned to the truck, Maman brought in the suitcase she had packed for Papa. "Be careful, *chéri*," she said, her voice tinged with anxiety.

Since the war of independence started, each time my father went on a job out of town, my mother waited in anguish until he returned. I worried, too. A lot. The thought that my papa might fall prey to a terrorist ambush and be tortured to death gripped my guts in a tight fist, and hard fingers pinched my throat so hard I couldn't even cry.

Zizou, the kids, and I stood close as Papa stuffed boxes of cartridges into the pockets of his sheepskin coat. "I'll be all right," he said. "In this cold, the *fellagha* aren't going to wait around. They know that people traveling at Christmas time join military convoys." He slipped the handgun Maman held out in his belt and grabbed the carbine. "Moreover, Debbah's a good man to have at my side. He's a fast learner; his aim improves with each lesson."

We followed our Pa and Ma to the door. "They predict heavy snow for the next few days; can't you postpone this job?" she asked, anxiety moistening her eyes.

"*Non*, I need to finish the Molineux's mausoleum cistern and cover it before the cement freezes or I'll have to break it all up and start from scratch."

"You'll be back on the twenty-fourth, right?"

"Early afternoon."

We all kissed Papa good-bye then stood at the top of the stairs and watched him drive away, Debbah sitting beside him in the cabin, the other workers hunched down under a canvas in the truck's bed.

Pinned onto the insipid-blue sky, the sun's pale glow did not dispel the bite of this December day, nor did it alleviate my worries. Once the truck disappeared at the bottom of the road, Maman hurried us back to the warmth of the kitchen's woodstove. "Come, children, we have a million things to do before Christmas," she said, failing to sound cheerful.

Christmas was the same every year, which felt good since it was one of the few times, along with Easter, when we were almost sure Papa would be in a good mood. To keep him this way, Maman served his favorite holiday dishes—which, Halleluiah!—also happened to be ours.

Our most prized Holiday pastries were *les oreillettes,* deep-fried pastry puffs smothered in powdered sugar and heaped in our large wicker basket lined with a bed sheet. The other delicacy that made me feel like I had died and gone to heaven were *les dates fourrées,* dates stuffed with a paste made of ground walnuts, rum, sugar, and a touch of rose water. Then, of course, *la pièce de resistance*: the goose stuffed with oysters— permeating every nick and cranny of our home with the aroma of its crackling skin.

We all went to work so that, upon his return on Christmas Eve, Pa'd find a house full of smells and tastes that would cheer his heart.

ON CHRISTMAS EVE'S AFTERNOON, I called from the dining room, "You can come now, Zizou, I finished the Manger."

My sister joined me at the sideboard.

I turned on the flashlight buried in the folds of the butcher paper I had shaped into the nativity grotto and focused the beam on the straw wad that would cradle baby Jesus. Zizou examined the white paint sprinkled over the grotto. "I did not know it snowed in Bethlehem."

"It's just that Christmas is not the same without snow." Feeling challenged, I added, "I like it better this way."

Zizou left a fingerprint on the round-mirrored tray I used as a frozen pond. "Catechism never said anything about frozen water either." She inspected the twigs that suggested a clump of trees. "And they had palm trees instead of these .... What are these sticks supposed to be?"

I blinked. "Well ... just trees. I imagine they could be ... olive trees or, maybe fig trees or ... date palms." Climbing on a chair, I stuck a cardboard star covered with silver chocolate wrapping on the wall above the scene. "And this is the North Star that guided the Magi."

Family portrait with Pépé Vincent, circa 1958.

"How can they see the star if it's snowing?"

I sighed. "It's Christmas, Zizou. Anything can happen on Christmas."

I glanced at the whitish-gray daylight beyond the window. "I really wish it would snow today. I can almost smell it."

She raised an eyebrow. "I wasn't aware snow had a smell."

"Oh, it does."

As if conjured by a magician's wand, snow began to fall. We ran to the French door and flung aside the curtains to watch the white flakes flutter like goose down. Zizou gawked at me. "You are a witch."

An inconceivable joy engulfed me. "It *is* Christmas!"

In the kitchen, the boys whooped and broke into a singsong. "It-is-sno-wing. It-is-sno-wing. Ma, can we go out?"

"No. I want you to be washed and dressed when Papa comes back from his trip."

She tried to conceal her worries about my pa, but I knew her well and heard the hitch in her voice. "He'll be cold and tired and if he arrives late, he will want to eat right away."

As I recalled my earlier wish for snow, the old cold fingers squeezed my guts. Just for a little while, I had forgotten Pa was on the road. Against the white thickening screen of falling snow, I pictured his truck on a remote mountain road.

Papa seesawing the wheel, trying to keep the skidding truck in check on the winding road. I heard the gears grind as he downshifted to avoid braking. I saw the chain-girded back tires glide sideways and drag the truck in a diagonal slide toward the snowed-in bank of a deep ravine. The men under the tarp at the back of the truck cried the beseeching mantra, *"Allahu Akbar! Allahu Akbar!"*

And I silently pleaded, "Oh, yes. God is great! God is great! *Allahu Akbar!*"

I opened the French door, stepped onto the balcony, and breathed in deeply. The freezing air burned my lungs and stiffened the small hairs inside my nose. I scanned the road. Not a single tire track marred the already thickening shroud of snow. I hung over the balustrade and stretched to see as far down as the bottom of the road, but Papa's truck did not round the bend. Tears slithered down my cheeks, and they weren't only the result of the cold air searing my eyes.

Maman called from the kitchen, "Nanna, you and Zizou have Mireille and the boys help you get some more wood. I want the house nice and toasty for your father."

We put on our coats and treaded to the woodshed at the back of the house. The sight of the fast-piling snow rekindled the boys' gripes. "Why can't we play in the snow?"

"Yeah, it's not fair—"

A faint bomb explosion reached us from a distance. No sooner had its dry bang faded than another followed, muted like a frail echo. Transfixed, we looked around, noses poking the air like hounds in search of a scent. But only fat flakes tickled our nostrils. Zizou's compressed lips dimpled her chin and her lashes quivered. "Nanna, do you think Pa's driving back through where the explosions were?"

"*Non,*" I tried to convince myself, to loosen the lump in my throat. "They seemed to come from Constantine, and Papa is driving from the opposite direction."

A bit reassured, Zizou nudged the boys. "Move it, *les gosses,* it's cold out here."

We carried armloads of splintered wood up the stairs, bounded down empty-handed and back up again with another pile, like a string of busy ants bringing choice morsels to their queen.

The logs stacked, we were standing at the *perron*, brushing wood dust and chips off our coats, when my ears perked at the familiar sound. Seconds later, the truck rounded the bend and, for the first time since Pa had left, I breathed freely. As Papa switched gears, the engine seemed to take a breath before charging up the snowed-in slope with a roar, exhaling oily smoke through its tail. Zizou's lips relaxed and her chin smoothed out. The kids pushed each other out of the way and raced to the kitchen. "Ma, Ma, Pa's coming."

Zizou and I hurried down the stairs, opened the gates, and stood guard with huge grins pulling at our cold-stiffened features until the truck turned into the yard and stopped. We pushed the gates closed and kissed Papa's frozen cheeks as he stepped off the cab. Zizou picked up his suitcase and we followed him up the slippery steps, along the corridor, and into the warm kitchen.

Stiff-fingered, Papa removed his fur hat, fur-lined gloves, and wool balaclava. Maman helped him shrug off his sheepskin coat and he plunked himself into a chair in front of the stove. "We made it through the pass just before the blizzard started to blow," he said through taut lips. His forest-green eyes glinted like two pools of melted snow reflecting nearby pines. His stubbled features seemed fossilized. Only his pale lips moved. "Nanna, take my boots off," he said.

I pulled hard on the cold rubber, almost falling on my ass as they came off, and peeled away two sets of those thick wool socks Maman liked to knit. Pa's feet were alabaster white, as if no blood flowed beneath the skin—glacial-looking and lifeless like the feet of the white marble angels at the cemetery—making my own toes curl in sympathy.

Maman ladled hot water from the stove's side tank into the blue enamel washbasin, cooled it with a dollop of cold water, set it down at Papa's feet then knelt in front of him and rolled up the cuffs of his pants. She gazed into his face. "Did you finish the job, *chéri*?"

He raised his chin to the ceiling and, whether from pain caused by his thawing feet or pleasure at their warming up, he closed his eyes and gradually lowered his toes deeper into the warm water. "*Oui*. That's why we left later than planned. Then we got caught in heavy snow halfway through the pass."

Maman rose to her feet and moved to the pantry, gathering ingredients for a *vin chaud*. "Did you encounter any problems?"

"None. But the cab heater didn't work, which didn't make a fuck of a difference since we had to keep the windows down—the only way to see where I was going. Drove most of the way with my head out my window, Debbah watching out his."

"Are Debbah and the men all right?"

"They were cold and a little shaken by the driving conditions but praising Allah by the time I dropped them at their homes in one piece."

While Papa spoke, Maman simmered a blend of red wine, cinnamon, orange zest, sugar, cardamom, and cloves until the sugar dissolved. Then, she strained the mixture into a glass and added a teaspoon of cognac.

The mulled wine soon worked its magic. Papa's skin regained color and he wiggled his toes in the cooling water, causing mine to relax in turn. Maman dried Pa's feet and sent Mireille for his slippers. He put them on and leaned back in his chair with a blissful sigh. Watching his handsome face relax, I nearly cried out, "*Oui*, God is great! God is great!"

Hung to dry over the stove's brass bar, the steaming socks, gloves, and hat exuded a wet wool tang that blended in with the opulent aromas of burning wood, roasting goose, and spiced wine.

Papa sniffed the air with a blissful smile. "It's so good to be home."

YESSS! My pa was home safe *and* he was happy.

Now we could surrender to the magic of Christmas and forget, for a while, the brutal world beyond our walls.

Papa Noël

FOLLOWING THE BOUNTIFUL MEAL, crowned with *la Bûche de Noël*—the rich, creamy, chocolaty Yule log—we cleared the dinner dishes and lined up our spit-shined shoes at the foot of the kitchen stove. "If you'd rather not have *le Père Noël* bring lumps of coal and old turnips instead of presents, you'd better shine those shoes," Pépé had warned, long ago.

Three years ago, though only nine years old, I had started playing along with Pépé's shoe-shine ritual and helped keep the belief in Santa alive for my brothers and sisters—that is until now, when Zizou and I knelt on the numbing tile and prayed, "Thank you, *Mon Dieu,* for bringing Papa safely home. Amen." We crossed ourselves and rose, ready to jump into bed.

Zizou whispered, "You know, Nanna, kids at school say that *Papa Noël* doesn't exist. What d'you think?"

Dying to instruct her on the realities of life, take her down a peg or two, I raised a scornful eyebrow, burning to say, "I think you're a little slow, *ma fille.* I have known *le Père Noël* doesn't exist since I was a year younger than you. Don't you think it's time for you to grow up?" Then I remembered my heartbreak at having to give up the jolly old man and his reindeers.

"Oh," I said, "I don't think those kids know as much as they think they do. Look at all the stupid things they tell about how babies are made—the stork, cabbages, getting pregnant by kissing boys, and other things that don't make sense. I can tell you: I know for sure *le Père Noël* exists. As a matter of fact I saw him, once."

"Are you teasing?"

I raised my hand and spat on the floor. "I swear I saw him. Thought I was going to have a 'heart'tack,' as Riri calls it."

The dubious set of Zizou's face said she did not believe me, but her searching eyes said she wanted to—making me take heart. She stood one foot forward, arms crossed against her chest, chin raised in challenge. "I'm listening."

I warmed to my task. *Better be good.*

* * *

"ET BIEN," I BEGAN. "It's like this. Remember that Noël when Papa, Maman, Yvette, Tonton Gilles, and Pépé Honninger went to midnight mass and dancing at *la Guinguette* afterward?"

Zizou nodded and I continued. "And Debbah babysat us? I think I was, maybe, eight and you, six. Before leaving, Maman said, 'Now, be good and listen to Debbah. You go to sleep now.'"

Thinking about that night brought back memories of how Ma looked standing at our bedside. So pretty in the green velvet dress Yvette had made for her. She wore the gold watch with the cursive digits under a domed glass Papa had given her when Riri was born, and the two rings that came from Mémé Honninger, her mother. One was gold with a Marquise-shaped ruby surrounded by small diamonds. The other a platinum octagonal Art Deco design with a diamond in the center from which radiated sixteen lines of diamond chips.

That was the ring I always felt had been created just for me. The ring which, from the moment of its conception, had longed to hug my finger.

Zizou brought me back to our conversation in her cavalier way. "That's all?"

"What's all?"

"How you saw le Père Noël?"

"*Ah, oui.* So, Maman told us to be nice and Tata Yvette laughed, shook a finger and added, 'Be careful. If, during the night, you hear noises in your room, it will be *Papa Noël* bringing presents.' She pointed at the row of shiny shoes set that year around the woodstove in our bedroom, then she said, 'Now, you have to know that *Papa Noël* is very shy and has been known to run off at the slightest suspicion of being observed. My goodness, once, in his rush to escape detection, he even broke a leg. You can easily imagine he never returned to the house; he fled in such a hurry.'"

I remembered that, at this horrible news, my heart had beaten a tattoo. "Never, ever?"

"Never." Eyes dancing, Yvette had stuck out her tongue at Tonton Gilles, who told her to stop her silliness, even though the smile stretching his mustache showed he adored her for it.

"So, how did Yvette's story end?" Zizou sighed.

"Well, she said, 'Above all, if you wake up in the middle of the night and hear noises, keep your eyes closed tight and do not dare move—'"

Impatient, Zizou snorted, "And *that* gave you a heart'tack?"

"But of course not. Even though I was excited, I fell asleep then something woke me up. I opened my eyes. By the dark gray light filtering through the shutters, I knew it was dawn. I turned on my side to go back to sleep, but caught a shift in the furniture's outline. Darker and rounder, it lumbered, heavy and slow, like the bear at the Amar Circus."

Zizou's eyes grew the size of award-winning bubble-gum bubbles. She panted, "What was it?"

Her fascination infected me and my voice turned to a whisper, "That's when I remembered what Yvette had said about *le Père Noël*. So I squeezed my eyes shut tight. Very tight. I breathed slowly through my nose and prayed *Papa Noël* would not hear my heart beat like the Boussadia's *tam tam* and make him run away and break a leg."

Zizou took a deep breath. "Do you think it was *Papa Noël*?"

I shrugged. "Who else could it be? After that, I didn't sleep a wink. I lay stiffer than Ma's ironing board and, I can tell you, nobody left or entered the room until morning."

"So, it *was* Him!"

"*Et bien, you* tell me."

Of course, I could not confess to my sister that, with each passing year since that night, I remembered piecemeal sounds of rustling paper and whispers. That I recalled shadows bumping into each other and a stifled giggle that sounded much like Yvette when she's up to no good.

However, proud of my white lie, I went to bed and tucked the blankets around my neck. "Go to sleep, Zizou. And remember; do not step into the kitchen tonight even if you're dying for a glass of water. Somebody might break a leg."

* * *

THE DAY AFTER CHRISTMAS, we learned that while we opened presents and basked in the comfort of our family holidays, other households grieved. News of the slain rolled off the daily's pages like rosary beads coursing through penitents' fingers.

The explosions we'd heard during our quest for logs while Papa was still on the road were only two of four that rocked Constantine that day. Killing nine people. During December 24th and 25th, attacks in Constantine and across the region resulted in thirty-one people slain and countless wounded. And, adding insult to injury, splashed across *Le Magrebien's* front page, French President René Coty grinned like he had just opened a wonderful Christmas present. The headline announced he had pardoned five Algerian terrorists on death row—*Good will toward men*. I gnashed my teeth. Who will pardon our slaughtered? Seal their slit throats? Restore their body parts? I wadded up the paper and threw it to the ground. Maman turned from the stove. "What is getting into you?"

"I hate Coty. Pardoning terrorists! They don't care who they kill. The things they do even to their own people." I wiped off tears of rage. A nauseous heat wave rose to my throat as I realized that, while I laughed and stuffed my belly with goodies, other children's guts blew apart. Still I shamelessly thanked God they belonged to other families. Not mine. Not this time. Then a certainty, hard and cold as an icy fist, punched me in the stomach.

The certainty that, never again, would I believe a kiss could turn a frog into a prince charming or a miracle free Lazarus from his shroud. A certainty that left me disoriented as I often am when exiting the cinema's snug hall—head full of images, sounds, and dreams, senses abruptly assaulted by the outside world. Transported from the safety of an artificial universe back to one where, for a split second, people and buildings, daylight and the air don an intangible, looming quality. A dissociation that makes my head swim and body seem to float like a kite in a sluggish wind.

ONE CONSTANT, THOUGH, THAT kept that kite tethered was the holidays. They marked the passing of the seasons, nudging us toward the next cycle of our lives as individuals and as a family. The predictable customs comforted even if they couldn't heal.

Whether religious or secular, celebrations served as a balm. When our native joie de vivre threatened to die, the holidays rekindled it. Killing the bold spirit engrained in the *Pied-Noir* soul would not prove as easy as our enemies believed ... not even after the FLN broadcast—"Hunt the infidels to take their land and their houses"—and its associated increase in terrorist attacks during the four months following Christmas.

Dimanche des Rameaux

Sidi Mabrouk, April, 1957

*W*HEN I WOKE UP, vision blurry with sleep, on Palm Sunday, I caught the faint glint of the *rameaux* hanging from the ceiling light. They looked like midget trees with trunks and bare limbs wrapped in gold foil. Each upturned branch held dangling tinsels and chocolate bells, eggs, rabbits, and chickens. I sighed. This morning there were only three *rameaux* gleaming in the morning light. At ten and twelve, Zizou and I were past the age when children were allowed to hold up the glitzy trees to be blessed at the ten o'clock mass.

Instead, we carried small olive branches Father Attar sprinkled with holy water. Later, we tucked them behind the cross above our parents' bed. The leaves dried there for a year until, on *Mercredi des Cendres*—Ash Wednesday— *le Père* burned them and rubbed their ashes on our foreheads in the sign of the cross. *"Poussière tu étais, poussière tu retourneras."*

At a younger age, the notion of "ashes to ashes" inspired me to stir the the cold cinders in our woodstoves, looking for signs of budding life—perhaps a baby. Finding none, I gratefully returned to the notion of cabbage patches and storks dropping babies down chimneys.

In later years, I found the prospect of turning to ashes after I died perplexing—what happened to Redemption and the promise to the righteous that they'd sit at the right hand of Our Father?

Better yet, how could God tell a pile of virtuous dust from a pile of bad dust? And, if saints and sinners ended up in an identical state, what was the point of being good?

After countless years of weekly Thursday afternoon catechism and Sunday morning ten o'clock masses, I made up my mind: I was born from nothing and would end up as nothing.

So ... what does that make me now?

I didn't even want to broach the subject with Zizou. She'd press her index finger against her temple and move it back and forth to imply I was crazy. I also knew better than to share my newly acquired conclusion that bringing a bunch of candies to be blessed at mass wasn't all that different from worshipping Aaron's golden calf. At the end of Palm Sunday mass, *le Père* appeared to agree with my reasoning. "Starting next *Rameaux*," he said, "I will bless only olive branches, as has been the Roman Catholic custom of this region."

Disgruntled exclamations rising from many of the assembled children and a few parents died away under the Father's withering glare. His strong voice rose into the restored silence. "This means that idolatry, in the guise

Two years later at Easter, 1959. House, front yard. Pépé Honninger, Mireille, Riri, Yves, Maman, Zizou, Nanna and two visiting friends.

of tinseled *rameaux's* blessings," he repeatedly struck the pulpit with a hard index finger for emphasis, "*will no longer be perpetuated in the church of Notre Dame.*"

Though I still harbored some resentment at *le Père's* banishment of First Communion frou-frous, and though it was painful to argue against chocolate—especially blessed chocolate—I felt *le Père* and I had become soul mates.

However, I dearly hoped he approved of Easter Sunday egg hunts as much as I did.

EACH *DIMANCHE DE PÂQUES*, my siblings and I galloped down the stairs to search for the eggs the stork had concealed throughout the garden. The grand black and white birds with long orange beaks and legs arrived in Constantine around springtime. They built bushy nests on top of the Kasbah's dwellings that threatened to spill over the edge of the Rhumel cliffs.

Of course, in addition to announcing spring and bringing chocolate eggs at Easter, the storks also brought good luck and babies. For years, Zizou and

I wondered how babies found their way home after the storks moved away in the fall.

"*Bien sûr,*" I had pondered, "cabbages must take over during the winter months."

"Unless it's real cold. Bad for the babies," Zizou mused.

"Then what?" I asked.

"I don't know!" she said.

ʙY THE AGE OF thirteen, I knew how babies were born and that Papa was not only Santa, but also the stork. I imagined him—a basketful of chocolate eggs swinging from the crook of his arm—as he tiptoed through flowerbeds like a mischievous djinn.

The image made me giggle. But what prompted him to give up his warm bed, early Easter Sundays, and steal into the cool outdoors? A flutter of guilt tickled my stomach. Papa was such an overwhelming force in our lives that I'd never realized how much he provided for his family, beyond the essentials. The realization of his secret caring washed over me, relieving the anguish that was kept alive by the constant outside threats. His love was more vital to me than food on our table, a roof over our heads, or even a gun in our hands.

If only Pa's caring could make the daily violence—the other constant in our lives—disappear. But that violence seemed to increase by the day, bleeding vitality from our communities like an ever hungry leech.

Yves and Riri at Jeanne d'Arc beach, 1961.

Chapter Twelve

Life Goes On

Spring, 1957

THE BLOOD-LETTING SPLASHED ACROSS the country's newspapers, echoed in the disembodied voices of radio broadcasters, the mouth-to-ear drone of *le Téléphone Arabe*, and the heartrending sobs of the victims' families.

I read the paper and listened to what I heard said around me and on the radio. The news buzzed inside my head like a swarm of killer bees, bringing visions of massacred European farmers and Arab peasants who had done nothing to deserve their death sentences. They toiled, day-in day-out, to scratch a living from the dry land and only wished to be left alone.

Learning the fate of seventeen kidnapped Arab families, I imagined terrified children crying out for their parents, the desperate wailing of their mothers and the swallowed moans of powerless fathers, husbands, and brothers. I couldn't understand their merciless mutilation at the hands of fellow Muslims.

Filled with unbounded pity for the victims and anger toward the terrorists, I reflected that, unlike the lambs sacrificed to the glory of Allah, the terrorists sacrificed to the glory of their cause the very brothers whose interests they claimed to serve.

I understood better, now, Papa's earlier explanation of terrorism: "Terrorists have a cause. They sacrifice everything, everyone—even their own lives in the service of that cause. They'll use whatever ploy necessary for that cause to succeed …."

Thus, a year earlier, three FLN women had placed bombs in our capital city, igniting a campaign aimed mostly at the French urban population. These bombings launched, the news had said, a blitz of eight hundred bombings and shootings a month that targeted cafés, cinemas, sports stadiums, buses, markets, and various other public places as well as increased attacks on farms. Even then, either out of habit, need, or defiance, the European civil population continued to patronize café terraces, sit in sports stadiums, ride buses, and shop at open markets as we used to before *Les Événements* started. Ultimately, the blitz resulted in what the newspapers dubbed, *"La Bataille d'Alger,"* during which French paratroopers hunted down the FLN cells entrenched in the city's Casbah.

Nevertheless, *fellagha* ambushes on country and mountain roads increased, forcing Papa to downsize his out-of-town business, restricting him to Constantine and its immediate surroundings. To make ends meet, Maman was soon forced to get a job as bookkeeper downtown.

After that, when I came home from school and opened the door, my house felt desolate and cold, as if I'd opened the door of a fireless woodstove in the middle of winter. Most of all, and even though I was thirteen, I missed my afternoon *café au lait* and *tartines* with Ma. My home felt like it had lost its soul.

As Maman pitched in to keep the pot boiling, Zizou and I picked up the slack at home. By the time our parents drove back late in the evening, we had fed the kids and put them to bed. These meals without our parents, and Pépé Honninger, when he was away, left a void inside me as empty as their vacant seats. I pined for Saturdays and Sundays when our home would be restored to its normal lunacy.

La Vie en Rose

ONE SUCH SUNDAY EVENING, Zizou and I were drying the dinner dishes, singing *"La Vie en Rose"* along with Edith Piaf. Everyone else lounged near the radio, waiting for *"La Nuit du Mystère,"* our prized Sunday mystery program, to begin. Maman knitted a sweater for Yves. Papa read one of his *"Le Saint"* mysteries. Pépé played *"Family"* cards with Mireille and the boys.

A radio announcement cut off Edith, leaving Zizou's and my mouths open in mid-song. A deep voice announced, "We interrupt this program for a newsflash." After a short silence, the voice trailed the sound of shuffled paper. "The FLN called for a general strike by Muslims to begin January 28 of the new year and made the following pledge: 'Moslem brothers, the partisans of the FLN will destroy and exterminate all Europeans, including their children.' "

All eyes zeroed in on Papa, who raised a hand to command silence while the deep voice continued. "Let's ask our station's political analyst what, in his opinion, prompted such declaration by the FLN."

A softer, more composed voice answered. "This is a new FLN terror campaign that is politically motivated."

"How so?" asked the deep voice.

"The FLN seeks to garner the attention of the Metropolitan French and the international community to their cause."

"Don't forget to mention the unconditional support of the FLN-ass-kissing communists," Papa muttered.

The radio host prompted his guest. "Can you expand on your allegation?"

"The FLN trusts the commission of atrocities will force the French military into harsh reprisals and torture to extract vital information from the terrorists, thereby fostering an international outcry substantiated by worldwide political and financial support to the benefit of its cause …"

I shut my ears to the ongoing dialogue. The evening glow was gone, "*La vie*" no longer "*en rose.*"

After a while, to my relief and that of my brothers and sisters, the regular programming resumed just in time for *La Nuit du Mystère*. We settled around the radio like chickens ruffling their feathers in preparation for a cozy night in the closeness of their coop.

We experienced this same closeness along with many others in our community when, at the end of the next Sunday mass, le Père Attar raised his hands aloft and preached, "Let us pray for the eternal salvation of the terrorists who burned the church in Vauban and those who bombed the church of Nedroma, killing ten of our brothers in Christ. Let us pray for the eternal peace of Dr. Brechet, indefatigable friend of the Muslim community, murdered in Bougie. Finally, let us pray for the souls of the slain Pères de Saint-Aimé and Bougie and for the grand Rabbi of Médea—that they may find their just reward seated at the right hand of our Lord."

The worshippers kneeled in a brouhaha of closing prayer books, displaced air, and creaking benches. Bathed in the sanctifying smell of burning candles and incense, we knotted our hands and bent our heads.

At the end of the Pater Noster, Père Attar raised his head. "And now, let us pray for our Muslim brothers slaughtered by their own brothers in Allah across our wonderful land, and for this month's latest victims in our beloved city of Constantine. Our sixty Christian and Muslim brothers who fell victim to terrorism earlier this week at the Négrier market. Finally," he added, opening his eyes, "let us pray for all grieving families that *Notre Seigneur,* in His great mercy, may bring them comfort in the prayer of our Lord. Amen."

Le Père dismissed mass and the congregation filed out in a quiet shuffling of feet. Outside, we took leave of each other in small, sober groups, our usual joviality muted in homage to the dead and polished Sunday shoes raising tiny puffs of dust.

My brothers, sisters, and I walked home, our stomachs growling from the morning fast in wait for the Holy Ghost, eager to shed the binding Sunday garb and dig into the dominical fare waiting on our kitchen table.

Changing into my housedress, I wondered once again how the prospect of a simple Sunday meal in the company of my family or even the worries I had about school could dim the suffering taking place every minute beyond the walls of my home. How could my life go on as if nothing was deadly wrong in our world?

Où il y a de la vie, il y a de l'espoir, People often said to soothe their worries. *Oui,* I gratefully concluded, where there is life, there is hope. It was no capital sin to allow life to go on by shoving aside other people's pain, at least for the space of a Sunday meal and—with luck and the help of neighbors like Monsieur Cavalier and his cinema—a little while longer.

Chapter Thirteen

Le Cinema de La Guinguette

Summer, 1957

ONE SUMMER EVENING FOLLOWING that Palm Sunday, Papa, Maman, and Pépé Honninger sat on chairs on the *perron*. The rest of us occupied the staircase like spectators on bleachers, waiting for *La Guinguette's* movie screen to light up and eating ice cream—a rare treat for us, even though we now had a *Frigidaire*.

Two months earlier, Monsieur Cavalier had opened an outdoor movie theater. He set up rows of folding chairs on his side lot. A tool shack served as projection room.

At first we joined the festive bazaar atmosphere in the company of people we'd known all our lives. Shared the comfortable cocoon of common experiences. We all wore our Sunday suits and were on our best behavior. Double-cheek-kissed close friends. Acknowledged acquaintances with a gracious incline of the head or doffing of the hat. Very proper. Very civilized.

Monsieur Cavalier sold tickets and candies from a round metal café table until the time came for him to start the show. No newsreels. Only the Saturday movie.

While black numbers and squiggles flashed on the screen, the spectators settled down in a rustle of shoes shuffling the gravel and throat-clearing coughs blurring the whisper of eucalypti and chirps of crickets.

I'd let out a sigh of contentment at the clack, clack, clack of the revolving reel and the dust-motted beam of the projector. Nothing can make you feel like one of the crowd the way sharing laughter during funny scenes does or holding your breath during dramatic moments. This laughter and breathlessness was shared by the Arab kids, who watched from the street side of the split bamboo screen in which they had cut viewing slits.

One evening, an Arab spectator sitting in the front row became so absorbed in the story that, to warn the good guy of the villain's creeping approach, he yelled and threw his shoe at the rogue. The screen heaved at the impact like a sail in a sudden squall, turning the spellbinding moment of suspense into comedy.

With *La Guinguette* entertainment straining our budget, Papa decided to take advantage of the screen's propitious location—its reverse side looked right smack at our stairs across an empty lot, allowing us to watch movies in homely comfort and *à l'oeil.*

While we watched our "free-of-charge" movies, Pépé chuckled, "Look at all these left-handed people." Yves opened his eyes wide in disbelief. "*Alors,* if so many people can use their left hand, why can't I?" Following a moment of amused silence and a few tics, Pépé teased, "And look at the cars; they're all driving on the wrong side of the street."

Watching movies from the reverse side of the screen didn't pose a problem until Monsieur Cavalier played a Swedish film in the original version and, read in reverse, the French subtitles became moot. Had it been an action movie, instead of mostly dialogue, we would've been able to follow the plot. But with this film, *Wild Strawberries*—a psychological drama by Ingmar Bergman—we quickly lost interest and one by one went to bed.

"Well," Zizou said. "At least we had our ice cream."

SADLY, WITH THE INCREASE of terrorist activities, people stopped going to *La Guinguette* cinema and Monsieur Cavalier folded the giant screen like a routed army folds its flag.

Chapter Fourteen

The Flies

That same summer, 1957

DURING THE SUMMER OF my thirteenth year, life went on—same as the previous one and the one before—leading us to search for entertainment whenever and wherever we could.

Weekdays, Maman worked downtown, leaving my sisters and me in charge of the house chores. Each day, before preparing lunch, Zizou and I washed and dried the previous evening's dishes and cleaned the floor. We found it faster to throw buckets of water laced with chlorine across the tiles and sweep it to the *perron*—the front door landing—and down the stairs. Once the floors dried, we closed the shutters and, in the penumbra, waged war on the perennial flies that, I could swear, spawned out of thin air.

We sprayed *Fly-Tox* throughout the house to eradicate invading insects. Later, heedless of the insecticide's acrid smell, we counted the flies lying on top of the bright kitchen table oilcloth.

One day, Zizou observed, "There are more today than yesterday."

"Yeah," I said, "but the day before we had a real hecatomb."

"What is that … etacome?"

"He-ca-tomb—means something like: lots and lots of dead bodies."

"Even for flies?"

"Why not?"

The flies lay flat on their backs, slender legs knitted in frozen ultimate prayers. Bodies so weightless, the slightest puff of air blown through pursed lips propelled them aloft like black snow flurries battered by crosswinds.

Most interesting were the few still left alive. Frenetic legs batting the air, frenzied wings buzzing against the gay oilcloth, they struggled in tight circles to right themselves. I thought of old men with lumbago striving to get up from their benches, reaching for canes that weren't there.

To help an insect turn its world right side up, I delicately picked it up by a single iridescent wing. Sadly, it refused to assist in its rescue. It batted its legs and free wing until the one I held detached from its body and remained stuck between my fingernails. The fly fell on its back again, traced taut circles using the lone remaining wing as a pivot point, and simply died.

I'm not sure why I felt guilty about killing the flies. After all, I'd seen them drink from sick eyes and runny noses, frolic among dead things, explore animal and human dung then alight on my marmalade. And there were so many of them—zillions. They drove me nuts.

Just the same, I felt sad that they had to die.

"Feeling sorry for dead flies?" Zizou was incredulous.

"It's not about dead flies. It's about killing them."

"Yeah. People are dying horribly every day and you worry about killing flies …." Her eyes glistened with tears. "What's wrong with you?"

At supper that night, Riri asked, "Papa, Nanna says she feels sorry for dead flies. Like it's wrong to kill them or something. Is it true?"

Papa studied me as if I were a fly drowning in his wine or, even worse, an unknown species from outer space. He shook his head. "What books have you been reading?"

"Just … books …."

"Books on Ahimsa?"

My face must have shown my puzzlement.

"That's the Hindu practice of non-violence and respect for life. Its original tenet is, do not injure, do not hurt."

"*Non* …. I haven't read about that."

Zizou asked, "What does that have to do with killing flies?"

Papa explained, "Hindus believe that all beings, and that includes plants and animals, are imbued with divinity. Because of that, all manifestations of life must be respected."

"I never read about that, Pa."

"Where, then, did you get that crazy notion of feeling sorry for dead flies?"

"I don't know, Pa. It's just that when things or people die, it makes me very sad."

Papa lit a cigarette, appraising me. As he inhaled, the set of his features and the expression in his green eyes seemed to say, "I understand how you feel, *ma fille*." Instead, words sharp as bee stings shot through the exhaled smoke, "You better keep a straight head on your shoulders, asshole, or you'll never make it in this world—"

At that moment Pépé Honninger entered the kitchen, unshaven, smelling of fish and sea salt. Papa's focus shifted from me to him. "What's wrong with you, Pierre? Are you looking for the *fellagha* to cut your throat?"

As long as I could remember, Pépé had always fished with his friend, Oscar, spending days on end at solitary beaches in Philippeville or Bône. *Les Événements* hadn't changed his rituals, which infuriated Pa and worried Ma.

Pépé's shoulders rolled in frustration. "I like to fish. I will not allow these murderers of women and children to control the way I lead my life."

I was so proud of him, I wanted to throw my arms around his neck and kiss him. But it was not our family's habit to hug and we only kissed our adults to say hello, good-bye, good morning and good night. Never to show affection. In addition, no matter how thrilling Pépé's heroic statement, kissing him on impulse would have led Papa to conclude that I preferred Pépé over him. That I was betraying him.

I often thought Pépé must be tired of sharing his house with our *shmala*—the crowding, the noise, and the ongoing antagonism between himself and Pa. I could see how fishing would be a good excuse to get away. Before *Les Événements,* I too looked forward to escaping to summer camp. To getting away from the crowds.

Maman turned from her cooking, lid in hand. "Papa, Riri is right. You might be killed or, worse, abducted. Then *you* tell the *fellagha* you won't allow them to slice you into bloody pieces." She banged the lid onto the pot. "And one of these days, you'll catch pneumonia"—she shook her head—"sleeping on damp sand!"

UNDAUNTED BY MAMAN'S REPROACHES, Pépé kept up his jaunts to the beach with Oscar. Once in a while, to placate my mother, he fished closer to the house, at *la Rivière des Chiens*. Since the start of the *événements*, fewer people hung around isolated spots and the Dogs' River's population of *grenouilles* and *anguilles*—frogs and eels—had exploded.

The very sight of *anguilles* made my taste buds salivate like a dog's when it ogles a marrow bone. Pépé hung the slippery eels by the gills, slit the black moiré skin from head to tail, and peeled it off inside out—like a glove—to reveal the firm, pink flesh. Once gutted, the eels were sliced into chunks, rolled into flour, and browned in olive oil till nearly cooked. After throwing in fresh parsley, minced garlic, and a cup of wine vinegar, Pépé covered the pan for the meat to simmer then served it with mashed potatoes or fried polenta. *Miam, miam!* There never was enough of it.

Les Grenouilles

THOUGH EELS MAY HAVE been the most mouthwatering of Pépé's dishes, his most spectacular one began that same summer with a bagful of live *grenouilles*. Hopping-mad, the frogs kicked at the inside of the canvas with even more gusto than Riri had exhibited while growing inside Ma's belly.

Zizou, the children, and I followed Pépé and his bag to the alley at the far side of our house. A thick hedge of dark green rosemary concealed the alley from the road below. I flinched when Pépé dropped the bag at the foot of the verbena shrub. My concern for the batrachians' welfare rose like mercury under the Sahara sun when Pépé snatched a frog from the bag he shoved into Riri's hands. "Here, hold the bag closed until I'm ready for the next one."

Six-year-old Riri gripped the canvas' opening so tight his knuckles blanched. Pépé wrapped his hand around the frog's back legs and we all inched closer for a better view as he brained the animal with the flat of the small axe, the one normally used to split kindling wood. Whack! We leapt backward.

Holding the upper body of the now dead creature, Pépé laid the still wriggling lower limbs on a woodblock and whacked them off at the waist. The boys gawked, I gulped, and Mireille's face turned white as Riri's knuckles. Zizou-of-the-batting-eyelashes stared, stone-faced.

We *all* stared, entranced, as one *grenouille* after another suffered the same fate—upper body thrown into the trash, severed wriggling legs into a bucket.

Puffed up with his duty as bag-holder, Riri warded off Yves, who insisted on grabbing frogs out of the bag and handing them to Pépé. I thought of my dead flies, their fate weighing little against this … this … animal version of the 1572 *Sainte Barthélemy* massacre in France.

The sweet verbena no longer perfumed the air. Not even the rosemary's bitter scent could mask the stench of river water, wet mud, and viscera. A sour tang swamped my tongue—a sign that I might soon add to the alley's slimy mess.

The last *grenouille*, a pretty one, brilliant green and bright-eyed, slipped from Pépé's grip. It hopped, erratic like a brainless spring, shifting course at sharp angles, the squatting boys in hot pursuit. Pépé chuckled.

Mireille cried, "Leave it alone!"

I echoed, "Just let it go!"

Zizou directed. "Over there, Riri. *Vite*, Yves, catch it. Oh, no, you missed again."

The frantic creature leaped blindly over the rosemary and landed on the road below. Zizou and I rushed to the hedge and looked over it. Eyes barely grazing the top, Mireille bounced up and down like a dribbling basketball.

Yves jumped on both feet like he was riding a pogo stick, "What's happening? I can't see!" Riri dropped to his knees and, ignoring Pépé's warning, tore a hole into the rosemary.

Down below, the frog bounded aimlessly then stopped in the middle of the road—flanks throbbing, eyes winking—unaware of the truck barreling its way. Riri shook the rosemary, releasing its strong scent. "Move, move."

Zizou clapped her hands. "Go, stupid. Go."

Mireille dropped into a crouch next to Riri. By the time Yves joined them at the viewing hole, one tire was closing in on the green beauty. Encouragement burst in varied pitches: "Run." "Jump." "Get away." "Move." "Go ... GO."

The creature remained stock-still. The exhortations dropped to an abrupt silence filled only by the truck's rattle. In a trance, I watched the wheel roll over the creature. Heard the pop of exploding skin. The squish of entrails. The crushing of bones.

My siblings' sudden ovation drowned out my heartbeat and yanked me back to the scene. I focused on the macadam. No exploded skin. No squished entrails. No crushed bones. Not even the live frog. I blinked. "Where is it?"

With a triumphant smile, Zizou pointed across the street, at the foot of the neighbor's wall. "Over there. See it?"

I squinted against the sun's glare. The frog hunkered in the wall's shade—flanks still throbbing, eyes still winking. I sighed, happy that my vision of the squished *grenouille* was only that—a mental picture.

After hosing down the alley, Pépé showed us how to skin frog legs—pulling the skin down like a pair of long johns, same as rabbit fur.

We followed him in solemn procession up the stairs and into the kitchen, where he prepared *Cuisses de Grenouilles à la Provençale*—frog legs sautéed in olive oil with garlic, parsley, thyme, and tomatoes. It was served with Potatoes in the Oven *à la* Elise—Maman's own recipe—and a side of braised endives.

The blood and gore should have curtailed my appetite, but the pretty *grenouille's* escape had taken the edge off my remorse. "*Ooh là là*. Was this good, or what?" the boys licked their fingers and Zizou asked. "Can I have more?"

Apparently, eating legs of butchered frogs didn't repulse her as much as Pépé's *Lapin Chasseur* after he broke her rabbits' necks. I couldn't resist giving her a poke. "*Yaa*, Zizou, don't you think frog meat tastes like rabbit?"

She set down the dainty bone she sucked on. "How would I know if I don't eat rabbit?"

Riri beat the rung of his chair with the heel of his shoe and grinned. "Yeah. It tastes just like fishy rabbit."

Yves stuffed his face. Mireille sighed dreamily. "I'm *so* glad the little *grenouille* got away."

Zizou said, "Me too." She picked another meaty leg. "It was too small anyway."

ZIZOU'S APPRECIATION OF BIG frogs came into focus weeks later when we discovered the father of all batrachians. It had sought refuge from the summer drought in the shade of the water meter niche. There it huddled under the leaky pipe like a starving puppy at its mother's tit. We crouched down and had a look.

Zizou wondered, "You think it's dead?"

"It looks like it's breathing."

Zizou rose to her feet, left, and came back with a twig. She poked the animal and it squeezed even farther behind the pipe. "It's alive and lots bigger than Pépé's frogs."

"Of course it's bigger. It's a toad."

"What's the difference?"

"Can't you see it's fatter than Pépé's frogs?"

"It looks more chubby."

"Chubbier. The biggest toad can be as big as twenty inches and the females even bigger than that." I indicated the tightly folded legs. "You can't really see them, but they are shorter than frog legs, too." I grabbed the twig and touched it to the bumps above the protruding eyes. "*Et là*, you have the parotid glands."

Her brows shot up. "What do they do?"

"HA." I let her hang on a little, for effect, then blasted, "POISON glands."

"You mean toads bite?"

"*Non.* Toads don't have teeth like frogs do but …." For once I had her undivided, perhaps respectful, attention. I stretched the moment. "They have"—I waved the twig like a magic wand and traced a couple of the brown bumps on the skin—"WARTS."

Her eyes dilated. I pushed my advantage. "They also have poison glands, but the poison is not as concentrated as in the parotid glands."

Her eyelashes batted. "How d'you know all that?"

"Science class," I preened, satisfied I had demonstrated my thirteen-year-old superior knowledge.

"*Oui*, but d'you think these legs are good to eat?"

My intellectual King Kong breast-thumping blown to smithereens, I spat, "Idiot, I just told you toads are poisonous. The glands' fluid is toxic if you swallow it."

She flicked her hand in the air. "Baah." Then she stood, took the stairs two at a time, and returned at a gallop, with Maman's big scissors.

I felt them cut into my guts. "What are you going to do?"

"These legs may be shorter, but they're lots fatter than those frog legs of Pépé's."

"Zizou—"

She knelt, reached into the niche, and pried the bunched creature from its sanctuary; held it by one back leg while the other pushed frantically toward freedom. She adjusted her grip and placed the scissor blades on each side of the toad's thigh, at the hip joint, just like when Maman carves a chicken.

"Stop that."

"I'll get you, little suck—" The frenzied frog released a stream of urine that hit Zizou smack in her yakking mouth. She let go of the leg and scissors.

"Spit, Zizou. Spit."

She spat. "Don't swallow. Spit." In a panic, I picked up the end of the garden hose and turned on the water. "Open your mouth and don't swallow." I flushed the inside of her mouth. "Don't swallow, you hear? Swish and spit." I shoved the hose into her hand, ran upstairs, two steps at a time. "Swish and spit, ma Zize." I dashed into the house, to the kitchen cupboard, back down, and gave Zizou the lump of sugar I had fetched. "Here rub your tongue with this."

She stared at me, cow-like.

I grabbed the sugar "*Allez, tires la langue.*"

She stuck her tongue out. I held it the best I could and rubbed it with the sugar, but her tongue recoiled into her mouth like a slimy snail into its shell. "Push it out, I told you," I screamed, hysterical.

Words rolled down her drooling tongue, "Eet heult."

"Spit! You have no idea how poisonous this can be. First you'll get HUGE warts and then YOU'LL DIE. Spit."

A none-too-sweet statement followed her last syrupy spit. "*T'es pas folle?*"

"*Non,* I'm not crazy. You better thank me for my fast thinking. I saved your ...." A horrible doubt assailed me. "You didn't swallow while I ran upstairs, did you?"

She shook her head. The water hose was still running, capital sin in these parched times. I turned it off. Zizou flicked her tongue in and out to cool it off. I pointed at it. "You may still get pimples on there, you know."

She immediately coiled her tongue back inside. "How d'you know about toads' poison and sugar?"

"I read it."

"Where? In Maman's medical books?"

"*Nonnn ....*"

She squinted. "Where, Nanna?"

"In a book."

"What book?"

My eyes searched the yard. "I wonder where that toad went—"

"Don't change the subject. What book, Nanna?"

"My wise woman's book, IF you want to know."

"What? My tongue burns like hell because you believe that stupid book of yours?" She paused, one foot forward, hands on hips, head tilted up, tongue back in its natural habitat, wagging. "The same book where you got the brilliant idea to use a coin on Mireille's forehead when she fell off the swing?"

I nodded, sheepish.

A spark that had nothing to do with the reflection of the white-hot sun above ignited her gorgeous hazel eyes. Her lips parted to display her perfect white teeth. And she laughed.

She laughed with gusto, mouth wide open, raw tongue dripping clear threads of saliva onto the sizzling concrete at our feet.

Water Shortage

THE SIZZLING WENT ON all summer, until a serious draught compelled the city to cut off the water from six o'clock in the morning to six o'clock in the evening, when people did some washing up, dishes, light laundry, and stocked up on water to last them through the next day.

Then there was no city water at all, and military cistern trucks had to dole out the precious liquid. Europeans and Arabs, young and old, queued like slow-moving trails of ants hoping to take a bite at a juicy scarab. They brought Jerry cans, pots, pans, buckets, earthen jugs, and who knows what else. Their containers filled, they carried them home with mincing steps—careful not to waste a drop.

One August day, Maman dispatched Mireille, Zizou, and me to a spot she knew in the field across the road where water welled from an underground source. When we arrived with our pails, Arab girls were already lined up. The oldest ones—about my age, thirteen—carried metal or earthenware containers atop their heads. A few bore toddlers slung across their backs or straddling their hips, while slightly older children clung to their skirts. The little ones wore short tunics, once white. Flies collected around their eyes and runny noses. Most were barefoot. The empty-handed little boys had shaved heads; the little girls, carting small pots and jugs, wore braids entwined with colorful rags.

I knew a few of the older girls by sight. They returned my nods as my sisters and I took our place at the end of the line.

Water collecting was slow and tedious—a girls-only job. They scooped up water with a cup as it gurgled out of the ground and emptied it into their containers. The teenager whose turn it was to kneel at the edge of the hole beckoned us to come down the line and take her place. I smiled and shook my head. "*Non, merci.*"

Zizou poked my back. "*Vas-y.* It's hot here."

I frowned. "We can't go." I motioned at the girls ahead of us. "They were here before us."

"Well, they want us to go first."

"How would you like to wait a long time in this sun and have someone go ahead of you?"

"Why do you think they want us to go first?" she challenged.

Mireille offered, "Because we are French?"

Zizou shook her head emphatically. "*Non.* That wouldn't be right."

I thought aloud, "Maybe … because they come here often, they believe the spring belongs to them …." I paused, trying to compose my thoughts.

"*Et …?*" Zizou prodded.

"And … They think we are their guests and guests always go first."

Mireille said, "I like that."

"I guess you're right." Zizou rolled her eyes and stepped back in line.

The heat sucked every bead of moisture out of our pores. "*Merde,*" Zizou said. "I feel like I'm turning into a dry date."

Eyes half-closed against the glaring sun, I watched the girl bailing water and realized we didn't have a cup. I squeezed Mireille's shoulder. "Go home and get a cup to scoop the water."

Zizou and I arrived at the head of the line before Mireille returned. The girl ahead of us moved her filled clay urn to the side and shook her cup at me. "*Tiens,* use this."

I asked, "Aren't you going home?"

She shrugged. "I can wait."

I thanked her and passed the cup on to Zizou. She had started filling her pail when Mireille arrived with our cup.

I returned the girl's cup. "*Merci beaucoup.*"

She tied the cup handle to her belt then bent down at the waist and, in a smooth, gracious motion, lifted her two-handled urn, balancing it on a folded cloth on top of her head.

"What's your name?" I asked.

With the back of her hands, she whipped her braids over her shoulders. "Amira."

"It's a pretty name."

"It means 'princess,'" she said, and added with obvious pride, "It also means 'prosperous.'" Then she walked away, her ankle-length skirt twirling around her legs. She glided on her bare feet, ankle bangles clinking, moving like a grown woman. Back erect, hips swaying. I watched her go, embarrassed by my flat chest and boyish hips.

Zizou posed beside her full container, fists balled on her hips. "Are you going to fill your pail or not? I don't want to turn into a dry date, you know."

Back home, we dumped our water into the oval zinc tub at the foot of the stairs.

The water sloshed in and swirled, conjuring wistful visions of the water bouncing over rocks at *La Rivière des Chiens*.

Chapter Fifteen

Mireille and the Tub

La Rivière des Chiens: The Dogs' River. That's where Papa took the family for a day to cool off the following Sunday. When we returned from the river, Maman went up to the house to start dinner. The rest of us unloaded the Citroën. Papa checked the carburetor and oil level.

While carrying the picnic things to the house, I glanced at my siblings. They had the rosy glow of turkey meat when you prick it and the pink fluid tells you the bird's not yet cooked.

Maman called from the kitchen, "Nanna, put the bathing suits and towels to soak in the tub, will you?"

I stepped down to the bottom of the stairs—our faithful zinc tub's quasi-permanent dwelling. It wasn't there. "Zizou, d'you know where the tub is?"

She marched down the stairs and searched the front and back yard, and the front yard again before yelling, "Anybody seen the tub?"

Eerie silence.

Done with his carburetor and oil level, Pa slammed the car's hood shut. He wiped his hands on a rag and lit a cigarette. While returning the pack of *Gauloises* and matches to his breast pocket, he contemplated his gathered brood through exhaling smoke. "Where's the tub?"

The unanimous answer came in various pitches. "I don't know," which translated into, "Don't even look at me. Whatever it is, I didn't do it."

Papa blew another coil of gray smoke. "Who used it last?"

I glanced at Mireille. Four different pairs of lips harmonized, "*Pas moi!*"

Papa zoomed in on she who hadn't replied. "Mireille?"

Her voice cracked. "*Moi.*"

"Where is it?"

She pointed to a spot in the front yard. "I left it over there."

We turned as one. "Over there" revealed nothing but patches of dry grass.

Papa picked a tobacco fleck off the tip of his tongue. "What was it doing there?"

Head down, Mireille whispered, "I was taking my doll for a ride, and Zizou called me to peel potatoes." She bent her head. "I picked up my doll and left the tub there." She pointed at the empty space again.

"You better find it." Papa spoke to Mireille but clearly addressed all of us.

Convinced the thing had found a self-anointed new owner, we searched with make-believe zeal. In desperation, smart-ass Riri explored the inside of the trashcan with a fervor that set off nervous giggles soon stifled when we realized the magnitude of the loss and pending retribution.

The tub had been in our lives since I don't know when and had always served whatever purpose was required—laundry, water tank, baby bathtub, even cradle. Once, before Pépé Honninger put a stop to it, it even served as a sleigh after a heavy snowfall one January day.

Zizou and I had plunked a delighted two-year-old Riri in it and dragged him through the snowed-in yard. The tub, valiant soldier and reliable servant, suffered a few leaks, which put it out of commission until the Gypsy tinker showed up in the spring. He added a couple of solder beads to the ones already there. They looked like tears of silver—testimonials to this faithful old friend's tormented saga.

Now, it seemed the tub's saga would go on in the service of strangers who'd have no idea of the sentimental loss they'd inflicted on us and of the immediate physical retribution Mireille was about to receive.

To his persona of Inspector Vincent, Papa added that of judge, jury, and executioner—Mireille had been neglectful. The tub was no more. The die was cast.

Pa shook his head as if powerless against the dictates of fate. He raised his hands to his belt buckle and moaned around the smoldering cigarette, "What am I going to do with these bastard kids?"

Even though we all stepped back to widen the space between him and us, we were not too concerned. We knew the drill.

First, he'd warn, "Don't force me to take my belt off." Meaning that once unbuckled, the belt had to come off and, in all fairness, he must wield it.

Typically, when Papa's hand erred toward his belt, one of us pleaded, "*Non papa. Non.*" His green eyes narrowed. The corner of his mouth pushed his cheek up a bit, then he'd nod. "Ah*, bon.* Behave yourselves, then. You hear? Because next time …." He'd let his hands drift from his waist to his breast pocket in search of a cigarette and would leave.

This time though, the belt came off.

The strategic circle widened, exposing the sacrificial vestal. Mireille begged, "*Non,* Papa. *Non.*" But this time, the plea held no magic. It was "*Maktoob.*" Preordained, as we say in these parts.

The belt struck.

Mireille screeched, "*Non,* Papa!" The poor soul wore the little white dress with red polka dots she favored. The thin nylon did nothing to absorb the blows, and her skin, already glorious sunset-red, sent distress signals like a frantic mirror. As for us onlookers, the goose pimples raising the hair on our skins had more to do with sympathy pains than natural reaction to sunburn.

We searched each other's faces. Amazed. Thrashed? Mireille? *Incroyable.* Hadn't Papa decreed that, because of her heart murmur, we must be tolerant and kind to her?

Convinced she used her affliction to get away with things, we often teased, "Oh, *la pauvre* Mimi, she has a *souffle au coeur.*"

I'd whimper, "I have a *souffle au coeur,* be kind to me."

Zizou clasped her hands upon her heart and say in sorrowful, accented Greta Garbo fashion, "Me toooo. Me toooo."

The boys mimed blowing into a balloon. "*Souffle, souffle.*"

And Mimi cried.

In time, the spontaneous spring of her tears won her the nickname of "Tsunami Mimi."

That day though, Mimi's stricken look and real tears inspired true pangs of empathy. As always, though, Papa's anger did not last. He threaded his belt back on, hiked his pants, and buckled up. He walked to the front gate and started up the road, saying to no one in particular, "Tell your mother I am going to *La Guinguette.*"

For a while, the skin on Mireille's limbs and back displayed stripes a hue darker than her sunburn. Riri smirked, "Hey, Mimi, if you wear your white dress with the red dots, then when these marks turn blue, you'll be just like the French flag—*bleu, blanc, rouge.*"

And Tsunami Mimi struck again. In time, Mireille's bruises turned blue, green, yellow, and then faded away—but not so the memories of our lost tub, tied forever to countless chapters of our lives. Most pleasant, some sad, a few funny, like the episode of the jumping liver, seven years earlier.

The Jumping Liver

Summer, 1950

THAT DAY, MY SIX-YEAR-OLD chest puffing up like the breast of the rooster in our poultry yard, I had helped Maman gather the dirty lunch dishes when lots of *pipi* ran down her legs. Grunting with the effort, she wiped the floor with a rag and called my pa, "It is time, Riri."

Papa and Pépé Honninger helped Ma down to the car. Then Pépé climbed back to the top of the stairs, where two-year-old Mireille, four-year-old Zizou and I stared anxiously at him. Pépé rolled his shoulders and his thin lips faked a smile. "Maman's going to have the baby."

I pulled at his pants' leg. "Did *le bébé* do *pipi* in Maman's belly?"

Pépé stared at me. His magnified eyes blinked behind the smeared lenses. "Hmm ...." He thought for a moment then licked his dry lips and bent down to pat my cheek. "*Oui .... Oui, ma petite. That's it. Le bébé* did *pipi.*" He took Mireille and Zizou's hand. "Let's take a nap. Come, Nanna."

"Can I finish cleaning the table, Pépé?"

He looked like he heard me but was thinking about something else. "All right, but after that, you'll take your nap."

The kitchen was dark. Forbidden to climb onto the window ledge to push open the shutters, I rose on tiptoe and flicked the light switch. Compared to the brilliance of the outdoors, the ceiling light was cold and sad, and the dirty dishes, stained oilcloth, and smell of fried fish made me feel miserable and lost.

I wanted to cry, but remembered Maman as she dried her legs, grunting as if she hurt. I contemplated the mess around me and, thinking Maman was going to be too tired to do the dishes when she came home with the baby, I pushed a chair up to the sink and climbed onto it.

How does Maman do it? The dishrag hung on the lip of the sink. The plug stood on its side against the wall tile. *Ah, oui.* I plugged the sink. Slid off the chair and, one by one, carefully dropped the dirty plates, flatware, glasses, and frying pan pell-mell into the sink. Then I climbed back onto the chair, turned on the water tap. It sneezed and coughed and shook like a wet dog, reminding me that the city cut off running water during the day. I climbed down and went to the water-filled zinc tub that stood beside the stove. I dunked the bailing pan hooked onto its handle into the water and emptied it into the sink again and again until it was filled and the front of my pinafore was dripping wet.

Once more, I climbed onto the chair. Great globules of fat floated to the water's surface like monster-fish eyes that darted and grabbed my arms as I submerged the dishrag. I yelped and quickly withdrew my hands, pinching my lips in disgust. Water washed over the slanted drying board, sloshed over the sink lip, soaking the front of my dress and my bare feet beneath. *It's not like this when Maman washes dishes. I don't know what I'm doing wrong.* I sniveled, wiped a fly off my nose, smearing the stench of fish across my face.

Maybe I'm stupid, like Papa says. Sobs bubbled up from inside my chest like hiccups when Pépé's voice made me jump. "What are you doing?"

"I'm washing the dishes, Pépé."

"Didn't I tell you to take a nap?"

"Yes, but I asked if I could clean the table first, Pépé, and you said yes."

He put his hands on his hips and nodded. "You're right. Now, why are you crying?"

I made a face. "I smell like fish."

He came to the sink and laughed. "*Bien sûr, ma petite*, you are using cold water and no soap." He dragged the chair aside, with me still standing on it. "*En plus*, you are not supposed to put everything together in the sink at once. The least dirty go first." He emptied the sink of dishes, pulled the plug, and set a pan of water to heat on the stove. Then he poured the hot water into the sink, explaining as he went. "And you add a little cold water." He grabbed the soap from under the sink, "And soap. Now, tell me, which of these dishes are the least dirty?"

I studied the sheen coating the heap of dishes. They all looked dirty to me, but I had to choose. "The glasses?" I clapped my hands when he nodded. He sunk the glasses into the soapy water. "Then you wash the flatware, the plates, and, finally, the frying pan."

When the washing was over, Pépé unfolded a clean dishtowel. I asked, "Can I help dry?"

He stretched his neck to one side then the other. "Maybe tomorrow. Go, take a nap, now."

My dishwashing attempt must have impressed Pépé as, when I woke up, he asked, "Want to learn how to cook liver?"

My chest filled again like the rooster's breast when he fluffs up his shining green, red, and purple feathers. I had never felt that important before. Now, I believed I could do anything.

I watched Pépé cut up the calf liver into pieces. While they soaked in milk, we gathered parsley and garlic from the garden and chopped them. "Now, be careful," Pépé warned. "These knives are very sharp."

I nodded.

* * *

A FEW DAYS BEFORE, THE tinker man had stopped at the roadside by our house and set up his grinding wheels. When he rang his bell to announce he was ready for business, Maman brought down all her knives and scissors. While she waited, my sisters and I sat on the slope at the roadside and watched the wheel grind against the knives and create flying sparks. They dashed in all directions like the golden hair of angels in a windstorm. I wondered whether the sparks burned or caressed, but they didn't seem to affect the tinker man either way.

The pull of the fleeting sparks became irresistible. I got up from the grassy knoll and approached the spinning wheels. The grating racket of the blades connecting with the stone along with Maman's stern warning stopped me near enough to the wheels to smell the hot metal and marvel at the sparks' orange, blue, and gold flickers. Spellbound, I extended a cupped hand to catch the lively fireflies, but Maman grabbed my arm and pulled me back to the knoll. "Sit down here or go back to the house."

Embarrassed at being scolded in public, I stomped toward the house, heavy-hearted, wondering what I had done wrong. *Now, I will never know if the sparks caress or burn.*

* * *

"KEEP YOUR FINGERS CURLED behind the blade, like this." Pépé's voice brought me back to the kitchen table, to the garlic cloves and bunch of parsley.

I kneeled on a chair and followed his instructions. "*Comme çà,* Pépé?"

"*Oui, comme çà.*"

Unconvinced that my chopping looked at all like his, I watched Pépé from the corner of my eye to discern whether he was serious. I concluded that he must be, since his thin lips seemed to smile and the rest of his face looked sincere. Reassured, I followed his lead and wiped my hand on his dishtowel, then crossed my arms on the table and sighed contentedly. "What do we do now, Pépé?"

"Now ...." He patted the liver pieces dry and spread flour in a plate. "We coat them with flour and fry them in olive oil."

The kitchen filled with the wonderful aroma of sizzling meat as Pépé browned one side then the other in a shower of spitting oil. The last piece he flipped on its raw side immediately jumped out of the pan into an arch and splashed into the water-filled tub at the side of the stove. I screamed and jumped back in surprise, then squatted, hands on the tub's rim, nose almost touching the water. My eyes searched beyond the faint reflection of my face and latched onto the half-browned liver, zigzagging lazily in its descent to the bottom of the tub.

Still crouching, I craned my neck and looked up at Pépé. He held his grease-dripping spatula aloft, glanced at the drowned meat then looked at my face and chuckled, "*Attention.* It's alive."

My head snapped back to the liver. It stirred. I jumped to my feet with a shriek and held onto his pants. "It's not dead, Pépé?"

"It was cut up into pieces. Of course it's dead." He laughed as I had never seen him laugh before and I laughed along with him. Then I asked, "What's funny, Pépé?"

"You, *ma petite*. You should have seen the look on your face when the liver jumped."

He raised his chin from side to side to stretch his neck. Then he bent down and grabbed the piece of liver. It dripped, gray and sad.

"What do we do now, Pépé?"

"We'll dry it and finish cooking it with the other pieces; then we'll throw in the parsley, the garlic, and add some vinegar."

I curled my lips in disgust. "But it's dirty, Pépé."

"On the contrary, *ma petite*, it got washed twice." Then with a twinkle in his eyes he whispered, "But let's keep it a secret between you and me, *d'accord*?" He chuckled again, making me giggle.

I never knew Pépé Honninger could be so nice and funny. His laughter made me feel so good that I wanted to throw my arms around his neck and kiss him.

But I knew I shouldn't.

I knew it wasn't right to love him because when he and Papa argued, Papa was always right. My heart told me so. He was my pa. He was beautiful and knew everything about everything. I wanted to please him all the time. And I wanted him to love me. But, even though I knew because Papa didn't like him that Pépé was not a nice man, today, like this, Pépé and me alone, I felt good being with him. Still, Papa wouldn't like me kissing him. So I didn't.

It was much better to love Pépé Vincent, Papa's Papa. Pa would never get mad at me for that. Besides, I loved my Pépé Vincent with all my heart.

Pépé Vincent

FROM MY FIRST MEMORY of him, Pépé Vincent had been *MON* Pépé. He was all mine and I was all his. In fact, I loved him even more than I loved the crunchy-honey *zlabeiyas*. I understood "Pépé" was his name like Papa was Pa's name and Maman was Ma's name.

In my heart, the name "Pépé" held the magic warmth I felt when my hand became lost in his rough paw or when he smiled at me. But then I met Pépé Honninger and was told to call him Pépé too. When I cried and stubbornly refused, they explained that a pépé is the papa of a papa or the papa of a maman.

But how could this be? How can a pépé be a papa? If Pépé Vincent is the papa of Papa and Pépé Honninger is the papa of Maman, *alors*, does that mean Papa and Maman are my Pépés too? I kept getting more confused as each explained in turn and then asked, "Do you understand, now?"

I'd poke a finger into my nose and shake my head. "*Nonnn.*" In the end they gave up. Papa turned his back on me and said to Maman, "She's bloody stupid."

I cried. Maman blew my nose and was mad. "How can you speak like this about your own daughter?"

Papa said, "She's your daughter. Not mine."

This was another thing that I didn't understand. When I was good, Papa said I was his daughter, but when I was not so good he said I was Maman's daughter. I tried hard to please Papa so I'd be his daughter all the time, but then things never seemed to stay the same and I did not know why.

Papa must be right, I am bloody stupid—even though I can't see any blood on me, I still must be stupid. Maybe I will understand when I am older, like Maman says.

I came to realize that the magic that made *my* Pépé Vincent unique was not in the word "pépé." Rather, it was that the magic lived deep inside him. It was in his warm eyes and in the smile that showed his big teeth underneath his square moustache. It was on his bulbous nose with the blue dot on the left side. It was the smell of his cologne, cigarette smoke, and dry cement.

IN TIME I UNDERSTOOD that even though there were lots of Pépés in the world, Pépé Vincent was unique. That he was still all mine and I was still all his.

I went on loving him with all my heart, still even more than the *zlabeiyas.* Until many years later when I was fifteen and he lay in bed, dying.

Chapter Sixteen

Une Glace à la Vanille

July, 1959

TWO WEEKS AFTER MY fifteenth birthday, I leaned my forearms against the railing of my bedroom's second-floor balcony. Behind me, Pépé Vincent dozed in his sick bed. In the yard below, my brothers raised sprays of gravel, playing soccer. My sisters took turns swinging one end of the jump rope, the other end attached to the gate.

From my window, I watched the rare car and the inevitable military vehicle speed along the street. Sitting in the back of the trucks, young soldiers whistled and waved at me. Though their rowdy calls led me to think I might be attractive, bolstering my ego, I feigned indifference.

I burned with the desire to wave and blow kisses back at them, but it was simply not done. Especially not under the averted eyes of our Arab neighbors, subtle as Abel looking upon Cain. Not unless I wished to scuttle my reputation and shame my family. More importantly, its male members. Most important of all, my Father.

There was a price to pay for such faux pas. Rumor had it that European men had sheared the hair of European women who had been "friendly" with *Patos* soldiers—the soldiers from France. I shivered at the thought of losing my hair that way and being labeled an "easy" girl. But then, as humiliating as this *Pied-Noir* equivalent of the *Scarlet Letter* might be, it was not as brutal as the Sharia law of stoning wayward Arab women.

My wandering thoughts raised the hair on my forearms. A chill that even the scorching sun could not thaw. I inhaled deeply, thankful not to have been born in a culture whose laws were much harsher than mine. Thankful that when the time came for me to be married, I wouldn't, as young Arab women did, have a mother-in-law waiting outside the nuptial bedroom to examine the proof of my broken hymen. To wave the blood-stained sheet amid ululations from the women's quarters, divulging my most intimate secret and inviting all to witness that my husband had picked the prized bloom of my maidenhood. Pronouncing me, and by extension, my family, decent.

Behind me, Pépé Vincent coughed. I turned and looked at the white sheet blurring the contours of his shrunken body. When Pépé had fallen ill with cancer of the liver, Papa, upon learning that hospital care wouldn't be better at this stage than homecare, had installed an extra bed in Zizou's and my bedroom.

I knelt at Pépé's bedside and touched his hand. "Do you want some water, Pépé?"

"*Non.* I would …." His unfocused eyes searched the room.

"Do you want to eat, Pépé?"

He seemed to search for what he wanted. Maybe look for the right words. "*Oui,* I would … I would like …." He licked his chapped lips. "*J'aimerais une glace.*"

Ice cream? "You want *une glace à la vanille ou au chocolat?*"

"*Vanille.*"

"I'll get it for you, Pépé."

I stood, closed the shutters and pulled the bedroom door shut behind me, looking for Maman.

"Ma, can you believe it? Pépé wants *une glace à la vanille.*"

"*Et bien?*"

"How am I going to walk one-and-a-half kilometers carrying ice cream in this heat? By the time I get home the only thing left will be a big mess."

Maman pulled a few Francs from her wallet. "Ask Abdullah to wrap it with butcher paper and walk fast."

Zizou and Mireille were still jumping rope in the front yard. I opened the little black gate with the mail box and called, "You coming, Zizou?"

She stuck the end of the rope into Mireille's hands and came running. While the gate slammed behind us, Mireille yelled, "Can I come too?"

"*Non,*" Zizou yelled back. "You'll slow us down."

Twenty minutes later we returned home out of breath and red as boiled lobsters from the heat. Zizou collapsed in the shade of the yard, next to Mireille. "You and Nanna always do things together and never want me along," she reproached.

She was right. Where Zizou went, I went and where I went so did Zizou. I hurried upstairs; not only bearing Pépé's ice cream, but also feeling a grating sense of unease for keeping our younger sister at arm's length.

Papa and Maman at Alger, where they drove Pépé Vincent to see an oncologist.

I gave Maman her change and opened the small ice cream container. "It didn't melt too much."

Maman held out a spoon and cloth napkin. "Take these along."

In the bedroom, I knelt at Pépé's bedside. His eyes were closed and his breathing shallow. I put the ice cream beside his leg and laid my hand on his heart. His barrel chest had withered to skin and bone and the strong lungs once mighty as a blacksmith's bellow now barely filled. I was wavering between waking him and losing the ice cream when he growled, "What do you want?"

"Here is your *glace*, Pépé. I got it for you. *Vanille*, just like you wanted." I spread the napkin under his chin and offered him a spoonful. "It's still hard."

"I don't want it." His voice exhaled in a raw whisper and his dull eyes closed.

I stared at the stubble on his hollow cheeks and, swallowing hard against his rejection, returned to the kitchen. Throat tight as a fist. Tears prickling my eyelids.

Maman sat, knitting, while the chicken cooked. "Didn't Pépé like his *glace?*"

I dropped the container of ice cream, spoon, and napkin on the table and croaked, tears in my throat, "He said he doesn't want it," but I thought, *He doesn't love me anymore.*

As if reading my mind, Ma locked eyes with me. "He is not himself, *ma fille.* The pain and drugs muddle his brain." Still knitting, she gave a curt nod toward the ice cream. "*Mange-la.*"

"*Non,* Ma. I can't eat it."

"Why not? It will only melt."

I shook my head. All my life, Pépé had spun a cocoon of love around me. Now that he lay in a bed that was not even his, in a house that belonged to others, his last vestige of privacy and dignity lost, I cringed and whined like a brainless puppy. Even worse—I was nothing but a squirming worm not even worthy of being fish bait.

"*Non,* Ma, I can't eat it. Do you think it'll keep in the *glacière* until he wants it again?"

"Not for long."

One reason we never had ice cream at home was that we didn't own a refrigerator. We used a *glacière*—a small wooden ice box, lined with zinc. Behind the two thick doors, a metal rack held the food above a block of ice, which, every other day, the ice man brought in—a chunk of ice clear as crystal with tiny air bubbles trapped inside. The *glacière* was not as efficient as a refrigerator, but we shopped almost every day, and it kept the food fresh until we cooked it.

I knelt in front of the ice box, hammered small chunks out of the block of ice, wrapped them around the carton of ice cream inside a dish towel and put the bundle into the ice box.

In the kitchen, Maman retrieved the cooked chicken from the oven, put it down on the stovetop, and covered it with a dishtowel. "I am going to lie down for a while until Papa comes home. Call if Pépé needs me."

Ever since Pépé's cancer had worsened, Ma was perpetually exhausted.

When he became bedridden, Pépé relied on Maman for all his needs. I could tell that his total dependence on his daughter-in-law was even more agonizing to his self-esteem than the relentless teeth gnawing at his liver.

* * *

Two days earlier, after carrying a pan of warm water to Pépé's bedside, I had waited there, wanting to lend a hand. Maman put down the towel and soap she carried and said, "You may go now."

"*Non*, Ma. I want to help."

"Later, *ma fille*."

Feeling powerless and rejected, I stood on the other side of the closed door and listened. In the midst of sounds of sloshing water, I heard Pépé weep, "Elise, I am so ashamed."

"Don't be silly, Eugene. You are like a father to me. Why wouldn't I care for you?"

The woeful sound of his voice raised the hair on my arms. "*Merci, ma fille*."

Unable to bear his pain, I took refuge in the kitchen until Maman joined me. "I think Pépé needs a little company, now," she had said, wiping her eyes.

* * *

While Ma rested in her bedroom, I returned to mine. Pépé had his back to the door, but his uneven breathing told me he only pretended to sleep. I wanted to tell him I loved him but did not know how. I wanted to hug him, but feared he might push me away. Instead, I retrieved my book from under my pillow and sat on the cool tile floor, leaning my back against the closed shutters so that the subdued summer light fell upon the pages and began reading.

"Cochons!"

Zizou's spat word cut through the bedroom door. I set my book on the floor and rose to my feet to check on Pépé. He had fallen asleep. I left the room, closing the door softly behind me, and stepped into the hub of a mini drama.

Zizou stared at Mireille and the boys the way Moses on Mount Sinai must have stared at the Children of Israel as they lay prostrate before Aaron's golden calf.

I put a finger to my lips. "*Shuut!* Pépé and Maman are sleeping. What's going on?"

Zizou hissed, "Look *à ces petits cochons*! Want to know what they did?"

Wide-eyed, I shook my head and nodded at the same time. Her outburst was so intimidating, I fell under her spell. Struck mute. Then I got my voice back. "What did these 'little pigs' do?"

One hand resting on her hip, Zizou leaned forward and shook a finger at the kids. "What happened? I'll tell you what happened. These three *petits cochons,*" she pointed at Mireille, Riri, and Yves, "ate the ice cream and didn't even share with us."

Crestfallen, I stared at them. "You ate Pépé Vincent's ice cream?"

Zizou's hazel eyes smoldered, challenging me to share her outrage while three pairs of anxious eyes—brown, blue, and gray—fastened to mine as to a safe harbor amid angry seas.

Mireille and the boys looked so wretched and, if one could believe it, so innocent and their sin seemed so minor. I pointed at Yves's mouth with mock wrath, "Sinner, the evidence of your crime betrays you. Repent!"

Zizou's chin quivered. Her lips pinched before parting in a chuckle. Mireille and Riri wiped their own upper lips before pointing accusing indexes at Yves. "Repent, sinner. Repent!"

Yves stepped back. "WHAAAT?"

He was feeling his mustache of crusted ice cream when a sharp explosion made him jump. The five of us grabbed one another in a protective cluster. Maman tore out of her bedroom and stopped short. Her glance skipped over each of us in turn like a pebble skips on water.

Reassured we were safe, she ordered, "Go to my bedroom."

Zizou and the kids scampered to the relative security of Ma's bedroom, but I followed her to Pépé Vincent's bedside. She touched his shoulder. "*Vous allez bien Papa?*"

He nodded. "I'm fine, *ma fille,* I'm fine," then croaked, "The blast came from up the street."

Maman went to the window, crouched, pushed the shutters ajar, and peeked through the balcony's scrollwork. "It's not Saiids' place." She straightened, leaned warily over the railing, and peered farther up the road.

Then she jerked around, hands flying to her mouth. "It's *La Guinguette.*"

Chapter Seventeen

Grenade

L *A GUINGUETTE?* SHARDS OF ice then sparks of heat stung my body. "Ma, Pépé Honninger's there." I took off down the stairs. Past the little gate with the letter box.

"Nanna!" Ma shouted.

I sprinted up the street.

I reached *La Guinguette*'s terrace, wheezing, ears whooshing like the inside of a conch shell.

A military patrol was already there. A soldier barred my way. "You cannot go in, *mademoiselle*."

I stepped around him. "My grandfather's in there,"

He grabbed my arm. "Sorry. You can't go in."

I jerked my arm free. "Why can't I go in?" Then, suddenly, I panicked. "Is he dead?"

"I don't know."

"I must see him!" I took his hand, my tears blurring his face. "Please."

He took a step back. "What does he look like?"

I sobbed, "He's old, tall, and he's thin and well dressed. He has gray hair and glasses, and his name's Pierre Honninger. They call him Pierro."

The soldier called another one over. "Keep her here." He turned and walked to the café's entrance.

I wiped my runny nose with the back of my hand and rubbed it on the side of my dress. My eyes dried up. The rims of my eyelids burned and I needed to pee. I crossed my legs. The *paimpon paimpon*, of ambulances rushing through the streets grew louder. I watched, hypnotized, as soldiers tramped in and out of the café, their boots splattered with blood coating the terrace. But, unlike the long-ago sacrificed sheep across the street, this blood wasn't alive. It didn't flow, but lay in wait, thick and unmoving like swamp water. I slapped a hand to my mouth to keep from throwing up.

"Are you all right, *ma petite*?"

I felt as if I were waking from a deep sleep. I didn't know which was true, the nightmare of my grandfather lying in a pool of blood, or the happy dream of his hand on my shoulder. Soldiers hurried about us. First responders loaded covered stretchers into parked ambulances.

"Pépé!"

Pépé lifted my chin. "*Çà va, Nanna?*"

At his back, the blinding orb of the early afternoon sun melted into the white-hot August sky, and beyond the racket of voices, heavy boots, and departing ambulances, the cicadas rubbed their wings. I threw my arms around his neck. "I thought you were dead." Then I got a hold of myself and stepped back.

Pépé's lips quivered, then he shook bits of plaster from his mussed hair and shoulders. "I was lucky." His pale lips ebbed into the ashen hue of his face and a long red scratch scored his cheek. His dusty clothes looked as if he had rolled in a mound of dirt like a horse trying to shake pesky flies.

Pépé chomped on his dentures to shove them back up his gums and turned to the soldier who had fetched him, "I'm taking my granddaughter home." He pointed down the road. "To that house."

The soldier shook his head. "We need your statement."

Pépé grabbed my hand. "Don't worry, young man; I'll be right back to help clean up. I'll talk to you then."

Pépé laid his arm across my shoulder and guided me home down the street.

ZIZOU SHOOK HER HEAD. "I tell you there was not so much blood as you say."

"There was too. I saw it. I saw the soldiers slosh in it. There was so much it reached over the soles of their boots." I vividly recalled the scene, felt that it was an insult to the sacredness of life. The recollection of these stained boots sickened me. Their trampling of blood—the essence of life—engulfed me in an immeasurable feeling of loss.

Zizou repeated, "*Oui*, there was blood on the terrace, but only from the soldiers tracking it from the café. Not the swamp you say it was."

"How would you know?"

"Because I was there."

"No you weren't. You were in Maman's bedroom with the kids."

"I was, but when I heard Maman yell for you to come back I peeked into the corridor and saw you racing out, so I went after you." Zizou left the room and came back with my shoes.

I grabbed them. "Where were they?"

"In the street. You lost them when you sprinted to *La Guinguette*." She pointed at my battered feet. "Couldn't you feel you were running barefoot on gravel and macadam hot enough to broil *merguez*?"

I shook my head. "I didn't feel anything."

She looked at me funny. "You really need to stay out of the sun, Nanna."

I SAT IN THE KITCHEN darkened by drawn shutters, feet soaking in cold water and a dollop of vinegar. I reflected on the images my mind had created, so vivid that I believed them to be true. The intense red—ruby droplets—leaping off boots that cut across a crimson pool. A pool that grew darker and more viscous under the sun.

That night, the owl woke me. I turned over and smirked at the empty warning. Papa said the night birds were portents of doom, but, in spite of this afternoon's attack on *La Guinguette*, Pépé Honninger lay secure in his bed, alive, and Pépé Vincent slept peacefully in the spare bed across from mine. *Hoot yourself, crazy bird.*

* * *

SINCE PÉPÉ VINCENT HAD moved in with us, whenever the owl hooted in the plane tree at the corner of the front yard, Papa gave it the finger and stole out in the dark, shotgun cocked. "Nobody in this house's going to die," he'd say.

Inevitably, Maman warned, "Careful, *chéri*, not to hit the power line." Inevitably, Papa shouldered his gun and shot at the tree, growling, "You think I'm an ass?" and inevitably, the hooting stopped.

The next morning, we'd find broken twigs and fallen leaves at the base of the old tree, but no dead owl. Not even a feather.

Jovial neighbors asked, "Did you get it this time?"

Papa peered into the tree; hands on hips, feet apart, head thrown back. "I know I got it. Must be stuck up there."

A few nights later, the hooting resumed, belying Papa's reputation as a fine shot, wounding his pride. Worrying him. "Keep away from my house," he'd curse.

But the bird always came back. And ten days after the attack on *La Guinguette*, the owl hooted. This time, I didn't smirk.

The Wake

"NANNA, WAKE UP."

"Pa?" Waking out of a restless sleep, I read the news in his red-rimmed eyes. "Is he dead?"

My father sat on the side of the bed. I had slept in my parents' bedroom while they spent the night in mine. The doctor warned that Pépé Vincent wouldn't last the night and they wished to be at his side when he died. Zizou and our three younger siblings were sent away to Yvette and Gilles' in Constantine.

"He died early this morning." Waxen under the tan, Pa's features were taut like a celluloid mask. I timidly touched his hand. He retrieved it and stood, searching his breast pocket for his cigarettes. "Your mother wants you to get dressed."

I got up and followed him into my room. Even though a glorious sun brightened the morning, the closed shutters swathed the bedroom in semi-darkness. Candles flickered on either side of my bed, where Pépé now lay. He wore his Sunday suit and tie. A white sheet covered his legs up to his knees. His hands rested folded at his waist, fingers entwined in a mother of pearl rosary. Two gleaming coins weighed down his eyelids. A length of white cloth passing under his chin was tied into a knot on top of his skull, giving his head the look of a beribboned Easter egg. The effect was comical. The indignity, heartbreaking.

I knew the cloth prevented his mouth from falling open until rigor mortis set in. "Can't we take this off, Papa?"

My father flinched. "Later."

I sat down on the side of the bed. The bedsprings shifted, buckling the mattress at its center, pushing Pépé's body upward. In the lurching candlelight, he seemed to levitate—straight and rigid like a wooden plank.

I nearly bolted, but Pa's gaze burning a hole on the back of my neck kept me rooted, eyes fastened to the body like flies on sticky paper.

Pépé's skin glowed, translucent like candle wax. A morbid curiosity moved my hand to his hands, clasped together in death. They felt neither cold nor warm, the flesh firm and smooth, powdery like driftwood—soulless.

An intense longing wrung my heart. A thirst to turn back the clock to that evening, long ago, when I gazed up into his face towering above me as he pushed my pram up the Route du Cimetière. Cocooned in blankets, I drank in the rugged smile that framed his strong teeth and the tiny blue dot on the side of his nose. He wore the full moon on the side of his head like a cockeyed beret, and the rest of him faded into the dark blue night. He made me feel warm all over. He created the word "Love" just for me. And now ….

Now he was a stranger who frightened me. A carcass that meant nothing.

Burning with revulsion and anger, I stood and walked around the bed to my wardrobe. The muscles of my buttocks cramped as I tried not to run, tried to hide my terror from Papa. To spare his feelings. I jerked open the wardrobe curtain, almost tearing it off the clinking rings, gathered clothes and shoes at random and speed-walked out of the room, fleeing from the deathbed in fear and from my father, in shame of that fear.

Over the next twenty-four hours, time passed—a sluggish, out-of-focus, motion picture in sepia. Strangers embraced and kissed us. Whispering friends gathered in an arc of chairs around the dead man's bed. Comings and goings caused the yellow candle flames to vacillate, sputter, and release sinuous threads of charcoal fumes.

Evening brought little relief from the August heat seeping through the shutters' slats. Minutes stretched like thick treacle. The smell of hot candles, food, and coffee, even that of disinfectant used to wash the floor, no longer masked the cloying stench of decay stemming from the bed.

By mid-morning, the body was transferred to a coffin resting on wooden trestles. The time had come to say good-bye. I stood at Pa's side. The mixed smells of rotting flesh and room disinfectant nauseated me, but to please my father, I followed his example and bent over Pépé for a last kiss. Almost brutally, Papa grabbed my arm and walked me to the other side of the casket. I looked up at him, fearful I had done something wrong. He pointed his chin at the trickle of black blood oozing at the corner of Pépé's mouth.

As we followed close behind the coffin being borne out of the room, Papa whispered, "Did you hear?"

"Hear what, Pa?"

"Didn't you hear Pépé say, 'Thank you Nanna'?"

I stared at my father. His pasty skin and red-rimmed eyes broke my heart. I wanted to say yes, to make him feel better, but I couldn't lie about something this important. I shook my head. "No, Papa, I didn't." Guilt and anguish pinched my throat. *What would Pépé thank me for, when I've been so spooked and rushed out of the room in disgust?* I wished with all my might he had spoken to me. Told me he forgave me. That he still loved me. But I hadn't heard him.

As the bearers maneuvered the coffin feet first around the front door jamb, a silly thought distracted me. *So, that's what "going feet first" means. I wonder why not head first?*

To my surprise, the bright sun flooding through the doorway made breathing easy again. I realized Maman was not with us and looked around for her. She stood at the kitchen door, shrunken in her mourning clothes, a dishtowel to her eyes. I stopped following the coffin to wait for her, but Papa eased me along. "Come. Your mother will prepare lunch while we are at the cemetery."

I followed him down the stairs, into a limousine. "Is she going to be alone?"

"No, Tata Yvette's helping her prepare lunch for after the funeral."

IT SEEMED THAT LUNCH would last forever. That people would never stop hugging us, saying how sorry they were. That Pépé's dying was "for the best." It seemed they'd never leave. But when they did, they left behind a vacuum. As if the house had ballooned from the inside out with us, minute specks, in the center—particles of cosmic dust trapped within an extraterrestrial bubble.

We sat, eyeing each other. Unable to stitch two words together. Strangers sharing a train compartment.

Finally, Pépé Honninger slapped his knees and pushed himself up from his chair. "Well, I don't know about you. But I'm going to *La Guinguette*. Anyone want to come?"

The room smoothly deflated, returning to its usual dimensions. I blasted out, "Can I come?"

Papa got up. "We'll all go."

Maman stood. "We'll be ready in a minute. Come, Nanna."

In her bedroom, she smoothed and pinned her hair on each side of her face with combs, applied powder on her cheeks and nose and a touch of color on the curves of her shapely lips.

I combed my hair while she held the black headband I had worn all day. Yesterday Ma had said to Papa, "We should buy a black dress for Nanna, but I don't want her to look like an orphan."

I envisioned Maman as an eleven-year-old girl in a black dress, mourning her mother. I could tell she still felt that loss and, for her sake, I would not have minded wearing a black dress. It would have been like holding that grieving girl in my arms, telling her, "It's okay, I'm here."

Papa said, "I don't want her in black either. Have her wear a small piece of something black."

Ma gave me a couple of francs and sent me to Guenassia's novelty store to buy a length of black grosgrain I sewed into a headband.

I put it on, and we joined Papa and Pépé Honninger waiting outside the front door. Pépé locked the door and handed the heavy key to Ma; then we all started for *La Guinguette*.

The Clock

AT THE CAFÉ, I gulped the cold glass of *sirop d'orgeat*, the barley water Pépé ordered for me, and scanned the plates of *kémia* that Mr. Cavalier, the owner, spread along the bar. Today, the appetizers were green olives in olive oil and garlic, curried fava beans, and peanuts in the shell. I didn't see my favorite—*sardines en escabèche*, the raw sardines marinated in spiced olive oil and wine vinegar. I picked up a few peanuts and crushed the shells while I studied the other patrons.

Two men leaned on the brass rail at the bar, revisiting with Monsieur Cavalier the grenade explosion of two days before. Four other neighbors played poker at a wood table still embedded with debris from the blast. Between hands they sipped *Pastis*—the anise-flavored alcohol that turns cloudy as water is poured—now and then cutting into the conversation at the bar. Monsieur Michelet called out, "*Dis-moi,* Cavalier, what did the doctor say about your foot?"

A flying piece of metal had hit Monsieur Cavalier's foot, and his usually sanguine complexion was now wan from pain and loss of blood. He leaned his forearms on top of the bar. "He said because of my diabetes I might lose it."

"I'm sorry, my friend. You tell us when you need help, *d'accord*?"

"*D'accord.*"

Monsieur Cavalier was a nice man who had lost his wife way back when I was little. He didn't have children but was kind to the neighborhood kids. I always thought how lonely he must be, living all by himself in the upstairs apartment. Now he was lonely, injured, and his café was in ruins. I watched him survey the damage and felt sorry for him.

The grenade had left a shallow crater in the grainy black-and-white tile floor and the concrete underneath. The bar mirror and most of the bottles were gone. Patches of missing plaster—some tiny as my thumbnail, others as big as my fist—pocked the walls down to the brickwork. It felt like I must be on the set of a Hollywood war movie, but here, the smell of old dust shaken off the building two days ago still hovered.

The clock that used to hang on the wall before the explosion had left behind the grimy, fly-speckled silhouette of its ogival-shaped case and a preserved swatch of the paper's original colors.

I'd loved watching the clock's round brass pendulum swing in the tempo of a slow heartbeat. Now the clock was gone. *Just like Pépé Vincent.* I was beginning to feel sorry for myself when I saw it—the clock—propped against the wall at the far end of the bar, glass shattered, face marred, big hand missing, small hand pointing to two o'clock. The time of the explosion.

"Papa," I touched his arm.

He shook my hand away. "I told you I don't like to be touched."

I stepped back. "What time is it, Papa?"

"Why?"

"What time is it?"

"Son of a bitch, these bastard kids won't leave me in peace—"

Maman whispered, "*chéri*, please."

He rotated his wrist and glanced at the watch. "Six o'clock."

I walked to the end of the bar and pointed the clock's small hand to the missing number six and asked, "Can you rewind the clock, Monsieur Cavalier?"

"It's broken, honey."

"Maybe it's not dead?"

"The pendulum is gone."

"Please?"

Mr. Cavalier opened the till drawer, took out the rewind key, and limped the length of the bar. He introduced the key into the clock's rewind hole, turned it a half turn at a time until it would go no farther and looked at me round-eyed. His pallid jowls quivered like gelatin as he said, "It works."

I put my ear to the clock and laughed at the halting tick-tock, tack-tuck—happy, for no reason.

Monsieur Voisin folded his hand of fanned cards. "At least this is one less casualty." He threw the cards to the green felt mat. "It's too bad about Hakim."

Although Hakim was Muslim, he drank alcohol and was a regular patron of *La Guinguette*. He worked at a government office in town and wore impeccably cut Western suits—looking more dapper any single day of the week than any of the European patrons on Sundays. His shirts and ties were immaculate, his shoes spit-shined. His smile—after he won at poker, or his snarl when, as a passionate FLN supporter, he engaged in heated political arguments with Papa—showed off a sparkling gold tooth.

Papa, took a sip of his *pastis*. "*Et oui!*" he sighed. "Even though we often disagreed, I'm going to miss the son of a bitch."

The other men nodded.

I recalled Pépé Honninger relating the details of the bombing. Monsieur Cavalier, Hakim, and two others were playing cards. Pépé was pouring a round of drinks behind the bar when three terrorists booted open the café's doors.

Two kept the five men in check with machine guns while the third pulled the pin off a grenade and lobbed it into the middle of the room. Then they ran out, pulling the doors closed behind them.

A split second before the explosion, Pépé dove from behind the bar into the back room. Two card players scrambled behind the bar, suffering only superficial cuts from the shattering bottles. Slower to react, Mr. Cavalier was wounded in the foot, while a projectile penetrated the underside of Hakim's chair seat, mortally wounding him.

Papa shook his head. "Fucking luck," he said. Then he picked up a garlic-coated olive and popped it in his mouth.

Silent up to now, Monsieur Nicholas left the card table, holding his empty glass, and walked to the bar for a refill. He put a hand on Papa's shoulder.

"Sorry about your father, Richard. I hope he didn't suffer too much at the end?"

Papa threw his hand up in the air. "What can we do? *Le maktoob, c'est le maktoob!*"

Monsieur Michelet agreed, "*Et oui,* 'Destiny is destiny.' The Arabs are correct—when you've got to go, you've got to go."

Everyone sighed as if to say, "Nothing we can do to change that."

Still wrestling with the inescapability of fate, Papa said to no one in particular, "You know that fucking owl in the plane tree?" Aware of my father's persistent feud with the night bird, Monsieur Cavalier shook his jowls while the other men nodded gravely. Papa took a sip of his cloudy drink. "It hooted three times, night before last. Woke me up. Early morning it was. 'Here, take this,' I told it." Reenacting his defiance to the prophetic bird, Papa slapped the crook of his bent left arm with a whack of his right hand—a hard blow, causing my own arm to sting in sympathy. "I yelled," he went on. " 'You won't take my father. Not yet, you son of a bitch.' But, just then, my father gasped. His bedsprings creaked and he expelled his last breath. I knew, then, the fucking bird had won."

No one spoke. Papa finished his drink and thumped his glass on top of the counter. "*Allez,* Cavalier, pour us a round," he ordered with a wide gesture encompassing the people in the room.

By ten o'clock, we said good night and walked down the deserted street. Under the full moon, our shadows—crisp as under an August midday sun—glided beside us like docile puppies on a leash. Gently rustling eucalyptus leaves anointed the evening with their clean scent, and the crickets' clear monotone lulled me into indolence. Then Pépé opened and closed the little black gate, violating the night's serenity with the sound of metal scraping against the concrete threshold. Papa said to Maman, "Lili, remind me to repair this door tomorrow." He always said that.

We trailed the path across the front garden and turned to climb the stairs. Graceful skaters, our shadows slithered along the wall. They mimicked our ascent, briefly erasing the handrail's lacey silhouette that clung to the moonlit house like phantom ivy.

We closed this long day with a quick bowl of onion soup and carrot salad before going to bed.

Until my room was free of the wake's cloying scent, I was to sleep on a mattress at the foot of my parents' bed. Maman and I layered sheets and a pillow atop my makeshift bed and the house settled into its comforting nighttime ritual. The creak of bed springs, the drip of a faucet, and the dry bark of Papa's smoker's cough lulled me into a drowsy sense of security. And yet, the stimulation of the day's events and moonlight filtering through the shutters' slats kept me awake.

As I lay on my side, my gaze skipped along the floor beneath my parents' bed, across the corridor, and into my bedroom. There, the full moon brushed the multihued tiles with a dulling silver glow. My heart raced. At any moment, now, I'd see the shadows of Pépé Vincent's shuffling feet ….

Papa's leitmotiv repeated in my head in a loop, "Keep your head out of your ass. Come down out of the clouds. Stop making things up." Heeding Pa's familiar command, I inhaled deeply and confronted my fear that Pépé Vincent might come back to haunt me.

I tried to be rational. All my life, Pépé had loved me, protected me, so why would his spirit hurt me now? If he wished to manifest himself to me, wouldn't it be simply to tell me that he loved me?

This soothing notion slowed the throbbing at my neck, pounding in my heart, leaving me to almost wish I could see the shadow of Pépé's shuffling feet ….

I don't remember falling asleep, but when next I opened my eyes, I had a vague notion I had come out of a nightmare—a nasty dream that clung to me like a swatch of thick, dusty spider web.

Chapter Eighteen

ONE AFTERNOON, AFTER PÉPÉ Vincent's funeral, I drifted to the hallway where Maman sat, holding Mireille between her knees while tending to her earache. The wide-open front door overlooked the garden and street two floors below, where the sun oppressed all that grew and breathed. The cicadas worked hard to drown out the buzzing bees and crickets, while grasshoppers and other hopping, flying, and creeping things went on hushed errands.

Maman sat in a chair near the open door where sun and shade drew a razor-straight line across the corridor's tiles. I rested one hand on the back of the chair and watched her count drops into Mireille's ears. Poor Mimi's ear infections stank to high heaven, making her the constant butt of the boys' sing-song teasing: "Mi-miche is stin-king! Mi-miche is stin-king!"

"Stop wriggling like a worm, *ma fille*," Ma said, losing patience with Mireille. Then, eyes and hands still focused on her task, she asked, "What is eating you, Nanna?"

"Nothing," I said, surprised she knew something was bothering me.

She glanced up. "It cannot be 'nothing.' You have acted like a scared mouse for days."

The sun poked slanted fingers of heat into the darkened house. Up to her knees, Maman's legs looked bleached under the blinding sun, while the rest of her and Mireille faded into the shade.

"Really, it's nothing, Ma."

She stuffed cotton wads into Mireille's ears. "Tell me anyway."

A cooling breeze swept the freshly washed floors with the mixed fragrances of late summer—the heat-exuded scent of acacia, the tang of cow dung dropped earlier by a small herd on its way to pasture, and a whiff of Mireille's sick ears.

"It's just a stupid dream."

Maman wrapped her arms loosely around Mireille. "Then tell me."

The anguish that, since the dream, had haunted my days and kept me awake at night surged like water through a failing dam and spilled past my lips.

"In the dream, I was at the little roadside market—you know, Ma, the one at the end of the Sidi Rached Bridge on the way to Sidi Mabrouk from Constantine?"

Ma nodded. Mireille exclaimed, "I know it. That's where they sell spices, and fruit, and vegetables."

I nodded and, as I began to tell it, the dream sucked me in, forcing me to live it all over again.

The Mirror

ARAB VENDORS HAD SET lean-tos under the shade of plane trees lining the band of packed dirt between the road and the Rhumel River below. The shelters, homespun blankets draped over sticks jammed into the ground, fused into a tapestry of vibrant geometric patterns.

I stood on the narrow band of ground between the back of the lean-tos and the deep gully dropping to the riverbed.

Between bouts of animated bartering, turbaned and skull-capped sellers sat cross-legged on prayer rugs and slurped piping-hot glasses of mint tea. Now and then, they leaned forward and brandished woven straw fans over stacks of fat, gooey dates to shoo away the flies.

Oblivious to their surroundings, hobbled mules milled their teeth over mouthfuls of oats.

Tied to plane trees, nose to the smooth bark, donkeys stamped their hooves against the packed dirt.

A mild breeze from the Rhumel cooled the shaded tents, while sunspots, patterned by the lobed plane leaves, played over pyramids of lemons, grapefruits, melons, prickly pears, and tomatoes adorned with mint.

The rich earth-colored paprika, cumin, and turmeric sent exotic aromas from the opening of jute bags, mimicking, in impressionist strokes, the lean-tos' colored blankets.

Sounds from the dusty road traffic mixed with laughter, animated bargaining, and the feeble bleating of a little white goat tethered to a stick in the ground.

Suddenly, tarnished-silver clouds roiled in, sucking away the dazzling colors, the smells, and sounds, as swiftly as a straw siphons a glass of lemonade.

A round silver-framed mirror hanging from a string at the back of a lean-to reflected the angry sky. I recognized Pépé Honninger's Art Nouveau mirror and approached it, wondering how it came to be here.

As I peered into it, a narrow, swift, blinding-white beam of light shot like an arrow from between the darkening clouds at my back and struck the mirror with the dry zap-zap sound of connecting electric poles.

The mirror shattered, but did not break apart, causing my reflection to look like a finished jigsaw puzzle. I jumped back, startled, but my fragmented image did not shift. I moved forward then sideways. Still, my face remained a static puzzle in the mirror.

I touched my face. My fingers found no nose. No mouth. No eyes. No ears. No chin.

My features ... my whole face was held captive of the mirror ....

THE TOUCH OF MA's hand on my cheek rescued me from the dream just as, long ago, she had rescued me from a spiderweb-filled greenhouse. I clung to the comfort of her quiet eyes, but Mireille grasped my arm. "What happens next, Nanna?"

My sister's question made me realize that I had not only relived the dream, but had also been recounting it.

"You had no face ...." Mireille's prodding thrust me back into the dream's maelstrom.

I HAD NO FACE. INSTEAD, a flat, smooth plane that felt like virgin clay.

I dug into the mirror to reclaim my trapped image. The glass splintered, shattering the puzzle sections of my features into even smaller pieces on the hard-packed dirt at my feet.

I dropped to my knees, frantically gathering the chips of my face. Pieces were missing; others were smudged with blood from the cuts on my hands.

I was sweeping what bits I could into the folds of my skirt when the wind picked up, tearing the tents from their tethers. Billows of stinging dust swept up the mirror fragments and the remnants of my face.

In a daze, I rose from my kneeling position. Reeled about—featureless face and hands raised to the clouds—and howled like a she-wolf calling for her litter lost in the desert of a frozen land ....

As I FINISHED RECOUNTING my nightmarish vision, Maman's warm hand took hold of my frozen arm.

"Come, Nanna," she said. "Let's have a hot *café au lait*."

Mireille followed us into the kitchen. Maman reheated this morning's leftover café, poured it into three bowls, and stirred in milk and sugar.

Mireille buttered slices of *gros pain*, the fat, crusty baguette I liked. "Nanna, you want sugar on your *tartine*?"

"Lots of butter and lots of sugar."

While we finished our snack, Maman searched my eyes. "Do you feel better now, *ma grande?*"

I swallowed my last piece of buttered bread and nodded heartily. "*Whoui. Merci,* Ma."

The table cleared, I retreated to my bedroom, feeling like a terrible load had been lifted from my very soul. I even summoned enough energy to work on my math—the school subject that had given me painful stomach aches all my life.

Chapter Nineteen

A LL MY LIFE, I had passed from grade to grade by the skin of my teeth. I liked geometry, but calculus was endless torture. I excelled at composition and dictation, but sentence diagramming was pure anguish. Continual reading enriched my vocabulary, taught me how words fit together, but I had no idea why.

By age ten, the gap between what I knew and what I should know had widened into an abyss. Every three months, I waited until the last possible moment to submit my progress report to Papa. The anticipation of his disappointment and rebukes pecked at my guts like an angry hen until he concluded his usual chewing out, "Good for nothing …" and, in disgust, tossed the signed report on the table.

The hen then retreated into semi-seclusion until the next report.

My Story

School year, 1956

B Y AGE TWELVE, I desperately wished composition were more important than calculus. If so, I'd really shine. I enjoyed writing short paragraphs on topics the teacher assigned in class and often wondered how authors came to spin whole stories. How they managed to whisk me away to unknown places, introduce me to extraordinary characters, and coax me into becoming one of them. By what sleight of words did they move me to laugh, cry, hope, and despair?

I came to wonder whether I, too, might be able to write stories. Touch others.

At night, before falling asleep, and in the morning, before fully emerging into the real world, I thought of storylines, rejected them, opted for new ones.

One day, I dipped the nib of my pen into an inkpot, set it on a sheet of paper and wrote, "Once upon a time …."

As it unfurled, the story took on a life of its own—an unmanned loom shuttle pulling dyed threads through the warp of a tapestry in progress—weaving new angles, guiding my pen to plait images, sounds, tastes, and feelings. It was magic.

I spent every minute after school and my house chores on my mission, locking myself in the bathroom for privacy. As it unfolded, the story seesawed between easy and hard, exciting and hopeless, tossing me in a maelstrom of highs and lows. But, as I penned the words, "The end," my mood settled on utter exaltation, taking my breath away as no book I'd read ever had.

Maman asked, "Are you all right, *ma grande?*"

I felt fuzzy as if awakening from a long sleep. "*Oui,* Ma. Why?"

"You have not been yourself these past few days."

I was all set to tell her about my story when Yves came into the kitchen, complaining that he had hurt his finger. Ma picked him up and cooed.

Zizou said, "You've spent lots of time in the bathroom, Nanna. Do you have the runs or what?"

I wavered about showing her the story, but she didn't care much for reading. Besides, she was more likely to make fun of my writing aspirations. "I needed to be alone to write a composition for school."

This explanation seemed to satisfy her. But what good was it to write a story if no one read it? Yvette would have been the perfect audience, but she and Tonton Gilles were in Italy for a month.

At recess, two weeks later, I kicked myself all the way to the classroom podium where Madame Denis, our teacher, sat at her desk. She distractedly looked up from her stack of handbooks. "*Oui,* Danielle?"

I placed my sheaf of paper on her desk and darted out of the room.

When class resumed, I sat staring at my marred desktop, hoping Madame Denis hadn't read my work. Praying she never would.

My story told the tale of a dashing prince, in the submerged kingdom of Atlantis, and his faithful companions riding herds of spirited sea horses. They collected pearls of unusual size and orient gifted by giant oysters. Hauled coffers of gold bullion and precious stones and casks of ancient wine from long-sunk vessels.

They raced their sea stallions to pay ransom. To free the delicate princess

Nanna, age 7, École Ferdinand Buisson in Sidi Mabrouk

doomed to wed the colossal octopus enthroned like a malefic spider in the hub of his submarine grotto.

Following the epic rescue, the prince and princess married in a forever-to-be-remembered ceremony, under shifting schools of baby sardines, swirling like silver clouds in a shimmering liquid blue sky. They swore to honor each other forever amid magical gardens of swaying seaweed softly lit by plump jellyfish that glowed like so many dangling moons.

Still under my story's spell, I equated the heady sensation that had swept me away as I wrote to the intoxication young swallows must experience while learning to soar into unending space—their first flight to freedom.

While I begged all the saints in Heaven that Madame Denis had set aside my story, she tapped her ruler on the desk to call us to order. "Mesdemoiselles." She brandished several sheets of paper. "I would like to read a story one of you wrote."

Friends searched each other's faces, trying to guess the author. They shook their heads in turn, pointing chins at each other, meaning *"Pas moi. Toi?"*— *pas moi.* What about you?"

Madame Denis' voice cut into the wordless stir. *"'Atlantis Sous les Flots' par* Danielle Bjork."

A rush of bottoms scooting on benches, shoes scuffing the floor, and twenty-nine pairs of eyes stung my face beet-red like a sudden gust of Sirocco sand.

The teacher forced the quizzical faces back to the front of the class. "Sit up straight, Mesdemoiselles."

As she read, I heard her words in a haze; they might have been broadcasted through layers of cotton wool. I stole glances at the still bodies ahead of me, lamenting, *Why did I ever bring this story to class? Why did I even have to write it?*

An ominous hush signaled the reading was over. I was doomed.

Madame Denis fanned the sheets in her hand. "Mesdemoiselles, this is how a story should be written."

The enormity of the compliment turned my whole body to jelly, compelled me to look down to hide my embarrassment. And my pride.

The teacher asked, "Danielle, tell us how you came to choose the subject of your story."

I stood up, hands at my back. "Uh … Uh …." Loud sneers from a couple of the beribboned spoiled girls channeled my thoughts. "My father said that nobody really knows how Atlantis was destroyed or if it even existed. But, uh … he read that scientists, now, say the continent of Atlantis was destroyed by the worst volcanic eruption and tsunami—that's a huge tidal wave—ever. He … he says …." I took a deep breath. "According to my father, some books say Poseidon, the Lord of the Ocean, became angry and destroyed Atlantis when … when its warriors lost against the warriors of Athens. My father says, also, that other books tell how Atlantis was totally destroyed when one of its scientists discovered the secrets of the Cosmos, which was not permitted by the gods."

Madame Denis nodded. "Thank you, Danielle. You may sit down."

I took my seat while she scanned the room. "Any questions or comments about the story I just read? She slowly rearranged the pens on top of her desk before breaking the continuing silence. "*Bien.* Now we will have dictation."

For the next few hours, I floated like a fluffy cloud in a clear blue sky and couldn't wait to hurry home and trumpet my triumph.

Maman read the story. "*C'est magnifique, ma fille.* I did not know you wrote stories."

"It's my first. You really like it?"

"*Oui, ma grande.* I love it."

After dinner, I hurried to hand my story to Papa before he left the table.

"What's that?" he said, sucking in his cheeks.

Blood whooshed into my neck. "It's a story I wrote," I blurted out. "Mrs. Denis said, 'This is how a story should be written.'"

My father picked up the sheaf, squared himself in his seat, and read.

Searching for the faintest hint of approval, I fastened onto his face like a sunflower locks onto the sun, and by the time his eyes reached the bottom of the last page, my nerves thrummed like viola strings.

Pa raised his head and brandished the sheets. "What kind of trash is this?"

The viola strings sagged. "But, Papa, Mrs. Denis liked it. She even read it to the whole class."

"I don't give a shit what she says. I want you to stop reading crap, let alone writing it. Better spend your time and energy on calculus." He tossed the sheets across the oilcloth. "This will not put food on your table later in life."

I gathered the jumbled sheets, averting my eyes to hide my disappointment and humiliation. On my way out, I wrung the pages in a wad, tight as the hurt closing my throat. In my room, I threw my balled story to the floor. Kicked it across the room and threw myself on the bed, soaking my pillow with tears and saliva from my gaping mouth.

When I had no tears left, I sat on the floor, picked up the crumpled sheets, smoothed and folded them on the cold tile with the flat of my hands. Then I rose to my knees and opened the lower doors of the china cabinet. The green tin box I had stashed away long ago was still there. I took it out.

L'oeil de Malika—the glass bobble gentle Malika had given me when I was a little girl—shone softly. A comforting touch of the moon.

I laid the folded pages at its side with the care I would a broken butterfly and closed the lid. I returned the box to the bottom of the cabinet and buried it under its stack of never-used table linens.

Two days later at school, one of the pink-frocked frou-frou girls laid a sheaf of paper on the teacher's desk. "I wrote a story too, Madame Denis." She turned around, shook her curls at me and waltzed back to her desk.

I was crushed. *The miserable bitch wants to take away my only achievement.* A sudden wave of anger filled my chest—an overwhelming resentment that made me want to hurt that girl.

The teacher read the piece, laid it flat under her spread hands and surveyed the hushed class. "Does anyone know what plagiarism is?"

I searched my mind and shook my head along with the other girls. *God, I hope it's bad.* Madame Denis stared at frou-frou. "Marie Terrine, do you know what plagiarism is?" Frilly's sausage curls batted her apple cheeks as she waved her head side to side, her cow eyes brimming with anticipation.

"The word 'plagiarism' comes from the Latin verb 'to kidnap.' By extension it means stealing someone else's work or idea and passing it as one's own. It is morally wrong and, in some cases, leads to criminal charges."

Marie-Curlies' angelic face turned crimson. *Halleluiah!* My heart rejoiced. My fists craved to thump the carved top of my desk with a celebratory tattoo.

Easy, Nanna. We shall be magnanimous now that the little angel had her wings clipped. The venomous sideglance Miss Plagiarism threw my way from across the room filled me with a satisfaction I could barely contain. Oh, the sweet taste of revenge!

My need to strike had vaporized and my lungs swelled with the same light-headed joy that once engulfed me as I stood in a field of poppies.

Papa could say I was stupid all he wanted, but I knew, now, I could be better than any spoiled and empty-headed Pappy's girl like this one. All I needed was prove it to him.

Chapter Twenty

THE OPPORTUNITY TO SHOW my father I wasn't so 'stupid' after all arose a few weeks later, while I watched him bend over his drawing board propped on top of the kitchen table and trace the outlines of a grave as part of a proposal to a client.

Back to the Drawing Board

Summer, 1956

"LOOK, *MA FILLE*," HE said, "I don't have time to work on these plans right now. Will you do that for me?"

Increasing road ambushes had severely curtailed Papa's out-of-town cemetery business. Money became tight, especially as he refused to lay off the older workers like Moustache and Debbah. However, thanks to his knowledge of the Arabic language and customs, he had found a job as investigator and interpreter for the police. In addition to this full-time work, Pa supervised jobs done during the week at the cemetery. He had put Maman in charge of customer service at the cemetery shop and let Debbah manage the work team.

My father asking for *my* help left me speechless. But I was all ears.

"All you need to do is trace the basic drawings. I'll take care of the embellishments and lettering." Interpreting my stunned silence as reluctance, Pa added, a tad vexed, "After watching me for twelve years, now, you'd think you'd know how to do it."

Unsure whether he was serious or making fun of me, I remained silent. He lit a cigarette and blew smoke at the ceiling. "I'll pay you for your work."

Yaa! This was the first time in my life that my father would not only trust me with important stuff, but also was prepared to pay for it. My delight and pride at Pa's thinking me worthy of his trust gave way to sudden panic. What if I couldn't perform to his standards? Was I just giving him an excuse to call me an ass, a good-for-nothing, again? "I watched you, Papa, but I've never done this before."

Pa turned on his charm. "*Alors, t'es pas la fille à ton Père?* Of course you can."

I certainly hoped I was my father's daughter. Otherwise, I'd be a bastard, which was entirely impossible, as Papa often said, "A husband can be certain the first-born is his, but there's always room for doubt about the legitimacy of younger siblings."

Pa relished retelling stories about females' unfaithfulness and cunning. His favorite was the Arab tale of a woman whose husband went away for months. When he returned, he found his wife pregnant. He counted on his fingers and, concluding there was no way he could be the daddy, confronted his wife. She answered, "How can you be so distrustful? So unjust, my beloved husband? Haven't I proven my love for you again and again?"

He shook his head, "*Laa!* I've been gone six months, there's no way I can be the father."

"*Yaa, Habibi!*" Struck with grief, the woman scratched her cheeks with hennaed fingernails and whined, "I missed you so much that I slept with your burnoose. And one night, when I missed you more than ever, it made love to me." She kissed the tip of her gathered fingers and swore, eyes brimming with love, "That's how I've become big with your child, my beloved husband."

WELL, PA HAD BEEN away at war when I was born. Nonetheless, not only was I the first-born, but also, the finger-counting test established without the shadow of a doubt that I was indeed my father's daughter.

Now I needed to establish I was his daughter in brainpower as well.

My eagerness to please, along with Pa's display of charm, gave me the push I needed to lend a hand.

Papa watched as I mimicked, tentatively at first, the steps I had observed him follow for years. All I needed to do was trace the basic drawings, wasn't that right?

I practiced tracing the lines of the three-dimensional monuments until I even became comfortable tracing the exploded drawings, which detailed the interior configurations. Papa then added the precise measurements that needed to be recalculated for each commission.

As I gained more confidence with each successful assignment, it occurred to me that I was amassing a fortune.

Yves had already set his heart on a mound of *Caca de Pigeon*—fly specks and all.

Riri put in a request for a *tawat*. A real slingshot from the store. Not like the ones the street urchins made from Y-shaped pieces of wood and strips of innertube.

Mireille said, "Nanna doesn't have to share. It's her money."

Zizou mentioned a silk scarf. "I'll get a red one." She batted her eyelashes at my stone face. "I know it's not your color, but I'll let you wear it, anyway."

I planned on keeping my income for something important. Didn't know what, but it would be big.

Proud as a chick that had laid a diamond egg but also trembling with apprehension, I submitted my tracings for Papa's verdict. "It's not perfect," he ruled, then concluded with a moue, "but it will do."

Relief flushed my cheeks. At the end of a fortnight, Pa elaborately searched his pockets and brought out a wad of Francs. "Here," he said, shoving a few bills in my hand.

My first earned money. Who said only calculus would put food on my table? I ambled out of the kitchen, counting my fortune. Zizou, Mireille, Riri, and Yves followed at close range—buzzards eyeing a road kill.

They were wasting their time. No way would I share. I earned this money. It was mine.

I had turned my back on them, counting the bills, when Papa's motto pricked my conscience. "If only a bread crumb is left, you'll share it with your brothers and sisters."

With a sigh and heavy shrug, I returned to the kitchen. "Thanks, Pa, but you better keep it to pay the bills." I handed him the loot.

He flicked his corner smile, the one that indicated he was pleased but didn't want to let it be known. Zizou and the kids, however, weren't smiling.

Boiling Hot

*M*Y BROTHERS' AND SISTERS' disappointment at losing my money didn't last long as they started to focus on the end of the school year and the prospect of summer trips to the beach.

For my part, a persistent fluttering in my stomach spoiled these prospects. Ruining my days. Spoiling my nights.

I was to present the compulsory exam *d'entrée en sixième,* which would propel me from the sixth grade primary at l'École Ferdinand Buisson, in Sidi Mabrouk, to secondary school at the Lycée Laveran in Constantine. Failing the exam would oblige me to repeat the sixth grade, while all my schoolmates went on, leaving me behind. The prospect created chaos in my stomach. It gurgled. It shrank. It burned. It quivered like a swarm of restless moths.

The day before the exam, needing to wash my hair, I set a pan of water to boil and later mix with cold water in the blue enamel washbasin. When the water bubbled, I grabbed the pan's handle, forgetting its wooden sleeve was loose. The pan twisted sideways and the boiling water spilled over my left thigh, down to my ankle. *YAA, that's freezing.* The bizarre thought melted like ice on a hot stove as my wet shorts clung to my thigh, further steaming my skin. I dropped the pan and jumped on my right leg as on a pogo stick, screaming at the top of my lungs, "Zizou, come, I burned my leg."

She sailed into the kitchen, flapping her lashes, sedate as Cleopatra. "What's your problem?"

"I spilled boiling water on my leg."

"What did you do that for?"

"Don't be stupid," I yelled, still jumping up and down. "What do I do?"

"I don't know," she said, wide-eyed.

What can I do? I grabbed my leg with both hands, causing white-hot needles to skewer it. *Water. I need water. COLD water.* I hopped along the corridor, down to the bottom of the stairs and dunked my leg into the new tub we kept filled with water. Tepid as it was, the water soothed my screaming thigh. As the pain abated, I realized Zizou stood close, scolding. "What are you doing, you idiot?"

"WHATTT?"

"You're supposed to put fat on a burn, not water."

"Oh, yeah, I forgot …." *Darn.* "Can you get butter for me, *ma* Zize?"

She took the stairs two at a time and was back in a flash with a chunk of butter in a plate. I grabbed the butter and tenderly touched it to the burns where it melted into an oil slick.

"What do I do now?" I whined, my greasy hand aloft.

Zizou leaned forward and examined my leg. "It's real red. It hurts a lot?"

"I don't know what 'a lot' is, but it hurts. What do we do now?" I snarled, losing my cool.

"Maybe we should call Ma?"

"I don't know, Zize. I don't think she'd like to be called at work just for a burn."

Zizou bent over for a closer look at the burn then straightened up. Hands on hips, she blew her hair off her face and announced, "I'll go to *La Guinguette* and call her. We'll see what she says."

When she returned, Zizou announced, "Maman says she's taking a taxi from Constantine and is calling Doctor Laurie to meet her here. She said for you to lie down."

Clothing littered the bed and floor of our bedroom, but by the time car doors slammed in the yard, we had shoved everything under the bed and smoothed down the bed sheets and blanket. I threw myself on top of the bed, forgetting my injured leg. "*Aïe aïe aïe!*" The bedsprings were still bouncing when Maman and Dr. Laurie entered the room.

He diagnosed secondary burns on my thigh and lesser burns on my shin. *Does it mean it's so bad I won't be able to take the exam, tomorrow?*

I kept my mental fingers crossed, letting my hopes rise. "But I will be able to take the exam, tomorrow. *N'est-ce pas,* Docteur Laurie?"

He shook his head. "I'm afraid this won't be possible. We need to watch for infection."

A blissful hymn unleashed inside my brain. "HALLELUAIAH, HA-LLE-LU-UUIAHH." Zizou skewered me with her evil stare. "What a bummer," she said, tongue-in-cheek.

For a few days, leg coated with unguent and sheathed in gauze, I relished the attention. Mireille and the boys thought it was cool to look part mummy. Papa was not mad at me. When he arrived home from work the day of the accident, Maman was tending my leg. He sat on the bed, examined the burn and asked, "What did Laurie say about scarring, Lili?"

"He said she has a second degree burn but, barring infection, the new skin will grow in smoothly."

Papa nodded. "Before coming home, I spoke to the Lycée's headmistress. She said she'll ask the board of exams for a special exemption, but we need to present a health certificate from the doctor."

"So, I won't have to take the exam, Pa?"

He locked eyes with me. I almost flinched. Then he shook his head as if fanning off an annoying mosquito—or the ugly suspicion, like Zizou's, that I might have had an accident on purpose to avoid the exam. But his frigid stare thawed. "You'll have to attend the make-up exam in July." On his way out the bedroom, he said over his shoulder, "You better use this reprieve to hit the books—the calculus books, that is."

I nodded. The napping moths stirred.

The Exam

THE WEEKS LEADING UP to the make-up exam became a blur of anguish. I knew. I just knew I would fail. Then my life would be a misery. I wished my leg had allowed me to take the exam on time. The nightmare would be a thing of the past now. *Fini. Kaput.* Over.

The day before the exam, Papa shoved a narrow black box into my hand.

"*Pour moi?*" Presents were for Christmas, new clothing for Easter, a cake for birthdays—maybe. I stared at the box, unsure what to do with it.

"Open it," he growled.

Maman nodded with a smile. The boys elbowed each other to get the best view. Zizou observed from across the room. Mireille crowded me. "Want me to help you open it, Nanna?"

I took a step back and lifted the hinged lid. It exposed a white chamois cloth. I removed it. My breath caught as the cloth revealed a black fountain pen ensconced in folds of white satin. An elegant thread of gold circled the bottom of the cap. The slick body, smooth as silk, gleamed softly like the eye of a dove.

The boys grabbed the pen. Riri said "It's a *stylo*." Before they had time to uncap it, Mireille snatched it. "It's Nanna's." She caressed the pen with her eyes before returning it to me. "Here's your *stylo*, Nanna. It's beautiful."

It was beautiful. Too beautiful to lay a hand on. What was I supposed to do with it?

Maman read my mind. "This is to make it easier to write, tomorrow. To make it so you won't waste time dunking your *plume* in the inkwell every other word."

I fell in love with the pen. Love at first sight. A love that quickly changed to aversion; Pa's gift made it even more imperative that I perform.

The days following the exam were a drone of relentless questions, "How did you do?" "Do you think you did well?" "You must have an idea how you did …."

Leave me alone!

I burned to shriek, "I failed miserably. Let everyone down. Let go of me."

I wanted to hide, but had no place to go.

TWO LONG, GUT-TWISTING WEEKS later, the Lycée and the Constantinois published the names of passing students. Mireille cut out the newspaper's article and pinned it to the kitchen wall with my name underlined.

On Sunday, Maman gave a family celebration dinner, including Pépé Vincent and Yvette and Gilles. Everyone fêted me. Papa boasted. "This is *MA fille*. She's her father's daughter."

I was happy for all of them, but secretly expected, any moment, now, to hear from the board of exams, informing me there had been a mistake. That I had failed.

While I died of embarrassment over undeserved credit, Papa offered rounds of drinks at *La Guinguette* and *la Boule Tricolore*, his Bocce club.

Day after day passed without word of my failing and I began to relax and enjoy what was left of summer.

BY THE END OF summer, the dread I previously experienced before the start of each school year gave way to the belief that a new dawn was rising for me. A conviction that *la sixième* would be the springboard that would propel me to the pinnacle of outstanding studenthood. That the daily bus ride to the Lycée in Constantine would carry me through the threshold of self-reliance and adulthood. For the first time—at least while I was away from home—my life would be free from the responsibility of caring for my brothers and sisters. Of dragging them like a cumbersome tail wherever I went. I would be free to be a unique, distinct individual.

Still, I wondered how brave I would be facing the world without Zizou at my side.

I did learn to manage without her and slowly made friends. Susanne was in *Classique,* with emphasis on Latin and Greek. I was in *Moderne*, stressing math and science—it had been my luck that the Lycée's *Directrice* and my parents decided that, math being my weak point, I must be schooled in it. How logical was this? How lucky could I be?

Math didn't make any sense to me. Math homework and tests were a nightmare. Reading the problems was like looking at a blank wall. Fortunately my other friend and classmate, Monique, excelled in math and, bless her heart, allowed me to copy her homework minutes before it was due.

I enjoyed English, loved French, and couldn't wait for the weekly Greek Mythology class.

"Why can't I change to *Classique?*" I asked.

"Latin and Greek are dead languages that will not put food on your plate."

"But, Pa, I'd be very good at it." I added with passion, "I know I would."

"The choice was made for your own good."

So I limped through *la sixième* and shuffled through the beginning of *la cinquième.*

Quarantine

ONE MID-JANUARY NIGHT OF my thirteenth year, I tossed and turned in bed. Math homework was due in the morning and Monique was home sick. *God, please, make me sick too so I won't have to go to school without my homework done.*

Zizou fumed. "Stop tossing. I want to sleep." She pulled the blankets her way. "And stop hogging the blankets. I'm cold."

I curled up on my side and cradled my misery in the tight space between my knees and elbows.

When I woke up the next morning, my forehead didn't even feel warm. Darn, *pas de fièvre*.

I dragged myself to the kitchen wishing something awful would happen to keep me home. I kissed Maman on both cheeks, "*Bonjour, Ma.*"

"*Bonjour ma fille.*" She felt my forehead. "*Tu es fievreuse.*"

My brows shot up in surprise. *I didn't feel feverish when I woke up.*

She held my chin. "Stick your tongue out." She opened the front of my pajamas, examined my torso, and ordered me to bed.

On the way to my room, I heard Ma say four more times, "Stick your tongue out," then she sent six-year-old Riri to my bed. She took our temperatures and compared our symptoms with those described in her home-care bible—the medical book she consulted when we fell ill.

The heavy leather-bound volume described symptoms of what seemed like every disease and deformity in the world, supported by large color plate illustrations—the pictorial details so vivid that whenever we peeked at them, Zizou and I squirmed and scratched for half an hour.

"*Scarlatine,*" Maman announced.

Scarlet fever kept Riri and me *en quarantaine*—four weeks of isolation in our parents' bedroom during which we had contact with no one but them.

After a while of such isolated, close living, Riri started to call me "Maman," which both flattered and touched me somewhere deep in my belly.

To make time move forward, I read and did school work Papa collected from my teachers. He brought in books and games. Still, days were long and nights, endless. *Well, Nanna, you prayed for it. Didn't you?*

More and more often, I got up and stared out the window. In the late January daylight, the trees' bare branches scraped the wintry sky, and the fields down the road and weeds lay flat and dull.

Even the pear and fig trees at the edge of the back garden stood barren of fruit and leaves. But the large laurel, darker green than in full summer, bore leaves that still perfumed Maman's cooking. And, best of all, it held a secret ….

Upon reading stories about the Barbary Coast corsairs and Sinbad the Sailor, I had become convinced that a treasure chest lay buried among the roots of our laurel tree. I was so certain of its existence that it might as well have stood in the yard, open for the entire world to behold, brimming with diamond tiaras, ruby rings, streaming garlands of pearls, and jewels of opal, emerald, and sapphire. They sparkled in my mind's eye as brightly as in a full August sun.

I didn't need to dig among the roots or pry open the lid to prove it lay there. It was enough for me to know.

I wanted to share my secret with my little Riri. But he played in his pen or slept, hugging his cowboy hat. *Well, he wouldn't understand what "treasure" means, anyway ….*

THE BLESSED DAY CAME when the quarantine was lifted. Hungry for fresh air, I ventured out the front door to the *perron* and its usual commanding view of the compound across the street and the surrounding fields. Today, a world oddly void of people and sounds greeted me and a bleak sky cloaked the still air with an eerie yellow haze. The ghostly mood filled me with a hard-to-define dread until a faint motion on the other side of the compound wall across the street breached the odd gloom. A glimpse of the old Fatima's solid frame vanishing behind her beaded door curtain.

Several families with common ties occupied separate quarters of the enclave. Most had known my mother since she was born. Fatima, the oldest living resident, owned a few cows she pampered like kittens. In return, they let her draw milk from their meager tits and provided the dung she shaped into flat patties and plastered to her adobe walls, drying them out for use as fuel for her *canoun* at cooking time.

* * *

EVERY MORNING FATIMA WADDLED across the street on her bowed legs and stout bare feet to our front door with her milk pail. We returned the previous day's empty container and counted change into the palm of her large hand, rough as a man's. She smiled her strong-toothed smile and dropped the change inside the bosom of her flowered dress.

Liver spots further marred the freckled complexion of a true redhead, the skin deeply crevassed and thick as the hide of her cows. As old as she was, she was still a force of nature, and when I visualized her as a young woman, I imagined the beauty and might of an Amazon.

"Tomorrow, I make *fromage blanc.* Your mother, she want some?" Fatima would ask.

"Ma, do we want *du fromage blanc*?"

Sprinkled with sugar, Fatima's home-made cottage cheese was the best summer dessert ever, and Ma knew we wouldn't leave her in peace until she said yes. She'd call from the kitchen, "Fatima, can you bring four *fromages*?"

"You sure you don't want six, Elise?"

After a beat, Ma would say, "All right, bring me six."

Fatima would waddle heavily down the stairs, the empty milk pail swinging from her fingertips, a glad smile on her face.

* * *

WHILE, FROM THE *PERRON*, I watched Fatima's lengths of beaded curtain sway behind her, Doctor Laurie's car drove up and parked at the roadside along our yard.

He shined a light in our eyes, checked our tongues, and, after pronouncing little Riri fit to return to kindergarten and me to step into the second semester of *la cinquième,* he knocked on Pépé Honninger's bedroom door.

"Is Pépé sick, doctor?" I asked.

Doctor Laurie patted my cheek. "We are trying to find out, Nanna," he said, and opened the door.

I tried to follow him in, but he gently pushed me back. Nonetheless, before the door closed, I stole a quick glimpse at Pépé. A very pale and gaunt Pépé. *What is wrong with him?*

Chapter Twenty-One

Shots

June, 1957

" "**I**F YOU PLEASE—DRAW ME a sheep!"

"What?"

"Draw me a sheep!"

It was Saturday. I celebrated the first day of summer holidays and my upcoming fourteenth birthday sitting on the floor, leaning against the foot of my bed, a book open in my lap. I had reached the part where plane-crash survivor Saint Exupery meets the little prince in the desert when Papa's car turned into the driveway. *Strange.* Every Saturday, his day off as police investigator, Pa checked on the work his workers had accomplished during the week. He wasn't due back home from the cemetery until much later. *Strange ....*

I closed my *Little Prince* book, met Papa in the corridor, and trailed him into the kitchen. Riri, who had spent the day with Pa, followed. Our father's pallor under the suntan, shortness of breath, and Riri's blue eyes big as Delft saucers, all suggested something bad.

Maman ogled her husband and seven-year-old son. "What happened?"

"They killed Gorman."

Maman's hands dripped with water as she filled two glasses at the faucet and set them in front of Papa and Riri. "When? Where?" She wiped her hands on her apron and pulled out chairs for them. "Why?"

"At the cemetery, Ma. And Papa ran out with his gun," Riri squeaked, the high pitch of his voice betraying his nervous excitement.

We all zoomed in on Papa like periscopes. He took a sip of water and put the glass down. "I was at the shop, planning the next job with Debbah, when

I heard gunshots outside. Someone yelled, 'They shot Gorman.'"

"*Oui,* Ma," Riri cut in, "and Pa drew his gun and ran out."

Papa snarled, "Didn't I tell you to stay in the shop with Debbah?"

Maman blanched. "Why? Did he follow you?"

"I didn't realize it until—"

"I wanted to make sure nothing happened to you, Pa," Riri broke in again.

Papa's dark look silenced him. "I ran to see what happened to Gorman and bumped into two armed terrorists running out of his shop—"

"They saw Papa and shot at him"—Riri's eyes pulsed a darker blue—"and at me, too."

We listened, mesmerized. Mireille spoke for all of us, "I'm glad they didn't hurt you, Pa, and Riri."

Papa took up where Riri had left off. "Their shots went wide—"

Still wound-up, Riri crooked his thumb and pointed his index finger at Papa. "Peeeve. Peeeve," imitating the sound of ricocheting bullets.

"Stop that. RIGHT NOW," Maman warned.

Mireille cut in, "Then what happened, Pa?"

"I took aim at them, but a bus showed up and let out a group of Arab women and children and the terrorists took cover among them. They took potshots at me from there and I couldn't return fire without the risk of hurting civilians." Papa took another sip of water. "I'm lucky. They must have run out of ammunition because they fled."

"That's when Papa went after them," said Riri.

Zizou batted her eyelashes. "Did you get them, Pa?"

"*Merde, non.* While I neared the cluster of civilians, I stopped, thinking, 'Hey Vincent, you old son of a bitch, what if another of these armed fuckers is hiding among them? He'd drop your ass before you'd know it.'"

A disappointed Yves asked, "So, you didn't kill them, Pa?"

Papa studied his four-year-old son with hard eyes then went on, "The crowd dispersed and I walked back to check on Gorman, but discovered," he gave Riri a pointed look, "that this little shit had been standing at my side all along." He shifted in his seat and lifted his arm to backhand Riri, but changed his mind. "When I tell you to hide, you hide." He stared at each of us in turn. "*Compris?*" His green eyes seethed with anger. "Or I'll beat the shit out of you all."

We all nodded in a hurry.

"Now," Papa's green gaze stabbed four-year-old Yves. "*Non,* I didn't 'kill' them. First, had I gone on shooting, I would have hurt innocent women and children. Second, by going after them I could have fallen victim to an ambush." He asked Yves, "Do you know what an ambush is?"

The kid bobbed his head. "It's like when Riri hides and jumps on me when I don't know he is there."

Papa nodded "Third, this is real life, *mon fils*. Not a cowboy movie. One kills only to defend one's life or protect someone else's."

Maman laid her hand on Papa's. "I'm sorry Gorman is dead. Do we know why they did it?"

Papa's neck pulsed and he swallowed hard. Monsieur Gorman had been his patron and friend. He shook his head. "Because he was there."

Chapter Twenty-Two

IN THE COURSE OF the next two years, bad times followed good times and good times followed … nothing old. Nothing new. Until, something *really* new heralded the year of my sixteenth birthday

Papa, Please

May, 1960

DURING THE WEEKS LEADING up to my sixteenth birthday, my father boasted, "*Ma fille* passed *le Certificat d'Étude.*" He offered rounds of toasts and threw a theatrical hand in the air. "How could it be otherwise?" he bragged. "She has her father's brains."

Sure I do—fair-weather friend!

The Examination of Primary Education diploma was promptly added to the box containing the other important family documents. Having no other recourse, I basked in Papa's pleasure and waited impatiently for the forthcoming summer holidays.

THE WEEK BEFORE THE last day of school, my friend Susanne said, "My parents agreed to give a party to celebrate passing *le Certificat*. Would you like to come?"

Would I like to come? I mean, to go? Hell yes. Overwhelmed with the idea of my first party—nobody had ever invited me before—"*Oui,*" spilled out of my mouth without first going through my brain. "I'll go."

"It will be next Sunday, starting at two in the afternoon." She nudged my arm and grinned. "There will be boys."

"Boys?" I echoed, pain in my voice.

Her index finger pushed her thick glasses back up the bridge of her stubby nose. "I tried to convince my parents they didn't have to supervise, but they said, 'Unless you want it to be girls only … and remember, no alcohol.'"

"That's all right; I don't drink." Even if I did, I wouldn't mind not being able to.

Going to this party became the single focus of my life. I agonized over how to ask Papa's permission. I lay in bed so worried he'd refuse that I twisted and turned, prompting Zizou to protest, "Will you let me sleep!"

I rehearsed one approach after another. But, whenever I was close to broaching the subject, my guts churned and I chickened out.

Two days before the celebration, Zizou warned, "You're running out of time."

"I know, but I'm afraid he'll say no."

"Well, if he does, he does." She gave me a wink. "But I'd suggest you don't ask and just go."

"I can't do that." *Could I?*

In the end, I approached Papa at his courtyard workbench. I often watched him work, initiating idle conversations to manufacture a warm togetherness moment when I'd have him all to myself. But this time, I doubted the moment would be so cozy.

I worked my mouth several times, like a fish out of water, until the words squeezed out. "Papa I …."

After a short hush broken only by the sound of blood whooshing in my neck, he said, "Yes …." his tone reserved—letting me know he was aware I needed something from him but was afraid to ask.

He kept his eyes trained on his task—reeling me in. I took a deep breath and blurted, "My friend from school, Susanne—you know, Monsieur Schroeder's daughter?—she's giving a party at her house next Sunday to celebrate passing *le Certificat* and she's invited all her friends who passed and her parents will be there the whole time and there won't be any alcohol. Can I go Papa?"

"*Non,*" he decreed, not even looking up.

"But, Pa, I passed *le Certificat* and I'll be sixteen at the end of the month. Can I go, please?" I cast all sense of pride to the wind and begged, "Please, Papa, let me go."

His eyes remained on his busy hands. His mouth twisted at one corner. "Will boys be there?"

I'm going to lie. I'm going to say there won't be boys at the party. It's my only chance. I'm going to lie.

I said, "Boys are invited," and quickly added, "but Monsieur and Madame

Schroeder will be there the whole time. Everyone else who passed the *Certificat* will be there. Say *oui,* Pa."

He remained bent over the workbench, intent on his work. "I said*, Non.*"

"Please, Papa, *sois gentil.*"

But he refused to be nice. "*J'ai dit non.*"

Defeated, I sidestepped around the bench and shuffled toward the house. I had nearly reached the bottom of the stairs when I heard "Psst!"

Zizou's head poked around the corner at the far side of the house. She beckoned with a crooked finger. When I joined her, she whispered, "What did he say?"

My faint side-to-side headshake was news enough. She plumped her cheeks and blew air out. "I knew it." She shoved my shoulder in anger. "Why don't you do like I do—don't ask and do what you want?"

"*Oui,* you can do that because you're younger and he thinks he doesn't have to watch you—not yet. He thinks I'm so stupid and gullible, boys could make me do whatever they want."

"Well, it's too bad. I really kept my fingers crossed for you to go." A quacking laugh escaped her lips. "I hoped the boys there would get to know you and stop calling you '*la princess de glace.*'"

My brows shot up. "They call me the ice princess?" I couldn't believe it. "What does that mean?"

"At the bus stop, you never answer their smiles and look away. They believe you think you are too good for them."

"But that's not true. I think they're making fun of me, because I have skinny legs and don't have big boobs like the other girls."

Zizou shrugged. "Well, I tell you how it is."

A deep anger roared inside me like a mighty wave crashing upon jagged rocks. I hit the stucco wall hard with the side of my fist. "It's not fair. It's just not fair."

Baited by Zizou's rising eyebrows, I squared my shoulders and gave her a withering stare. "I don't care what HE says. I'm going."

She threw me a dubious look. "You're sure that's what you want?" Stunned by what I had just said, I remained silent. Zizou sighed. "You know there will be hell to pay."

"I don't give a fig." I lifted my chin and proceeded to tighten the noose around my neck, "I'm going." Then pounded the last nail in my coffin, "Nobody or nothing will change my mind."

She snorted. "Well, hopefully, one of the boys will 'defrost' you with a kiss and you won't have to ask me how it feels to be kissed ever again."

I shoved her shoulder and cracked a smile. "*Idiote.*"

During the thirty-six hours left before Sunday afternoon, I felt relieved that I had been brave enough to ask Papa's permission, but sorry for my rash pledge to Zizou. I vacillated hourly between defying my father's will and giving in to it.

On Sunday, I helped clear the lunch dishes until Papa retired for his siesta then changed into my Sunday clothes. Maman asked, "Where are you going, *ma fille?*"

I glanced at the kitchen window framing the two miles of road leading to Susanne's building. "To Susanne's party."

My mother paled. "You can't, Nanna. Your father forbade it."

I resisted stamping my foot. "It's not fair and I'm going."

Mireille and the boys' eyes shifted from Maman to me as if watching a fascinating game of ping pong.

Zizou, however, studied me like a cat would a trapped mouse scurrying for a way out.

Maman's hands flew to her face. "Nanna, your father is going to kill you for challenging him and me for letting you go."

"I don't care." I spun on my heels and left.

Angelo

THE INTOXICATING BRAVADO THAT had sustained me grew fainter as my Sunday shoes trampled the road dust, whittling away at the distance to Susanne's place. Guilt at leaving my mother in a bad spot nagged at me. The distracted glance I cast at the Arab adobe houses lining the road at my left glided to the plowed fields at my right.

Soon, wheat would conceal the dry clods with a mantle of gold. The hairy ears would rustle and sway in the summer breeze, unveiling blood-red wild poppies.

Zizou and I used to pluck the buds hanging from the tip of their skinny spiked stems like shepherd crosses. We peeled back the green sheaths to reveal the tightly folded petals. Then we unfurled them, careful not to tear their delicate velvet membranes, and stuck them to our lips and cheekbones—a natural makeup that would leave no trace for Papa to get mad at.

The brief respite from worry provided by musing on the golden harvest and blood-red poppies vanished. *What am I doing?*

It would be just my luck if Papa decided on this of all days to cut short his siesta. He was like that. Seemed to have a sixth sense about things. He'd drive down, pluck me from the road by the scruff of my neck and bring me back home.

Nanna, age 16.

Susanne's building loomed, blinding-white, against the ultramarine sky. *Can't go back now.*

I dusted my shoes with my handkerchief and climbed the few stories to Susanne's apartment. Through the door, I heard music, the buzz of conversation, and laughter. I patted my hair and rang the bell, for the first time concerned about meeting girls outside of school grounds and boys I had never spoken to. Wondering whether I wore the right clothes.

The door opened and Susanne took my hand. "I was afraid your father wouldn't allow you to come."

"He didn't."

"He didn't? I'm impressed, Nanna. It's not like you to go against him. Hope there won't be hell to pay."

That expression again. Sharp fingernails pinched my guts. I forced a bland smile and cast a shy glance across the crowd. A blur of bodies writhed to the beat of rock 'n' roll. Reluctant to make eye contact with others, I focused on the back of Susanne's head as we waded through the crowd to greet her parents.

Madame Schroeder had been very nice to me the two times I had *goûter* at their apartment after school. Monsieur Schroeder was an acquaintance of Papa's.

My friend's mom smiled. "We are glad you came, Nanna. Susanne thought your father might not allow you to come."

I inclined my head, thus acknowledging her comment without having to lie.

Susanne took my arm and marched me to the buffet. Her hand swept over the laden table. "Help yourself," she said, and in a smooth motion, turned to a cluster of boys standing close by, drinks in hands, and introduced me to one of them. "Nanna, this is Angelo. Angelo, this is my friend, Danielle."

I was struck stupid.

Susanne's discreet poke moved me to take Angelo's offered hand. He shook mine with a firm grip. "*Bonjour,* Mademoiselle Nanna."

My eyes traveled from our linked hands to the scarf folded in the opening of his shirt's wide collar, spread over the V-neck of his Argyle sweater. He looked more mature than the other boys who surrounded him like a prince consort's retinue. His bright smile and black velvet eyes struck me even more stupid.

Susanne poked me again.

The room temperature rose sharply and I blushed.

I tried to pull my hand away, but he held onto it. I averted my eyes. "*Bon—Bonjour,*" and not knowing why, added, "Thank you." *What was his name?*

His entourage watched with the keen eyes of vultures perched on the twisted limbs of baobabs.

One boy snickered and the room temperature plummeted. My blood rushed ice crystals down to my toes. *Great! Not only am I "la princesse de glace," but now I've become "La STUPIDE princesse de glace."*

Angelo—*Oui, that's his name*—released my hand. "Would you like some punch, Nanna?"

I nodded, relaxing a tad as the other boys dispersed.

Angelo offered me a glass of ruby-red punch and raised his. "*Santé.*"

I steadied my drink with both hands, and avoiding his eyes, focused on his drink. "*Santé.*"

When our glasses clinked, a weird, painfully delicious shiver ran up my legs, forced my knees together. It almost felt like I wanted to pee. *What's happening to me?*

I was thinking I might need to go to *les toilettes* when Angelo took my glass and set it on the table along with his and grabbed my hand. "Let's dance."

I had learned to dance with my sisters, mimicking the adults doing the *paso doble* and *tango* on *La Guinguette*'s dance floor during the Fourteenth of July's celebrations. I'd also slow-waltzed holding my baby brothers in my arms. Yvette had taught us the One-Two-Three-Four-cha-cha-cha, One-Two-Three, and Zizou and I had made ourselves dizzy, whirling to the One-Two-Three tempo of Johann Strauss' waltzes. But none of these tutorials had prepared me for Angelo.

Angelo—*Ange* or Angel—danced with wings on his feet. My feet were made of lead. He patiently guided me to move in rhythm, encouraging me to dance on two feet instead of one.

When a slow number replaced a twist, he pressed me to his strong body. The scarf at his neck brushing my cheek released an unfamiliar peppery scent. Stirred, I breathed it in, when a boy on the dance floor winked at him. This signal of connivance felt like a slap in the face. *They are making fun of me.*

I stopped in mid-step.

Angelo frowned. "What's wrong?"

I stepped back. "I don't want to dance with you anymore."

He squeezed my hands, his dark eyes setting my cheeks ablaze. "Danielle, I want you to kn—" A thundering blast shook the building. The record player's needle skittered with a whine across the forty-five disc, and for an instant, everyone in the room froze as if they were mannequins in Madame Tussaud's wax museum.

Voices rising from the street below revived our petrified figures. We searched each other's eyes, connected through the conduit of common plight—the inimitable current that binds total strangers into fellowship and allows them to feed off one another's inner strength.

Angelo hugged me then laid a comforting forearm across my shoulders.

Monsieur Schroeder looked out a window, his voice almost lost in the din of police sirens. "Sounded like a bomb. Looks like it happened across the street." He turned around and gave us a warm smile. "It's all right; you are all safe here." He waved a hand to signal that the party should go on.

Someone started a new record. Couples resumed dancing, but the music, louder now, couldn't cover up the thuds of three more explosions, each one sounding farther away than the preceding. And yet the dancing continued as if nobody heard anything.

Up to that point, the novel satisfaction of being with people my own age had fogged Zizou's sober prediction of "hell to pay," but the successive reports, police and ambulance sirens revived the flutter in my belly.

I was in deep caca. Better go home *fissa.*

I pushed away from Angelo. "I have to go."

"I'll walk you home."

Yeah, all I needed was to show up at our house with Angelo in my wake. Hell, Papa would really *love* this. "Thanks, but my father is picking me up."

His lustrous eyes caressed my face. "Want to go to the movie next Sunday?"

I blinked slowly like a sticky-tongued lizard that caught a butterfly in mid-air and swallowed it.

Yeah, you, and me, and the shmala. Say yes, Nanna. Say yes.

I looked at my feet. "I don't know …." and left abruptly to find Susanne.

She hung onto her partner's neck. I glanced, bug-eyed, in the direction of her parents, but other couples sheltered *les amoureux*.

Siamese twins linked from pelvis to chest, they swayed to the pulse of the slow dance. Embarrassed, perhaps with a pinch of envy, I closed in on them. "Susanne—" they gazed into each other's eyes as if sharing secrets only they could read. "Susanne—" Her hand signaled I should leave her alone. "Susanne!"

"What do you want?" she barked, her eyes, magnified by thick lenses, devoid of their usual gentleness.

"My parents must be worried. I have to go."

She broke away from her friend. "You can't go out now. Let's call them." She slapped a hand to her forehead. "You don't have a phone."

"I have to go. Thanks for inviting me." I stepped closer and whispered, "It's been the best party of my life." I kissed her on both cheeks. "You don't have to walk me to the door. I'll say good-bye to your parents. Have fun."

Monsieur Schroeder asked, "Isn't your father picking you up?"

"*Non*, but that's all right. I don't mind. I can walk home."

"You can't walk home." He glanced at his wife. She nodded. He said, "I'll drive you. Let me get my car keys."

On the short drive home, Monsieur Schroeder frowned. "I don't understand why your father isn't picking you up."

I worried the hangnail on my forefinger. "Uh … I think—uh … I think he's mad at me."

"Why would he be mad at you?"

I brought the finger to my mouth and tore the loose skin with my teeth. "He didn't want me to go to the party."

A drop of blood replaced the pulled hangnail. I licked it.

Monsieur Schroeder swerved to avoid a chicken crossing the road. "Why not?"

The chicken scurried away, neck extended, wings flapping. "Because he asked if boys would be there and I said yes."

Monsieur Schroeder shook his head, mumbling, "Ah, Vincent, *mon ami*."

Silence settled as we arrived and parked the car along the curb. In the semi-darkness, my house crouched like a giant cat ready to pounce.

Facing the Music

I WAS SO GRATEFUL FOR Monsieur Schroeder's presence, I almost slipped my hand in his.

When we entered the kitchen, the family sat at the table, faces hovering over their soups as if searching for the meaning of life. Pa's spoon hung halfway to his lips. The stab of his green eyes burned like the puncture of a falling icicle. "Go to your room."

"Papa—"

The faces no longer stared at their bowls. They stared at Papa and me.

"*Ferme ta gueule.*" His voice was serene as a subglacial lake, but his words held the promise of the harsh chill to come.

"But, Papa, Monsieur Schroeder is here—"

"I said, 'Shut your trap.'"

Monsieur Schroeder stepped around me, into the light. "Calm down, Vincent, everything's all right." He scanned the weary faces around the table. "The party guests were good kids."

Papa's expression darkened like roiling clouds gathering before a tempest. Only, Monsieur Schroeder didn't see it coming. "In addition, my wife and I were present every instant."

Papa studied his spoon. He dipped it into his bowl and lifted it to his lips. But the soup spilled back into the bowl.

Papa warned, "Leave, Schroeder."

Monsieur Schroeder shook his head. "I'm sorry you're taking it this way, Vincent." He nodded to Pépé Honninger and addressed Maman. "I apologize for butting in without being invited." He turned around and left.

I fled the kitchen and went to my room, leaving the door ajar and standing in the dark—listening.

Amid the clinking of spoons against bowls, Maman asked Zizou to make room on the table for the next dish. Lone words strung into short sentences as she served the food.

Papa's challenging tone broke into the dining sounds. "Where are you going?"

"Taking food to Nanna," Maman replied.

"Bring that plate back here."

"But, Riri, she needs to eat."

Maman's plaintive pitch did not mollify him. "Let her starve." Silverware clanged against a plate and Papa snarled, "And you shut your trap too. You're responsible for what happened."

Anguish choked my mother's voice. "What did I do, *chéri*?"

"She defied me with *your* permission. *Tu fais la maquerelle à ta fille.*"

His accusation of my mother playing "Madam" to me cramped my stomach.

"How can you say this, Riri?" she asked, the tremolo in her voice, a sign of imminent tears. "I did not know she was going until she left—"

A chair scraped hard against the tile floor, followed by Pépé Honninger's voice. "I've had enough of this."

He stomped out of the kitchen, his shadow gliding ahead of him along the corridors' floor. I silently closed my door.

I LAY ON MY BED, staring at the dark 'til I was blind and my eyes closed. Bad move. Thoughts of what surely happened here after I left popped up. I envisioned Maman's anguish in expectation of Papa's fury while *I* danced.

On this day I had shaken off my father's yoke with the bravado of a Don Quixote, dismissing the key point that Papa was anything but a helpless windmill. I'd selfishly defied his authority without weighing the consequences to others.

My eyes flew open at the sound of the turning doorhandle, but immediately squeezed shut under the sudden glare of the ceiling light. I lifted a hand against the brightness. Zizou stood at my bedside bearing a tray. She pursed her lips and blew a soft "Shush," then pushed the door closed with her hip. "I brought you something to eat."

I swung my feet to the floor and sat up on the side of the bed. "I'm starving. *Merci.*" I set the tray on my knees and shoveled soup into my mouth with the fervor of a dog digging up a bone.

Zizou studied me as if she'd never seen me chomp on chunks of vegetables before. I swallowed. "Why d'you look at me like that?"

"Like what?"

"Like I'm a bug under a microscope."

"Well." She sat on the floor and rested her chin on her knees. "You know, until you left I didn't think you'd have the guts to go through with it."

I dipped my spoon into the bowl and grinned. "Me neither." I finished the last of the potage and set the spoon down. "But I'm glad I did."

"You can't believe how angry Papa was," she whispered. "He paced like a caged wolf then sat and stared at the kitchen wall." She leaned forward. "You know—the one with the indent from the bottle he threw at me, years ago, when we came back from Saint Arnaud after '*La Toussaint Rouge*'?"

I nodded. "Then what happened?"

"Nothing for a while, but you could tell he was planning something dreadful for you." She batted her eyelashes, relishing the tale. "He had the same look in his eyes as Torquemada, you know, the bad guy in the movie on the Spanish Inquisition."

Aïe aïe aïe! This is NOT good. "Then what?"

"Everyone was walking on eggshells." She framed her mouth with cupped hands, as if telling a secret. "Even the boys didn't squabble."

"What about Ma?"

"She stayed quiet too, even when Papa accused her of being your *maquerelle*."

"*Yaa*, I'm sorry about that. I should have thought of her before I made up my mind to leave."

Zizou scooted closer to my feet. "So, tell me about the boys you met at the part—" her mouth clamped shut as we watched the door handle move slowly. Mireille's nose poked around the doorjamb. She whispered, "Can I come in?"

Zizou asked, "What d'you want?"

Mireille shoved a small plate ahead of her like a white flag of truce. "I'm bringing this to Nanna."

I motioned she could come in. "And close the door," Zizou said.

Mireille set the plate beside me. I gave her the tray with the empty soup bowl and picked up her offering, a piece of *gruyère* cheese and slice of bread.

While I ate, she shifted from one foot to the other as if deciding whether to stay or go, then murmured, "Did you find a boyfriend, Nanna?"

My heart missed a beat. Zizou growled. "Mimi! Are you trying to make things worse?"

"I was just wondering, that's all." Mireille looked about to cry when Riri and Yves sneaked into the room. Six-year-old Yves held out a piece of cake. "We brought you dessert, Nanna." He stepped up and put it in my hand.

I examined the crescent-shaped bite in the cake. "What happened to it?"

Yves puckered his lips and rolled his gray eyes. I took hold of his chin and forced him to look at me. "Did a mouse take a bite out of it?"

He pulled away and licked chocolate frosting off his fingers. "It wasn't a mouse. It was me." He flashed his crooked smile. "I couldn't help myself."

Riri gave him a playful shove. "What this little twerp doesn't say is that he already had his dessert. This one was yours, Nanna."

I held Yves' eyes, broke the cake in two, and gave one piece to Riri, the other to Mireille. Yves yelped, "*Et moi?*"

"Didn't you already 'help' yourself?"

He shrugged and opened his mouth to reply, but a light knock on the door silenced him.

Pépé Honninger walked in. His neck and shoulders did a couple of stretch-and-rolls at the sight of the mob gathered in the room. "What are you all doing here?" A chuckle belying his stern words, he laid a hand on Yves' head, pointed his face toward the door, and gave him a tap on the *derrière*. "It's time for bed." He wordlessly showed both Riri and Mireille the door. "You, too."

Mireille made a long face and left with the tray, holding the empty bowl and plate.

Pépé stared at Zizou, still seated on the floor. "Don't you have to brush your teeth?"

She stood, stomped to the door and stuck out her tongue at his back.

Pépé stretched his neck right and left, then drew a chocolate bar from his pocket. He put it on the bed and left before I could thank him.

I knew the chocolate came from his armoire. The unexpected gift moved me because he dug into his treasure chest only on special occasions, mostly for the young ones.

I had just slipped the chocolate bar under my pillow when Maman came in with a bowl of soup and buttered bread.

As much as I needed to make it up to her, I couldn't eat any more. "Thanks, Ma, but I'm not hungry."

Her eyes roamed from the bedspread to the floor at my feet. *Breadcrumbs.*

She ignored the signs of the clandestine meals and beamed. "Did you have a good time at your first party, *ma fille*?"

"*Oui*, Ma." I burned to tell her about Angelo, but didn't want to create new worries for her. "I'm sorry Pa is mad at you. It's all my fault. I'm *so* sorry, Ma."

She tucked a strand of hair behind my ear and sighed. "Don't worry, *ma grande*, this too shall pass."

LATER ON IN THE dark, Zizou asked, "Nanna, you're awake?"

"I can't sleep. What is it?"

She chuckled. "Papa's the only one who didn't sneak in to give you food. What d'you think he'll bring?"

I frowned into the darkness. "He's going to bring … hmm … *Zlabeiyas* … *Makrouds*—with lots of honey—hmm … *Beignets salés … et sucrés*." Zizou added to the list of mouth-watering Arab sweets, "*Caca de pigeon* ....." The mattress bounced as she shifted position. "Will you give me some of your *Caca de pigeon*, Nanna?"

"I don't know. Have you been a good girl, listened to Papa, and stayed home?"

The bed double-bounced. "Yeah. *Alors*, tell me—how did it go? Did you meet a gorgeous boy? Who's he? Do I know him?"

I gave her the short version of what happened at Susanne's, knowing full well she'd pester me for days to squeeze more details out of me. And she was right on track. "So, why are you annoyed with Angelo? It's not his fault if a jerk winked at him."

"I think he bet he'd be first to go out with me. I think they all think he's won."

Zizou challenged me. "So what?"

"I'm not a stupid trophy."

"I've news for you, my girl. Boys bet against each other all the time. In sports. Who'll grow the first beard. Who spits the farthest. Girls, everything. So, let it go." She took a deep breath as inspiration struck her. "Do you like him?"

"Well. He's not very tall but he has a nice smile and his eyes give me the shivers."

She cackled. "So, *la princess de glace* will be thawed, after all." She faked a quivering voice. "Wait until she gets kissed."

I turned my back on her. "I don't want to talk about this anymore. Go to sleep, *idiote*."

Long after Zizou had fallen asleep, I furtively unwrapped Pépé's chocolate and let one small bite after another coat the inside of my mouth.

For days Papa gave me the silent treatment, dismissing my presence, even when I was in his direct line of vision, compelling me to be as quiet as a sparrow in the hush of a pending storm. I would have much preferred a slap in the face or his belt. Insults, even, rather than this endless, nauseating silence that made me feel like I didn't exist.

That summer, as time went by, my father and I learned to interact one cautious step at a time, like two strangers discovering each other's quirks and learning to live with them.

When he was home and my chores were done, I withdrew to my room, read or sewed or leaned on my balcony's railing.

Watching the world go by was like turning the familiar pages of a majestic book, bustling with Algeria's colors, sounds, and smells. It filled me with the exhilarating joy of belonging and gave me strength.

One familiar scene I watched from my balcony that summer of hostilities with my father was the Boussadia.

Chapter Twenty-Three

Le Boussadia

IN TIMES OF DROUGHT, the Boussadia appeared out of the dust at the top of the road. An impalpable ghost growing into a colossal ebony-skinned creature, he boogied down the road.

A flock of squealing Arab kids trailed him while the beat of his drum called for the desperately needed rain.

His helper followed, a flour sac over his shoulder, collecting *kessra*—the flat, unleavened Arab bread—and small coins from children sent by their mothers or from women, faces averted, slipping alms from behind partly open doors.

Shards of mirror speckled the towering fur hat, which emphasized his stature and lent him the appearance of a mystical force that delighted and terrorized the children.

They formed a respectful ring around him while he paused at door stoops. I held my breath as he closed his eyes, rose to the balls of his feet, and gyrated on bent knees, picking up speed with the increasing beat of his crooked stick against the drum's hide.

The paler soles of his feet slapped the hot macadam in a frenzied whirl that rattled the bells at his ankles and caused the animal pelts at his belt to lift away from his body like a furry tutu while the chips of mirror on his hat scattered blinding sparks of sunlight like a revolving ballroom orb. The delighted children hopped to the throb of his drumbeat, clapped their hands, and shrieked—their fun contagious to Riri and Yves, who clapped and hopped on our side of the fence.

Boussadia's body blurred like a whirling djinn raising a sand funnel, then he abruptly stilled and, flashing a set of strong teeth as dazzling as the white of his rolling eyes, he lunged at the kids with a roar. They screeched and burst into flight like sparrows at the sound of gunshots.

One day, after the frightened children scattered, the goliath took a step forward and lifted up a child who had tripped in his rush to flee. Terrorized out of his mind, the snot-drooling kid squealed, *"Ahbouiya-bouiyia, bouiyia …"* and scampered like a mouse on hot coals the instant the man released him.

With a last roar, *Boussadia* swaggered down the road and around the bend, towing along the haunting echo of his drum.

The young children dispersed while their older brothers began a game of sticks.

They placed a short piece of wood on the road and hit it with the end of their sticks, causing it to flip in the air where they hit it again into the distance.

Clearing the road to let the sporadic car or military vehicle pass, they then resumed their game with gusto. They rushed, elbowed, and shoved each other, yelled warnings and laughed in the midsummer scents of stirred dust, cow dung, and eucalypti.

My brothers looked on, yearning, I knew, to join the game, but they were strictly forbidden to step out on the road. I called, "Are you ready to have your *goûter*?" and left the *perron* for the kitchen.

Yves joined me right away, Riri lingered at the fence.

In the kitchen, I cut thick slices off a large baguette. I rubbed their crusts with a garlic clove then split each slice open, dribbling olive oil on the doughy part and sprinkling it with salt—my preferred summer snack.

Yves made a face at my garlic-smothered bread. "Nanna, can you make me bread with *du lait Nestlé,* instead?"

I retrieved a can of Nestlé's condensed milk from the pantry, punched two holes in the top, and trickled the gooey syrup on his bread.

"One for Riri, too, Nanna, please?"

"Is that what he wants?"

"That's what he wants."

Yves carried both snacks to the *perron* outside the front door and called, "Riri, come get your *goûter.*"

I started to return the can of milk to the pantry, but the temptation was too great. I tilted my head back and let the sweet syrup fill my mouth. *Mmmm. The only way to enjoy condensed milk—sticks to the taste buds.*

I licked my lips and joined the boys, bringing my snack with me.

Face and hands sticky with milk, Riri mused, "If we practice sticks, maybe the kids in the street will let us play with them?"

I sat between the two boys. "I don't think so."

Riri turned his sky-blues on me. "Why not?"

"First, because you are not old enough. Second, because you might lose an eye from that flying piece of wood—"

Riri, 1959.

"I'm nine. How old do I have to be?"

I plucked a number at random. "Twelve. And you know you're not allowed to set foot in the street." I frowned, trying to look fierce. "Remember what happened last time you disobeyed the rules?"

* * *

THE YEAR BEFORE, THE family had waited around the lunch table for Riri to arrive home from school. Time went by, but no Riri. Clearly upset, Maman served lunch. Pépé Honninger shrugged his shoulders and stretched his neck this way and that. Zizou and I hitched eyebrows at each other, guessing Riri would get the what-for as soon as he came in. Mireille stared at her plate. Yves stuffed himself.

Papa conjectured, "This little bastard *doit jouer aux billes* and forgot the time." But a doubt seized him. Maybe his son wasn't playing marbles. He turned white as candle wax. "Son of a bitch. They kidnapped him."

Maman moaned. "*NON! Non, non, non.* Don't say that, *chéri*. Please don't even think it."

Pépé's tics disappeared and he turned to Yves. "Did your brother say anything about going somewhere after school?"

Yves kept on chewing his food and shrugged.

Pépé's voice strengthened, "Did he say he was going to be with a friend?"

Yves swallowed. "He didn't say anything like that."

Papa zeroed in on him like a snake on a field mouse. "If 'nothing like that,' what else did he say?"

The seriousness of the situation seemed to sink in. Yves' eyes grew bigger and glistened with tears. He dropped his fork on his plate. "I swear, Papa, I don't know anything."

Papa stood, almost losing his balance. "I think they took him. To get at me."

It wouldn't be the first time the family of a police officer had become a terrorist target. A payback for arresting their acolytes.

Papa lurched out of the kitchen. "I'll go look for him." He glanced over his shoulder. "The rest of you stay home. No school this afternoon."

Maman ran after him. "I am coming with you."

Pépé left the table. "I'll go to *La Guinguette* and get a search party together."

Stories of horrible tortures inflicted on hostages flooded my mind. Mireille cried. Zizou locked herself in the bathroom. I stalked from room to room in anguish, pinching myself to make the hurt in my chest go away. *Not my Riri, please, God, not my Riri.* Then I paused. Yves sat on the floor, leaning against the wall, hugging his legs, forehead propped on his knees. He sobbed with the abandon of a six-year-old. I forced him up. "*Viens, mon petit.* Let's sit and wait on the stairs. Don't worry. Papa will bring him back."

And he did.

Yves and I rose from the stoop and warned our sisters, "Riri's back."

The car had not yet come to a full stop before he flew out the door like a sparrow before a hawk.

Papa stepped out of the car and paused to light a cigarette. He struck a match. It broke. He struck a second one. It, too, broke. The third one flared. With shaking hands, he brought it to his face and muttered around the cigarette, "That little shit. That son of a bitch. I'm going to kill him."

Maman rounded the car. Some color had returned to her face. "Calm down, *chéri*, please. Let us thank God he is all right."

Deaf to her plea, Papa walked up the fifteen steps to the front door—deliberately—like Burt Lancaster at the O.K. Corral. His face was still pale, but had lost its waxen hue.

I was so grateful Riri was back in one piece that I didn't care if he got the whipping of his life.

He received a few wallops of the faithful belt without a flinch. *Way to go, little man.* But when Papa dragged him to the bedroom and handcuffed him at the foot of the bed, he cried out, "*Non*, Papa, *s'il te plaît*, don't do that."

"How many times have I told you to come directly home from school? Do you understand: *maison-école, école-maison?* Just as I've told you to stay in the yard and not step across the road?" He turned and glared at the rest of us. "Just as I warned all of you not to walk close to doorways where someone might hide and grab you." His raw voice broke and he stomped out of the room, slamming the door behind him, fuming, "Little fuck."

He glared at Maman, standing with the four of us in the corridor. "Your bastards will be the death of me." And left for *La Guinguette*.

Maman cooled Riri's face with a wet towel and brought him lunch. He ate sitting on the floor, one hand manacled to the foot of the bed. Zizou and I lounged on top of the blanket. Mireille and Yves sat on the floor. Mireille asked, "Where did you go?"

"I was coming home for lunch and when I passed the road that goes up on the right, I got the idea to follow it."

Zizou asked, "How far did you go?"

"Not too far, because I saw a bunch of Arab kids *qui jouaient au foot*. I asked if I could play and they said *oui*." He lifted a shoulder. "And I forgot the time."

So, while we all worried he might be dying in a horrible way, Riri was playing soccer—I couldn't blame Papa for being so angry. "But what made you decide to go up that road?" I asked.

His blue eyes, clear as an angel's in a stained-glass window, widened as if stating the obvious. "I wanted to see where it went!"

* * *

THAT'S MY RIRI, I had thought. I still wanted to kiss him for his answer but asked with what was meant to be an angry frown, "Remember what happened last time you disobeyed the rules?"

He nodded.

I bit on my bread. In spite of the sweet aftertaste of condensed milk, I savored the mixed fragrances of olive oil and garlic. *Hmm, could do with a lot more garlic.* I rose to get more and said, "Lucky you spent only a couple of hours tied to the foot of the bed. I would have kept you there for a week."

His impish smile angered me. "Wipe this smirk off your face. Do you think you'd have been smiling if the *fellagha* had taken you and hacked you into small pieces?"

No longer hungry, I stomped away before he could answer.

Night fret

A FEW EVENINGS LATER, WHILE the rest of the household slept, Zizou and I sat in bed, sharing pages of *Le Maghrébien*. The French doors to the balcony stood open. Through the slats of the closed shutters, a breeze tinted with the sweetness of acacia carried in the dreamy song of crickets. Suddenly, gunshots shattered the peaceful night. I started and looked at Zizou. Her pupils were dilated, reflecting my own dread. A bullet clanged against the balcony's ironwork. The room went dark and the shots stopped.

A tap, tap, tap sound broke the eerie silence. I felt around for Zizou's arm and whispered, "What's that noise?"

She shoved my hand back. "It's the newspaper, you *idiote*."

"What do you mea—?"

The sensation and sound of my knee beating a tattoo against the newspaper cut short my question. Panicked by the bullet's clank against our balcony, I'd dived under the sheets, dragging the newspaper with me.

I fished it out and dropped it to the floor. My heartbeat filled the darkened room. "Do you think a bullet cut the electric line?"

"What's wrong with you?" she snapped. "Don't you remember? You jumped out of bed and turned off the light. You flew across the room like a ballerina doing entrechats. Are you stupid or what?"

"I did that?" *Wow.*

"Just shut up and keep down, Nanna."

New volleys of gunshots rang in the street. Papa hollered above the racket, "Everyone, on the floor. Head down. Crawl away from the windows."

Zizou clambered over me and dropped to the floor. I rolled off the bed and crashed on top of her. "*Aïe*," she cried. "Can't you watch where you're going?" She shoved me off. "I got your knee right in my guts."

"Shut up," I said. "Get to the wall."

While we scurried across the floor, the door creaked open. In the near darkness, the corridor's nightlight outlined Papa's crawling shape and glinted off his handgun. "Are you all right?" His raspy voice resounded as if from the inside of a crypt.

"*Oui*, Papa," we said in unison.

"Keep your heads down and follow me."

We joined the rest of the family sprawled on the kitchen floor. In spite of the warm air, I shivered—my skimpy nightgown a poor barrier against the cold tile.

The gunfire stopped. Creaks and scraping from our rusty yard gate filled the ominous silence. Boots stomped along our garden path, followed by orders in French, "Kneel. Hands on your heads." Heavy steps tramped up our stairs. Loud knocks shook the front door. "French army. Open up."

Papa walked in a crouch to Pépé Honninger's bedroom for a furtive peek at the *perron* to ascertain the callers were who they claimed to be.

Then he returned to the kitchen and shoved his gun at Maman. "Hide this."

She hurried to their bedroom while he opened the door.

Soldiers rushed in, turning on the lights, searching every room. When they were done, Papa vented his anger. "What do you think you are doing invading French citizens' homes without their leave?"

One very handsome soldier with marks on his sleeves said, "*Je suis désolé, monsieur*. We are only following regulations. Terrorists could have forced themselves into your house or you could be sheltering them."

While he spoke, his eyes swept over everyone in the room, briefly lingering on me. Papa barked at me. "Get dressed." He glared at Zizou and Maman. "You too."

When we returned to the kitchen, wearing dressing gowns, the soldier was saying, "Our foot patrol was ambushed by terrorists hiding in your front yard. At first, we could see their silhouettes against the light filtering through your shutters, but then it went dark."

Zizou and I glanced at each other. I made big eyes at her, but she couldn't shut up. "Yeah, Nanna turned it off."

My ears burned with embarrassment. "I heard gunshots, and I think a bullet hit the balcony." I pointed at Zizou. "She says I got out of bed and switched the light off." I glanced at my father. "A normal thing to do, I guess, when one hears shooting. But I don't remember doing it."

The soldier said, "The attackers must have shot at your window, hoping someone would do just that." Seeing my discomfort, he smiled. "You had no way of knowing, *mademoiselle*. We still got them."

For Papa's sake—or, rather, mine—I lowered my eyes until the soldiers left the room, Papa at their heels. Zizou cast me a knowing glance. I stuck my tongue out at her and returned to bed.

The next morning, Papa used the tip of his pocketknife to extract pieces of shrapnel that had become embedded in a shutter after a round hit the balcony's wrought-iron railing and disintegrated. If not for the balcony's interference, Zizou or I might have been hurt, maybe killed. *Is that Maktoob or what?* Destiny must have had better things in store for us—like allowing me to see Angelo, even though Papa still confined me to the house and fenced yard.

Papa Meets Angelo

THE FENCED YARD. THAT'S where Angelo called on me when Papa wasn't home. One Friday afternoon, as we met on opposite sides of the fence, my father's car rounded the bend at the bottom of the road. My stomach did a somersault. Papa wasn't supposed to be home until much later.

My first reaction was to bolt up the stairs and into the house, but either pride or pigheadedness kept me rooted.

Angelo and I watched Papa park the car and amble toward us, a frown creasing his brow. He snarled, "Who's that punk?"

The insult burned my cheeks and I struggled to keep calm. "Papa, this is Angelo. I met him at Susanne's party."

Papa zeroed-in on Angelo, his green glare venomous. "What do you want here?"

Angelo grinned. "Bonjour, Monsieur Bjork. I was passing by and stopped to say hello to Danielle."

Were it not for the fence between them, Angelo would have offered to shake hands, I thought, filled with admiration for his pluck.

Malice greased Papa's voice. "'Passing by, *hein*?" He stuck his balled fists on his hips. "Do you take me for an asshole?"

Angelo's eyebrows shot up, but he remained silent as my father barreled on, "That's what I did when I came to see her mother and have her fall for me: 'passing by.'" He took a pack of Gauloises out of his breast pocket. "Where do you live?"

"Sidi Mabrouk Inferieur, *monsieur*."

Papa leisurely tugged out a cigarette and turned toward me. "Did he ever touch you?"

To hide my humiliation and stifle the urge to scratch out his eyes, I stared at my feet. "*Non ....*"

"Didn't you dance?"

"*Oui ... Oui*, but we didn't get too close."

He studied me while striking a match and lit his cigarette. "Not too close ... Right." He shut an eye against the rising smoke and turned to Angelo. "What's your name?"

Mischief danced in Angelo's eyes. "D'Amore, *monsieur*. Angelo D'Amore."

"Italian." Papa shifted from one foot to the other. "What does your father do?"

"He's a commercial contractor."

Papa nodded as if pleased Angelo's family seemed respectable. He threw the half-smoked cigarette at his feet and ground it into the dirt, then, heading for the house, he spat over his shoulder, "Stay away from my daughter, you hear?"

Papa climbed the stairs and disappeared into the house.

Angelo defiantly pointed his chin at the empty doorframe. "I guess I'd better go."

I nodded.

"*À bientôt*," he said.

"*À bientôt*." I smiled, heart in my throat, fearing "soon" might turn into "never again."

Au Revoir

SINCE THE DREADFUL ENCOUNTER with my father, Angelo had not come back to see me. Seven days of sitting on the kitchen windowsill, making believe I read a book while casting covert glances at the road. Seven days of dashed hopes.

I tried to read, but after half a page, I cut an eye toward the scorched road to Sidi Mabrouk Inferieur. No Angelo. Zizou nagged, "You're letting in the flies. Close those darned shutters, for heaven's sake."

I pulled the shutters, leaving enough open space to keep an eye on the road, and returned to my book. Not a word stuck to my brain.

On the eighth day, at last, a faraway speck emerged from the road haze. My ears pricked like a puppy's at its master's voice.

As the speck grew, I recognized Angelo's gait. I jumped off my perch. Maman looked up from her knitting and teased, "*Amor, Amor, Amor* …." The old popular song making my heart flutter, I hurried to comb my hair and ran down to the front yard to stage an accidental encounter. I lingered over the weeds in a flowerbed when Angelo called up from the fence.

"*Bonjour*, Mademoiselle Nanna."

"Oh …." I turned with raised eyebrows and a handful of weeds. "How long have you been here?"

"I just arrived." He grinned. "Are you going to say *bonjour*?"

I dropped the weeds behind a calla lily and ambled to the fence, let out a breathy *bonjour* and laced my fingers through the wire. Angelo traced them with the tips of his. The shine of his black curls competed with the glow of his velvet eyes.

I looked down at our touching fingers. Blood raced to my face, adding to the heat of the blazing sun, but Angelo's next words hit me like a bucket of ice water. "Nanna, I came to say good-bye. We are leaving."

My heart skipped a beat. "You're leaving Sidi Mabrouk?"

"We are leaving Algeria." He wrapped his fingers around mine. "Nobody's building nowadays and my father's business has gone down the drain." His features dimmed as if under the shadow of a passing cloud. "An uncle in Italy offered him a job and we are moving there."

"Italy …." I murmured, "When?"

"Next week."

"Next week?" A vein at my neck marked time like a runaway metronome.

"We've known this for a couple of months," he added. "I hoped plans would change, but …." He retrieved a piece of paper from his shirt's pocket. "This is my address in Italy."

I unfolded it. "Siena. I've never been to Siena."

"I've been there on holidays. It's in Tuscany—where Florence is." He closed an eye against the sun. "Maybe, one day you'll come and see me?"

"One day ….?" I tried to keep a squeak out of my voice. "Maybe …."

He shoved his hands in his pants pockets, sidestepped until he reached the road and said, "I'll write." Then raised a hand and left.

I raised mine and followed him the length of the side fence along the sloping road and called out, "Angelo."

He stopped and looked up, shielding his eyes with a cupped hand. My heart hopped to my throat. "Did you …." I wavered, but had to know. "Did you bet with your friends that I would fall in love with you?"

He grinned. "I did." Then he sobered. "But I discovered I liked you … a lot … then all bets were off." He studied the toe of his shoe, tracing squiggles in the dust and looked up. "It's too bad we didn't have time." He flashed his cocky grin. "I would have loved to be your boyfriend."

Air filled my lungs and I beamed. "For sure?"

"For sure." He blew me a kiss with the flair of a plumed d'Artagnan and strolled down the road.

I rushed upstairs and leaned out the kitchen window. I held onto the sight of him until his silhouette dissolved into the shifting haze; then he was gone. Sadness at a friendship's lost potential and regrets at an unfulfilled romance followed in his wake.

I stood vigil at that window for days, wishing Angelo would come for one more good-bye. I waited with the same fervor and ache with which, as a five-year-old child, I had waited for Malika's return. But, unlike Malika, Angelo never turned up at the end of the road.

Angelo D'Amore had blazed through my life like a shooting star and no wish, however fervent, would ever bring him back.

Chapter Twenty-Four

—∾—

IN THE FOLLOWING MONTHS, no hope—however fervent—for the survival of *Algérie Française* had ever seemed more futile.

"Listen to this, Pa," I said, and read aloud from *Le Constantinois*. "'Recanting on the pledge of *Algérie Française* he made to the Algerian French and the army who brought him to power, General De Gaulle announced in his September 16, 1959 address that the fate of Algeria would be determined by a referendum on Self-determination.'"

I set the paper down beside Papa's plate and asked, "How can there be any chance at all that Algeria will remain French when millions of Arabs will surely vote, *Algérie Algérienne*?"

Papa pushed the daily aside. "Most Moslems will vote for *Algérie Française* if France assures them it will stand firm in its resolve to remain in Algeria. Short of that, in fear of the FLN reprisals, once they come to power, they will vote, *Algérie Algérienne.*"

"So, which is it going to be?"

"De Gaulle doesn't want to keep Algeria," Papa said. "That's your answer."

I seethed at De Gaulle's betrayal of his promises to us.

So, apparently, did thousands of other *Pieds-Noirs*.

Les Barricades

January, 1960

THE INSURRECTION EXPLODED ON January 24, 1960. Civilian *Pieds-Noirs* erected barricades in the streets of Algiers and seized government buildings. General Challe, commander of the Army in Algeria, declared a state of siege and announced a general twenty-four hour curfew.

Unable to venture outside, we gathered around our kitchen radio, holding our breath. In spite of General Challe's order to the army not to fire and the scattering civilians pleading, "In the name of France, don't shoot!" the French soldiers fired, leaving twenty unarmed insurgents dead in Algiers' Boulevard Laferrière. Nevertheless, in defiance of curfew, the insurgents in the capital held on to their barricades until De Gaulle made an appeal for the people's support and the army's loyalty to France.

To my bitter disappointment, the barricades came down, putting an end to the one-week rebellion the media dubbed *La Semaine des Barricades*.

Meanwhile, De Gaulle's betrayal of the *Pieds-Noirs* and of the Muslims loyal to France fueled bitterness and rage, causing some *Pieds-Noirs* to form *l'Organization de l'Armée Secrète*.

The *OAS* took action against the proponents of De Gaulle's auto-determination and FLN supporters, thus becoming the champion of most *Pieds-Noirs*, gaining in the process their unconditional loyalty and, in many instances, their complicit support.

The Bottles

March, 1960

"PAPA, I'M CONFUSED," EIGHT-YEAR-OLD Riri said, a few months after the Barricades came down.

"Confused about what, *mon fils*?"

"Who is for or against the *Pieds-Noirs*? And why?"

"Time for the old bottles," Zizou chuckled, eyes brimming with mischief.

This thing with the bottles had become a family joke when, needing to illustrate a complicated matter, Pépé Honninger lined up bottles on the table, each representing one of the points in question.

Papa's green eyes fixed on Zizou. We expected him to ram her for being flippant. Instead, he bit the inside of his cheek and motioned with both hands, "Right, bring in the bottles."

I asked, "How many?"

"Four should do it."

Brouhaha ensued as we spread out to grab bottles and set them on the tabletop.

Papa lit a cigarette and spoke around it. "I will explain this only once." He closed an eye against the smoke. "Because, if you haven't gotten the picture by now, you are all a bunch of assholes."

He set the cod-liver oil bottle apart. "This is the FLN—the Arab activists who seek the independence of Algeria from France through terrorist acts."

He fingered the bottle of red wine. "Now, this is the French government, represented by President Charles De Gaulle."

"You mean *La Grande Zohra*?"

A smug grin stretched my lips at Zizou's mention of De Gaulle's disparaging nickname. The Pieds-Noirs started calling De Gaulle, *La Grande Zohra* after a cartoon that depicted him wearing an Arab woman's garb and earings, suggesting that he was prostituting himself to those in favor of *l'Algérie Algérienne*.

Papa cast her a withering look then addressed me. "You saw him when he toured Algeria after he became President."

I nodded. The newly elected president, Charles De Gaulle, had pledged to thousands of ecstatic French and Arabs gathered on the Place de la Brèche that "*L'Algérie restera française!*" Algeria would remain French.

I was only fourteen at the time, but Papa had allowed me to accompany him and Maman to the gathering. "I remember," I said, and mimicked the president's famous index finger pointed upward and gravelly voice. "*Je vous ai compris.*" I understood you, he had said. And, "*Vive l'Al-gérie Fran-çaise.*" I could still hear the distinctive speech pattern resound among the buildings that framed Constantine's central square.

The recollection of the shameful lies, the betrayal of us who had led him to power, filled me with bitterness and anger.

While I reminisced, Papa had moved the red wine bottle next to the cod-liver oil. Now that the two bottles touched, the cod-liver oil's dark gold and wine's deep ruby overlapped over the oilcloth into a telltale muddied pool.

Pointing to the contiguous olive oil and vinegar bottles, Papa said, "These two represent the French Army. Its duty is to protect France against its enemies and follow orders from its government. In this case, that duty is to enforce De Gaulle's policies in Algeria."

Little Yves asked, "Why does the Army get two bottles?"

"I am getting there. Just shut your trap and listen. Better yet, make yourself useful and bring one more bottle."

Yves came back with the water pitcher. "I can't find any more bottles," he said.

Papa returned to the oil and vinegar bottles.

"Now, remember, De Gaulle was elected with the help of generals," he said, indicating the oil bottle, "who wanted to keep *l'Algérie Française.*"

He lifted the vinegar bottle. "This represents the generals who will follow the president's order no matter what." Moving it to the side of the cod-liver oil and red wine, Papa continued, "However, now that De Gaulle changed his mind and recommends self-determination, I predict that these generals ...." He held up the olive oil bottle by the neck and set it beside the water pitcher. "I predict that, in the near future, these generals will rebel against the new policy and take the side of the *Pieds-Noirs*," he tapped a finger on the pitcher's rim, "meaning us."

My guts tightened at the sight of the two separate sets of bottles and pitcher. They glowed under the kitchen light like a malefic portent of things to come. A gathering of forces of Evil against outnumbered forces of Good. A battle of epic proportions that didn't bode well for the *Pieds-Noirs*' future.

Riri laid his hand on the bottle siding with the pitcher. "So, this olive oil army is on our side?"

"*Oui*. It's on our side."

"And what is the *OAS*, Pa?"

"It stands for *l'Organization de l'Armée Secrète*. A group organized by *Pieds-Noirs* and a couple of generals. Its goal is to keep on fighting for *l' Algérie Française* by eliminating FLN terrorists and their supporters here and in France."

"By the way," he grabbed his empty glass and upended it on top of the cod-liver oil bottle, "this represents the French and international Communist Party, which gives the FLN its unconditional support."

Our father looked around the table. "Do you understand my explanation?"

We all nodded, except for Yves, who said, "Kind of."

"Right," Papa said. "Now get off my ass and let me eat in peace."

THE *BARRICADES* DOWN, CURFEW was raised and our life went on as if no hopes had been dangled then dashed. Our parents returned to work. We went back to school and home chores.

Some days brought little pleasures, others little miseries such as *petit* Yves soon came to experience.

* * *

La Trottinette d' Yves

June, 1960

THURSDAY AFTERNOON. HALF-DAY OFF from school, I sat at the kitchen table, gutting a chicken for dinner. Mireille washed lettuce from the

Yves, age 6, at La Boule Tricolore.

garden and Zizou peeled potatoes. Nine-year-old Riri stood at her side, flicking the peels across the oilcloth to the floor.

"Stop that." Zizou rapped his fingers with her knife handle.

He wrinkled his nose at her and sent another peel skittering over the table's edge. She pointed the knife at him like an accusing finger. "Pick that up."

His reply died before passing his lips when she fired him a blistering glare. He dropped to his knees and gathered the scattered peels, making faces at her once out of her line of sight.

I plucked feathers into the bucket between my feet and noticed only four of us were in the room, "Where's Yves?"

Riri rose from the floor and threw the potato skins on the table. "He's playing with his *trottinette*."

Not surprising. My little brother loved his new scooter.

Six years earlier, Yves had become the last addition to our family. He grew up a quiet, pleasant little boy with a crooked grin and winning sense of humor. Although he rarely got in trouble, I felt guilty for not keeping track of him. I marched in near panic to the front room balcony and checked the garden below.

Yves stood at the fence, fingers hooked through the wire. He looked up and down the sloping road, but his eyes didn't rest on the man straddling his donkey and his trailing black-veiled woman or on the passing cars and military trucks raising dust along the road.

Squinting under the blinding sun, I leaned over the balcony railing. "Yves. What're you doing?"

He didn't respond. His head swiveled from side to side like a mechanical toy—as if looking for something or someone to appear up or down the road. Reassured that he was safe, I shrugged and returned to my chicken.

Later, I returned to the front balcony. Yves stood at the same place, hands welded to the wire fence, peering up and down the road. Once in a while, his eyes rested on Fatima's cows clustered across the street then resumed their scanning.

"Yves, what're you doing?"

He did not turn around, but slowly shook his head.

I left the balcony and strode along the corridor, down the stairs to the front yard and joined him at the fence. As he didn't acknowledge my presence, I turned him around and forced him to look at me. His usually mischievous gray eyes didn't sparkle. "Yves, what's wrong?"

"I am waiting."

"Waiting for what?"

"For my *trottinette*."

"What do you mean you are waiting for your *trottinette*?"

He clenched his fists. "I am waiting for my *trottinette!*"

I straightened up. "All right, what happened to your *trottinette*?"

A thud from across the road checked his answer. Big, bowlegged old Fatima had stepped out of her walled-in yard and let the metal door slam behind her. We exchanged nods of greeting with her before she rounded the corner of the mud wall of her enclave. She waddled to the stone trough and her waiting cows, slapped them on the rump to open a path to the trough's water tap.

I turned to my brother. "What did you do with your *trottinette*, Yves?"

Resigned that I was not going to let the matter drop, he sighed, "I lent it to a kid."

"What do you mean you lent it to a kid? What kid?"

"An Arab kid."

"What Arab kid?"

He bowed his head and murmured, "I don't know."

"What do you mean you don't know?"

No answer.

"Are you saying you let a kid you don't even know take your *trottinette* away? What is wrong with you?"

Avoiding my eyes, his skittered to Fatima, who had gone and come back with a milking pail. "Well …"

The cows at the trough slurped the water, their skinny tails swatting at clouds of flies.

"Well, what? Look at me."

When he did, his eyes held something like resentment. "He said he did not have a *trottinette* and asked if he could play with mine, so, I lent it to him."

I stared at him without a word. He defensively added, "*He said* he would bring it *right* back."

"And how long have you been waiting here like an ass?"

He pinched his lips.

"You *know* you will not see him ever again, don't you? And you can say good-bye to your *trottinette*."

His shoulders sagged. He bit his lower lip, scraped the dirt with the tip of his shoe and shook his head sadly. "I know."

"Papa's going to kill you."

He acknowledged my prediction with a slow fatalistic shrug and, when I attempted to coerce him upstairs, shook his hand free.

He remained in futile expectation till dark, when I forced him to come up, wash his hands, and have dinner with the four of us.

Amid the clink of silverware against china, we stole glances at Yves who, eyes downcast, played with his mashed potatoes. At last, responding to Riri's attempts to cheer him up, he flashed a crooked grin and showed his spunky sense of humor. "I guess I should have waited for Papa's car."

I couldn't help smiling as his comment brought me back to three months earlier.

* * *

THE FAMILY WAS HAVING its midday Friday red snapper and oven-roasted potatoes, when Yves asked with a frown, "Papa, when you die, can I have your car?"

Reading while eating, Papa didn't hear the question.

Yves insisted, "Pa? Yo, Papa?"

Papa lifted his eyes from "Pecos Bill," his preferred illustrated magazine. He chewed his food, staring at Yves.

"Papa, when you die, can I get your car?"

Papa swallowed. "How soon do you want me to die, *fils?*"

"*Non*, Papa, not right now, but when you die, a long time from now, can I get your car?"

"And what makes you think you will get my car after I die?"

"Well, when Pépé Vincent died, you got his things."

Papa glanced at his empty wine glass and, with a motion of his index finger, signaled Ma he needed a refill.

While she poured, he asked, "Why do you think I would leave my car to you? What about your brothers and sisters? They have a right to the car as well."

"I know, Papa, but I asked first."

The rest of us had been watching the exchange like a game of ping-pong. It was now Papa's turn to hit the ball. He set his fork on his plate and frowned, apparently considering his son's point and rendered his verdict, "Look, son, I don't want to die just yet, so why don't you take my car now and let me enjoy my life a while longer?"

"I cannot drive the car right now, Papa, my legs are too short. I guess we can wait a while before you die."

"Thanks, *mon fils*, I'm glad to hear that."

Papa returned to his meal and magazine hero. Maman finished frying the last snapper and served the remaining roast potatoes while we passed the bread around.

Not allowed to speak at the meal table, we communicated among ourselves with waggling of the eyebrows, eye squinting, twisting of the mouth—any expression that would convey our feelings about whatever the matter at hand.

We were, thus, wondering how Yves was allowed to get away with breaking the rule of "children are meant to be seen, not heard," when he asked with a deep frown, "Papa?"

Papa turned a page and looked up without raising his head. "*Oui, mon fils?*"

"Since it will take a long time before I can get your car, why don't you buy me a *trottinette*—now?"

The only noise came from Maman's stacking the dirty dishes into the sink and the clanging water pipe.

Papa raised his chin, appraised Yves through half-closed green eyes, pressed his lips together, bobbed his head up and down, as if in a private dialogue, and returned to his reading. Zizou and I exchanged signs that meant, "That's that." But, several days later, Yves became the *very* proud owner of his own set of wheels—a *trottinette.*

Now it was gone.

* * *

AFTER DINNER, AND THE dishes done, I found Yves slumped on the *perron's* top step.

Under the vastness of a starlit summer sky, I searched his brimming eyes. "Yves, losing your *trottinette* is not the end of the world, you know."

"You tell that to Papa."

I spoke off the cuff. "Listen, I understand you feel cheated, but the one to really feel sorry for is that little kid."

"How can you say that? *He's* the one who stole *my trottinette,*" he cried in vexation and tears of anger, "I am a stupid idiot."

"That's true."

I did not have the heart to leave it at that, so, I fudged, "But think of it this way: the little thief will have to fight the other kids until another takes the *trottinette* away from him."

Yves' eyes shone grayer. And, getting the hang of it, I fudged further. "Now, tell me who will be stupid, then. *Hein?*"

"You think so?"

As he began to savor the sweet nectar of revenge, his face relaxed and a slow, knowing smile spread from his lips to his roguish eyes. "*Yaa,* but *you* tell that to Papa."

As it happened, our parents came in late that night and the issue of the lost *trottinette* took second seat to heartbreak.

Adieu

AT BREAKFAST THE NEXT morning, Yves' eyes drilled into mine, silently begging me not to spill the beans. I shook my head and made a rotating motion with my index finger to signal the matter of the *trottinette* would be addressed later. Then I gathered my schoolbooks and headed for the bus stop.

IN THE AFTERNOON, ON my way home from school, I planned my *goûter* with the relish of a child of six instead of a mature sixteen-year-old, picking and rejecting possibilities until I settled on a slice of *gros pain* slathered with a thick layer of churned butter sprinkled with loads of sugar. *Aïe aïe aïe.*

I opened the front door to my house, smacking my lips, and stopped in my tracks. White sheets shrouded the furniture.

The hair on my forearms bristled. *Pépé Honninger's dead.*

The blood test the doctor had done last January had revealed lung cancer. The disease progressed steadily until he became bedridden. On weekdays, with us children at school and Papa and Maman at work, Pépé was home alone all day.

Oh, God, make it so he didn't die alone.

"I checked on Pépé before leaving for work," Maman said after I held her close.

"I asked if he needed anything before I left …." Her voice faltered. "He only grabbed my hand and said something I couldn't understand. 'What did you say, Papa?' I asked. He squeezed my hand and garbled a few more words …." Blood leached from my mother's face. Her voice weakened and she took a halting breath. "We gazed into each other's eyes and … and he died."

The light in her own eyes had dimmed. Feeling her pain, I hugged her tight. "I'm so glad he didn't die alone, Ma."

"Thank God," she sobbed.

I nodded. This would have been so horrible for him. Imagine sharing your house with a crowd and dying without a living soul at your side. Ma's guilt would've been unbearable.

PEOPLE CAME AND WENT for last good-byes. People I knew. People I had never met before.

During a short afternoon lull, I heard a knock on the front door. Maman and I went to open it at the same time. Oscar, Pépé's fishing friend, stood on the *perron*. He hugged Maman with a fierce grip. "*Mon pauvre Pierro. Mon pauvre Pierro*," he bawled. The old man's grief sounded so melodramatic that a giggle bubbled out of me. I slapped my hands over my mouth, but the giggle spilled in between my fingers. I stepped behind Oscar and cast a mortified look at Ma. She returned the sobbing man's hug, patted his back, and made big eyes at me over his shoulder. "*Stop that*," they said.

Her face took on the tortured look of a constipated person with no hope of immediate relief. Then a bark of contained laughter slipped by her tightly pressed lips. Faking a cough, she let go of Oscar and escorted him to Pépé's bedside.

I rushed down the stairs, to the back of the house. Bent forward to hold my aching sides, I laughed. Laughed until I bawled.

I cried for Maman who had lost her father.

I cried for Pépé who had never had much love in his lonely life.

I cried for me who had not loved him.

It had felt as if Pépé Vincent had used up all the love I would ever be able to give a Pépé.

It had also felt as if loving Ma's father meant choosing him over my father and risking the loss of my pa's love.

I should've loved Pépé Honninger anyway.

Now, it was too late.

AT NIGHT, MOURNERS TOOK turns keeping company with Pépé. I sat on Mémé Aimée's settee, at the side of Pépé's bed, and watched the candlelight play hide and seek over people's features—beautiful, ugly, mysterious, serene, sad, sealed ….

I studied Oscar's creased face and opaque irises, his sparse gray hair flattened by the cap he doffed before entering the house. Though he and Pépé had spent lots of time together since they retired, I didn't know whether Oscar had a wife, children, grandchildren, a dog, or even a goldfish.

I looked away when he produced a handkerchief as big as a dinner napkin and blew his nose with the sound of a trumpet swan. This time, I didn't giggle but wondered what his thoughts were as he viewed the body of his old friend starting to rot. *Do you recall the blustering fish stories and personal woes you shared while you sat on the damp beach sand, pole in hand, waiting for the catch of the century? Or do you wonder how long before you'll set foot on the trail he is now mapping out for you?*

Oscar fell asleep in his chair. I felt like sleeping also, but rose from the settee and followed the smell of coffee. Maman and Tonton Gilles sat at the kitchen table, lost in private thoughts. Papa smoked, eyes looking at nothing. Yvette refilled coffee cups. I sat beside Maman and whispered, "I'm sorry I laughed when Oscar came to the house. It's just that I couldn't help it when he bawled so hard."

Maman played with her cup. "I know, *ma fille*. I too had a hard time not laughing." She took a sip of coffee. "The poor man," she added. "He and Pépé were life-long friends. He is going to miss your grandfather something awful." She tucked a strand of hair behind my ear. "Don't worry. It was just nerves."

She rose and put her empty cup in the sink. On her way out to Pépé's bedroom she said, "Go to bed, Nanna. Tomorrow will be a long day."

I nodded, but realizing I would not be able to see him after tomorrow, I returned to the settee and scrutinized Pépé Honninger's face. Same wooden look as Pépé Vincent's, but this time, I wasn't scared or angry. Instead, an unexpected memory flashed through my mind, pinching my guts—a moment, in August of the previous year, between Pépé and me.

* * *

THE KITCHEN WINDOWS WERE open, but no breeze came in through the half-closed shutters. The heat of the iron added to the heat of the day and aggravated my bad mood. Starching my percale petticoat always put me in a bad mood. The canons of fashion were adamant. One needed a starched petticoat to balloon out one's full skirts and, like every fifteen-year-old, I submitted to the trend.

The starch's sharp smell rose with the steam, burning my eyes, scratching my throat. Pépé walked in, holding out a shirt. "Would you iron this for me?" he asked, unsure if I would agree. I resented the imposition but put the petticoat aside and grabbed the garment. I dunked my fingers in the water bowl, sprinkled the shirt, and ran the iron back and forth without a word.

Pépé stretched his neck on one side then the other. "If you did nice things like this for me once in a while, I could do nice things for you," he said.

I looked up and was surprised by the fleeting vulnerability skimming his features. Until that moment, I had thought my grandfather was tough and didn't need other people. Now, I discovered a loneliness and need so intense that he was ready to barter for a bit of attention, a crumb of affection. I wanted to say, "D'accord, Pépé, just tell me when I can do something for you." But I wouldn't betray my father. Couldn't bear his resentment.

To my everlasting shame, I refused the olive branch and finished the shirt without a word.

In the kitchen's penumbra, a sad smile tugged at the corners of Pépé's thin lips as if he had read my thoughts and was making peace with them.

* * *

NOW THAT HE WAS dead, the chance to set things right had passed. Pépé's lips appeared to twitch under the candle flames, and a dull pain poked my guilty heart.

I didn't know then that a sharper pain lay in wait for us all.

Chapter Twenty-Five

Mouloud

July, 1960

"PA, WE NEED MORE paint." Zizou, Mireille, and I had run out of the green mix to finish the kitchen walls. The kitchen remodel started with the addition of a sleek gas stove that booted out the old wood-burning behemoth. Maman delighted in the change. I mourned the old stove. Felt like we had exchanged a classic locomotive for a bicycle. No history. No soul.

The boys played in the yard and Maman attended to her ironing.

"I'll mix more paint." Whistling a light tune, Papa left the kitchen with two empty pails. He had reached the front door, when his whistling gave way to shouts. "*Non,* Riri. Stay."

The pails clattered down the stairs. The squeal of brakes brought me running to the *perron.* I stopped, transfixed, taking a series of mental snapshots. Papa rushing through the gates. Riri lying like a broken doll on the hot macadam. Our nineteen-year-old neighbor, Mouloud, rising slowly from a prone position. Little Yves, frozen-faced, holding onto the wire of our gate. On the periphery, my eye caught a soldier jumping out of the driver's side of a military truck.

Maman had followed on my heel to the top of the stairs. She gasped at the sight before us and bounded down the steps, sobbing, "God, *Non.* God, *Non.*"

Papa kneeled at my brother's side and shrieked, "*Mon fils. Mon fils,*" like a man being skinned alive. My Riri lay inert, pale as the Holy Ghost, his beautiful blue eyes closed to the world. With a hand on his son's chest, Papa turned to Mouloud. "Are you hurt, *mon fils*?"

Mouloud drew to his knees and staggered to his feet. He limped to my father. He examined the cuts and scrapes on his own arms and hands, reached up to his bleeding cheek and concluded, "I don't think so, Monsieur Riri."

The truck driver came running as Papa picked up Riri and carried him to his car, calling over his shoulder. "Come, Mouloud, you need to go to the hospital."

Pale and out of breath, his young face a study in grief, the soldier shadowed Papa. "I'm so very sorry, *monsieur*. I couldn't stop in time." He hurriedly opened the rear car door for Papa. "Can I help?"

Maman pushed past him and sat on the back seat, extending her arms to receive her son. The door slammed on an image of Mary cradling a limp Jesus. Mouloud joined Papa on the front seat and they sped down the road.

My sisters and I stood transfixed at our front door. It was hard to believe that only a few moments earlier Papa had been whistling, on his way to get more paint.

"Come, Yves," I called. Little Yves climbed the stairs, wiping tears with a dusty forearm, smudging his nose and cheeks with dirt. From the yard below, the anguished soldier called out, "Do you need help? Is there anything I can do?" His metropolitan accent fanned my gut-wrenching resentment. I shoved Yves into the house and slammed the door.

Inside, I asked, "Why was Riri in the street?"

Yves sniffled. "He wanted to play with the kids in the street. I told him," he sighed, gray eyes imploring, "I told him he wasn't supposed to cross the road." He shrugged. "But he didn't listen."

"What happened to Mouloud?"

"He jumped after Riri and pulled him away from the truck."

It was a long time before Papa came home. My siblings and I rushed to the car as it turned into the yard. My heart stopped. Only Papa and Mouloud stepped down. Mouloud wore bandages on his forearms and head. Papa laid both his hands on the young man's shoulders and gazed into his eyes. "I'll never forget you saved my son's life, *mon fils*. Anything I can do for you, just ask."

Mouloud smiled his wide, forthright smile. "It's nothing, Monsieur Riri. Allah is great; your son will be all right." Then he limped across the street to the rough accolades of the other males waiting outside their enclave.

"How's Riri?" I asked, a lump in my throat.

Papa rasped, "He has a head injury and was still unconscious when I left the hospital. It will be a few days before we find out if there is any lasting damage. Your mother's staying with him."

"Did you see what happened?"

"He was across the street playing bounce the pouch. He glanced toward the house just as I stepped out on the *perron*." Papa lifted his hands to his hips and shook his head as if shaking off a cloud of flies—wishing he could turn back the clock or deny the accident ever took place.

"So he knew he would catch hell for crossing the road," I hinted.

"I told him to stay put, but, once more, the little bastard didn't listen." He shook his head again, his voice cracking, "The little son of a bitch just wouldn't listen."

My heart broke at the remorse concealed amid the volley of swearwords. I stifled an urge to hug him—Pa wouldn't like that.

That night, between spurts of dozing, I saw images of eleven-year-old Riri flash against the room's darkness, pulsing in rhythm with my heartbeat. Riri laughing. Riri crying. Riri full of mischief.

Riri, after my Djebel-Ouach encounter with a spider-covered tree trunk, throwing a dry leaf at me, warning, "A spider, Nanna." Laughing like a hyena while I went bonkers.

I woke up from another doze, bathed in sweat. On the screen of my throbbing eyelids, I replayed the moments when four-year-old Riri had climbed into the cab of Papa's truck.

* * *

THE TRUCK HAD ROLLED forward without the benefit of a purring motor—its silent progress more threatening than the rippling muscles of a skulking tiger.

I jumped onto the truck's running board, wrenched open the driver door, and slithered up the slick leather seat. My eleven-year-old's feet couldn't reach the pedals. I crouched to push the brake with my hand. Three pedals. I thought back to the family car for a clue. My mind screamed, *Which is the brake?*

Things outside the truck moved backward. At a loss as to how to stop the unrelenting advance and scared out of my wits, I jumped out and fell on my hands and knees. I looked up. Framed in the opening of the swinging door, Riri jumped up and down on the seat. Laughing. Loving the game. I picked myself up, brushed the gravel embedded in the heels of my bleeding hands and knees, measuring the truck's steady progress. It would push through the gate, come to a rest perpendicular to the middle of the road, and be speared by a barreling military truck.

Crying with frustration, I jumped back onto the running board and slithered back up the slick leather seat. I studied the foot pedals, shoving aside my playful brother, when my hand found the stick with a round knob. *Non. That's not it. Papa moves it when he wants the car to go faster or slower.* Then my eyes fell on the horizontal handle behind the stick.

That was the last thing Papa pulled before getting out of the car. *That* was the brake. I wrapped both my hands around the handle and pulled up with my whole body. A grating/moaning sound followed and the truck stopped.

Tears running freely off my chin, I pulled Riri out the door and shook him by the shoulders. "How did you manage to get into the truck?"

"I climbed through the window," he said, as if I should have known. It was hard to imagine a six-year-old kid could perform such gymnastics, but he had. My eyes rested on the wooden wedges Papa always put in front of the back tires. "Did you move these, Riri?"

"*Et bien, oui*," he said with pride. "That's what Papa does before going into the truck."

I replaced the wedges in front of the tires and towered over my brother. "And why did you get into the truck?"

"I wanted to go for a ride."

"For heaven's sake, Riri." I rested my hands on my hips and shook my head. "Papa's going to kill you."

"You're going to tell him?"

"Do you think he won't notice the truck moved?"

* * *

Reliving the ordeal must have exhausted me. The next time I awoke, daylight peeked through the shutters—a new day that might see my Riri back home.

Papa returned from the hospital at lunchtime. He sat with the four of us at the table we had moved to the corridor while we painted the kitchen.

We'd just started lunch when the soldier who'd driven the truck rapped timidly on the open door. Papa set down his knife and fork and inquired with a raised chin, "*Oui?*"

The soldier doffed his cap. "*Monsieur*, I'm Jean Dupuis. I drove the truck that hit your son. I came to find out how he's doing and tell you how sorry I am."

Papa motioned him in and indicated the chairs lined up against the wall. "Pull up a chair."

The soldier carried a chair into the space between Papa's place and mine. He sat at the table and Papa said, "Nanna, bring a plate."

The soldier raised a hand as if swearing on the Bible. "Merci, *monsieur*, I already ate."

Papa signaled with a flick of his hand that I should get up. "Bring a glass."

I remained rooted to my chair. Unblinking eyes glued to the center of the table.

"Didn't you hear me?" he demanded. "Bring a glass."

I'd rather die than welcome the man who hurt my Riri. Almost killed him. I set my jaw in a mulish clamp and shook my head.

The soldier intervened, "That's all right, *monsieur*. I am not thirsty."

Papa glared at me. "Are your ears so stuffed with shit that you can't hear?"

I pushed myself up with clenched teeth, fetched a glass, and plunked it in front of my brother's assailant.

The soldier nodded, averting his eyes, then turned to Papa, who poured wine in his glass. "*Merci*." The man fiddled with his drink. "*Monsieur*, I need to know your son's condition."

Papa reclined in his chair. "He woke up this morning and answered questions, but my wife says he doesn't remember anything from before the accident."

"Riri's brain-damaged?" My throat squeezed so hard it hurt.

Zizou's chin quivered and Mireille began to cry. Yves' eyes roamed from person to person, looking for cues on how to behave.

My father glared at me. "What are you talking about, asshole? Of course he isn't brain damaged. He has amnesia. The doctor says it might last a few days or weeks, but he should be fine in a couple of months."

I was so thankful I almost didn't hate the soldier any longer. He took a small sip and said, "I'm so relieved your son wasn't more badly hurt, *monsieur*." He stood and faced Papa. "You must believe me, *monsieur*, your son stepped in front of my truck so unexpectedly there was no time to avoid him."

Papa gave a magnanimous nod and the man glanced at me. "I'm so sorry," he said with a bow of his head. He squared his cap on top of his head and walked across the threshold. When he was out of earshot, Papa surprised me, asking in a soft, measured voice, "Where were you going there, being rude to a guest?"

"He wasn't a guest."

"Anyone who's allowed in this house is a guest."

"I didn't invite him," I spat. "I hate him."

Patiently, almost sadly, he said, "Your brother crossed the road in front of the truck. This young man is right. There was no way he could have avoided him."

"Riri got scared when he saw you," Zizou charged. "That's why he crossed without looking. He was afraid of *you*."

The jagged barb found its mark. Papa dropped his napkin at the side of his plate. He stood in the deadly silence, his chair scrapping the floor, the sound like fingernails against a blackboard. Then without a word he shuffled to his room like an old man.

I knew well how he felt. I too bore a load of guilt.

Guilty

ONE EVENING, EIGHT YEARS before, Papa was on his way back from an out-of-town job and Pépé Honninger was fishing in Philipeville. Maman was preparing the evening meal while Zizou and Mireille played with their dolls under the kitchen table and seven-month-old Riri teethed and shrieked. Ma said, "Nanna, *ma fille*, pick him up, will you?"

Riri's crying subsided as I heaved him out of his crib. He was getting heavy for my almost eight-year-old arms, but I folded him in a blanket and cradled him in the crook of my arm. I walked him around the house, rocked him and crooned, "*Mon bébé chéri, ne-veut-pa-ha-do-ormir-reux ....*" In-between bouts of crying, he displayed a toothless smile full of enflamed gums.

He grew heavier and I shifted him from one arm to the other, but my hands tangled in the blanket. I lost hold of the baby and he fell to the tile floor. Panic-stricken, I screamed and dropped to my knees. He'd stopped crying and didn't move. I reached to pick him up. "Don't move him," Maman snapped as she knelt by my side.

"I dropped him, Ma," I shrieked.

She listened to the baby's chest. "He's breathing." She probed his tongue and quickly felt his arms and legs. "Where did he fall?"

"On the floor, Ma."

"What part of his body touched the floor first?" she urged.

"His head, I think."

She bundled the baby and tore out of the house. "I'm going to *La Guinguette* and have someone drive me to the hospital. Watch your sisters."

The enormity of what I had done was crushing. I wandered about the house like a mechanical toy, bumping into doorways and furniture. My skin felt stiff and cold as tin. I was filled with horrendous remorse. And grief. Oh, the overwhelming grief.

I wrung my hands and cried like a sheep whose throat was being slashed. A tortured face, red, and gaping mouth, leapt from my bedroom tilted mirror. I froze at the eerie sight. The black hole of a mouth. Eyes big as saucers and disheveled hair.

I approached the mirror. My crying stopped as I curiously examined the alien face and saw it was mine. I felt the drying tears stretch the skin over my cheekbones, making my face feel hard and numb. My eyelids burned. Eyelashes glued in clumps.

Then, I remembered my sisters. I found Mireille asleep on the floor, hugging her doll. Zizou, I realized, had followed me throughout the house bug-eyed, sucking her thumb, her index finger hooked onto the end of her nose.

I woke Mireille. Cajoled and threatened her and Zizou into eating the food Maman had prepared, coaxed them to bed and lay beside them, waiting ....

Maman took a long time to come home.

I arose when she turned on the bedroom light, Riri gurgling in her arms. I rushed to her. "Did I hurt him a lot, Ma?"

"Don't worry, *ma fille*. The doctor says he will be fine."

I stretched my arms to hug him then dropped them to my sides. I had vowed never to touch him again, but still felt a desperate need to hold him. "Can I kiss him, Ma?"

She bent down. "Gently," she whispered. When my lips grazed his forehead, his baby smell filled me with overpowering warmth that reached all the way to my heart. "I'm so sorry I dropped him, Ma. So sorry. I wanted to die," I sobbed.

"Don't ever say silly things like that. Hear me?" Her eyes were severe. "It was an accident. He will be fine. Come. Help me change him."

Later on that night I went to bed but, worried about how mad Papa would be, couldn't sleep. After a long, long wait, I woke up to the sound of tires on crushed gravel. The truck door slammed. I listened hard but couldn't follow my father's progress up the stairs. Even though the crepe soles of his shoes made him silent as a cat, my skin felt him draw closer. One step at a time.

The front door opened. Closed. The latch clicked. Locked for the night.

My parents' voices blended as they traveled from the kitchen to their bedroom and, I was sure, the cradle.

I was straining to make sense of their murmuring, when my door opened. Papa's backlit shadow came into view—sharp-edged and flat like a paper doll. I shut my eyes tight and stopped breathing. The side of my bed dipped. The heat of Papa's body coursed across the covers, wrapped around me like electric current from a stripped wire. "Are you awake?"

My eyelids quivered.

"Tell me what happened," he whispered. "Don't be afraid."

I opened my eyes. Tears ran freely. "Riri was heavy and I wanted to change arms and my hands got tangled up in the blanket and ...." I sobbed, "*Pardon*, Papa."

"It was an accident, *ma fille*." He wrapped his hands around my shoulders, sat me up. "Here, kiss me good night."

I threw my arms around his neck and buried my face in his shirtfront. Inhaled the smells of dry cement, cigarette, and *brillantine*—the smell of my papa.

He unlocked my embrace, eased me onto my back and straightened my blankets. "Don't worry; your brother is all right. Go to sleep now." He rose and left, closing the door behind him.

I rubbed my eyes and relaxed. My world was right again.

* * *

YES, EVEN EIGHT YEARS later, at sixteen, I too carried guilt. It was like an old injury that seemed to be healed until a rainy day came along.

Chapter Twenty-Six

Referendum

January 8, 1961

Papa and Maman dressed in their Sunday clothes and drove to Constantine. It was January 8, 1961, when French citizens everywhere would cast ballots on De Gaulle's referendum for Algeria's self-determination. I watched the car disappear behind the bend, wishing bitterly I were a year older and eighteen so I could also cast my vote.

The previous day at *La Guinguette*, Papa had declared, "The metropolitan French will vote for self-determination. No doubt about that." He pulled on his cigarette and faced Monsieur Cavalier. "I think De Gaulle is right to call for self-determination." He waited for a rebuke that didn't come. "Want to know why?" he challenged.

Monsieur Cavalier's jowls bounced up and down.

Monsieur Fournier, who played poker at a nearby table, snarled, "Because you are a traitor to the *Pieds-Noirs*, Vincent. That's why."

Monsieur Cavalier studiously wiped the bar.

Papa allowed a pitying grin to pull the corner of his mouth and cut into the patrons' frosty silence. "Oh man of little brain, listen to Vincent's genius." He took a sip of *anisette* and turned sideways to lean against the brass railing. "If Algeria remained a French province, France would have no alternative but to grant French citizenship to six-and-a-half million Arabs." He threw a fatalistic hand aloft. "In that case, within twenty years France herself would become Muslim."

The men at the poker table gave grudging nods of ascent. Papa raised his glass in a victorious salute and downed his drink.

I WAS BOTH PROUD AND despairing when Papa was again proven right. Three-quarters of the voting French citizens in the Metropole and abroad approved Algeria's right to self-determination. But then, how could it have been otherwise? The *Pied-Noirs* numbered only one million-and-a-half souls—a handful of confetti in the ballot box.

On the heels of the referendum, the French government and the FLN Provisional Government of the Algerian Republic held secret negotiations in Evian on the terms of Algeria's independence.

"Why the secrecy?" Papa asked as I stood next to him at the bar. "Why is only the FLN represented? Why not the French from Algeria? As a matter of fact, why not the *Mouvement National Algérien*? They are also involved in the fight for independence." Papa glared at *La Guinguette's* other patrons.

"I'd like to know that," Monsieur Voisin said, breaking the preoccupied silence.

Monsieur Michelet hit the counter with his fist. "We ripped this country out of the thirteenth century and yet have no say in its future?"

The ticking of the new clock on the wall underscored the men's seething silence. Each tick, each tock, a rosary bead marking time 'til our fate was sealed.

Papa drew wet rings on the counter with the bottom of his glass. "And what of the one million Muslims who pledged their loyalty to France? *Les Ancients Combatants* who fought in our ranks during two world wars and the *Harkis*, at this very moment? What about the Berber and Kabyle tribes France armed for self-defense and territory control against the FLN?"

Tick-tock. Tick-tock. In the weighty silence, the clock marked my own anguished pulse at the ghastly fates in store for these Muslims aligned with the French.

Monsieur Cavalier wrung out his rag and leaned his hands on top of the bar. "We're all part of the equation with no say in its resolution. We are all expendable livestock."

Papa pushed himself away from the bar and took a seat at the table where a new poker game was about to start.

A cigarette clinging to his lower lip, he shuffled the cards and flicked them, one at a time, toward the other players. In the process of fanning his own dealt hand, he closed an eye against the rising smoke and mused around his cigarette, "I'm wondering. We know that as a member of the United Nations, France will observe the letter of the treaty. Right?"

The other players studied their cards, nodding.

Papa went on. "But what guaranties do we have that the FLN's Provisional Government, a self-anointed group, will observe the terms they agree to?"

"We all know the answer to this question, *mon ami*—" Monsieur Voisin threw a card on the table with a flourish. "Let's hope history will prove us wrong. Let's hope that both sides will observe the terms of the Accords."

I mentally made the sign of the cross. *Oh, God in Heaven, let him be right.*

WHILE CLOUDS OF OUR uncertain future gathered, a fantastic, breathtaking feat took place high above earth. Following Laika, the little Moscow mutt sent into orbit, the Soviet cosmonaut, Yuri Gagarin, launched into outer space.

On a restless night, I stood at my balcony and peered into the sky, looking for Yuri's capsule. A bright spot, which might be Sputnik 2, glided smoothly high across the sky—slow shooting star.

I imagined the first man in space, ever, in his tight pod, with a smile of incredible wonder and pride, looking down through hundreds of kilometers, beyond zones of gauze-like clouds, at the earth, its oceans, mountains, and rivers. Could he see the great metropolises' lights, all at once? Could he see a balcony with my cutout shadow lit from behind?

Could he see me wave? Could he, like a god from Olympus, observe us, despicable humans, murdering each other in acts more vile than beasts would ever wreak upon each other? Would he, then, keep on smiling?

The far away light dimmed out of sight in a smooth arc and I returned to bed, dreaming I was up there, above the fray, dissolving into the firmament. Unaware that further events would bring me back to earth and its worsening conflicts.

The Putsch

April 22, 1961

"RIRI, WAKE UP, *CHÉRI*." Maman's panicked voice reached from the kitchen, snatching me out of my serene dream. Zizou and I sat up in bed like wooden puppets with sagging strings. "What time is it?" Zizou moaned.

I glanced at the clock. "Seven."

"It's Saturday. Why can't she let us sleep?"

Ma's voice traveled from the kitchen to her bedroom. "Riri, there has been *un coup d'état à Alger.*"

My sister and I bolted out of bed, rushing barefoot and sans robe to the kitchen. Our parents had arrived first. They nearly hugged the radio, listening to a robot-like voice spill the sober message, "Last night, in an effort to overthrow President Charles De Gaulle and put an end to his policy of negotiations with the political branch of the FLN over Algeria's independence, French armed forces under command of Generals Zeller, Salan, Challe, and Jouhaud, seized control of Algeria and the Sahara along with its Hassi Messaoud oil fields."

"What's going on?" Yves staggered in, yawning and rubbing his eyes.

"Shut up," Papa barked. Pale and bushy-haired, he pulled up a chair and sat.

Yves joined all of us at the table, chewing his lips while the announcer concluded, "We'll return to the air with further reports."

Static trailed the disembodied voice, followed by solemn military music. Maman moved to turn off the radio, but Pa slashed the air with his hand. "Leave it on."

The bitter smell of scorched coffee filled the kitchen. The pot Ma started earlier before turning on the radio had run out of water. She distractedly picked it up barehanded and dropped it on the range with a yelp. Coffee grounds splashed about. "What are you doing, Lili?"

Ignoring Papa, Ma held her hand under the tap water.

My excitement over the generals' rebellion—the hopes they raised for a French Algeria in spite of De Gaullle's betrayal—transported me to heights of joy I had rarely known.

"Aren't you going to help your mother?" Papa's question called me back to a more down-to-earth present. I toweled away the coffee grounds and helped prepare breakfast.

While we ate, the radio whistled and the station identification reintroduced the lugubrious voice, "… now dubbed, 'Le Putsch d'Alger' or 'Le Putsch des Généraux.' The command of the coup d'état took control of government buildings and military installations in Algiers, with the further goal to seize Paris and depose President Charles De Gaulle …."

The sound of rustling paper replaced the interrupted report, then the deep voice resumed. "We'll return with the latest bulletins in a moment along with the names of the putsch's co-conspirators."

Brass instruments filled the ensuing silence and Papa twisted the tuner, but the needle gliding along the lighted dial produced more disjointed words interspersed with sputtering and whistling sounds. He returned to the initial radio station and toned down the volume on the martial music.

We were about to finish breakfast when the military trumpets and drums retreated, yielding the airwaves to a song that froze my spoon midway between my bowl and lips as I drank in the words.

> *C'est nous les Africains qui revenons de loin.*
> *Nous venons des colonies*
> *Pour défendre le pays ….*

> We are the Africans who hail from afar.
> We come from the colonies
> To defend the country ….

I jumped up and hurried to the radio. "Can I turn it up, Pa?" He nodded and I blasted the volume, swallowing hard at the patriotic words.

> We left behind family and friends
> And bear in our hearts an invincible ardor
> For we mean to hold high and proud
> The noble flag of our France.

Seated around the table, we communed in the absolute silence that attends the distribution of the Holy Ghost.

> And if someone attempts to hurt Her,
> We shall be there to die at her feet.
> Roll-on the drums for our loves,
> For the country, the Motherland,
> Dying afar,
> We are the Africans.

I could neither swallow nor breathe. This was much more than a song. It was a hymn that pierced my heart. A wake-up call. This was the love of country my father talked about. Pride in the flag. Courage to fight for my country's freedom. Die with honor to safeguard the dignity of family and friends.

The love. Pride. Courage. Honor. Dignity that carried my forefathers through the historic battlefields of Malta, the Roussillon, Alsace-Lorraine, the Dardanelles—that drove them to toil and die of fever and malnourishment until orange and olive groves, fields of wheat, grape vines, and pastures replaced the North African swamps.

"What's that song, Pa?"

"'*Le Chant des Africains*.'"

Ardent patriotic fervor gripped me. "Now, it's '*Le chant des Pieds-Noirs*.'"

From then on, radio became the focus of our lives. A magnet we were drawn to with bated breath. It slaked our thirst for promising news at the shallow pool of sporadic broadcasts, causing my heart to race in ardent hope that the coup would succeed. That *La Grande Zohra* and his deceitful policies had been defeated.

Sadly, the news began to spoil. The military commanders of the departments of Oran and Constantine had declined to join the insurrection. Anguish etched my parents' faces and my heart sank.

The following day, my father and mother decided to join the downtown demonstrations supporting the coup.

"*Non, ma fille,*" Maman said. "You cannot come with us."

"Why? I'm seventeen. It's *my* right to fight for my rights."

"It might be your right, but I cannot let you play with your life. The army here is against the coup. There is no telling what might happen."

For a moment, my mother's unbending pronouncement shook me. She had never sounded so firm. Feeling betrayed, I turned to my father. "Pa?"

He stood feet apart, hands on hips, green eyes fastened to mine. He glanced at my mother then back at me. Weighing. Then he gave a curt nod.

Like an eager flea jumping on a passing dog, Zizou announced, "I want to go, too."

Mireille and the boys parroted, "Me too."

"The rest of you stay here." Papa glared at Zizou. "You take care of your brothers and sister."

Zizou stomped to our room and slammed the door. I rushed to get ready and galloped down the stairs, leaping into the car as the motor started.

My enthusiasm at being able to stand up for my beliefs made the silent eleven miles to Constantine seem like one hundred. We parked at the entrance of *La Boule Tricolore* and joined the meeting already in progress at the *Place de la Brêche.*

Casserole concerts and chants of *Al-gé-rie Fran-çaise, Al-gé-rie Fran-çaise,* intermingled with megaphone speeches.

From streets beyond the gathering, automobile klaxons underscored the beaten saucepans' *Algérie Française* mantra. My zeal soared in tune with the chaotic rhythm.

Familiar faces dotted the festive crowd. Friends and families greeted each other with handshakes and hugs. The feeling of warmth and kinship gave me wings. Longing to reach the heart of the gathering, I forged ahead, but Papa pulled me back. "I want to be in the middle of things, Pa." Almost drowned out in the racket, my words didn't escape Ma's well-tuned ear.

"We'll stay right here, *ma fille.*" Her set features left no room for argument.

Jeeze, what's gotten into her? Crestfallen, but not disheartened, I remained on the outskirts of the crowd, singing along and shouting along with the pack whenever exhortations to overthrow De Gaulle, the betrayer, the turncoat, whipped-up the crowd.

Resentment mounted like a wave riding a deep undertow. The saucepan banging shifted from playful to hostile. Enraged scowls replaced cordial smiles. The good-natured *Algérie Française* chant swelled into heated slogans then rose into passionnate clamors of "*À bas De Gaulle!*" Raised fists pounded the air.

A trumpet sounding the first bars of the *Marseillaise* cut into the fiery shouts of "Down with De Gaulle." The national anthem rippled from mouth to mouth with amplifying fervor, engulfing the crowd, sweeping me in its wake.

> *contre nous de la tyrannie,*
> *L'étandard sanglant est levé*
> *L'étandard-ard san-anglant est levé.*
> *Entendez-vous dans nos campa—*

> Against us from tyranny,
> The bloody flag is raised.
> The bloody flag is raised.
> Do you hear in the countrysi—

In our corner, the mighty words froze on open lips as an older Arab man riding a Moped plowed into the crowd. No one other than those immediately around us noticed. The anthem carried on,

> … roar the savage soldiers
> Who come in our midst
> To slit the throats of our daughters and companions ….

The terrified-looking rider dragged both feet on the ground to stop his mount while, in panic, he accelerated. Papa jerked me out of the way. A man toppled the bike, causing it to spin on its side until another switched off the engine and pulled the old Arab up by the scruff of his neck. The unsuspecting crowd roared on,

> To arms, citizens
> Form up your battalions
> Let's forge ahead, let's forge ah— "

The hymn's call to arms seemed to fire up several men. Fathomless anger distorted their features as they closed in on the biker—their purpose obvious. Horrifying.

Maman moved closer to my father. I couldn't hear her amid the mayhem, but I read her lips, "Let's take her out of here." She pushed me ahead until we cleared the mob.

I glanced back in anguish at the spot where the angry men pummeled the old man. Hot tears dripped down my chin.

"Let's go, Nanna." Maman jerked me by the hand.

After a few paces I looked back. Through gaps between the milling bystanders, I saw several people push into the circle surrounding the old Arab. Their vehement body language conveyed their efforts to appease the angry men. Maman pointed me forward again. Steps later, I looked back again and spotted the old man limp his moped away while the throng gradually melted back into the demonstration.

"Ma, I need to *pipi*," I whispered through tears of relief.

A light danced in her eyes. "You mean that after all those tears you still need to pee?"

I nodded with a giggle.

"We'll stop at *La Boule Tricolore.*"

On the ride home, after a trip to the bathroom and a cold drink, I said, "I don't understand why the old man ran into the crowd, Pa."

"My guess is the poor bastard was trying to ride around the demonstration, but lost his wits and grip on his bike. When the crowd became restless, instead of stopping or turning around, he accelerated."

"I didn't realize nice people could become so mean. It was horrible," I squeaked.

Maman shifted in her seat and glanced at me. "Do you understand, now, why I didn't want you to go?"

Papa cut in, "It was time she got her head off her ass and learned the facts of life." His sharp eyes held mine in the rearview mirror until he needed to focus on the road again.

TWENTY MINUTES LATER ZIZOU said, "You're home early. What happened?"

While I changed clothes, I described the morning's events, the replay helping me organize my thoughts and feelings.

"It was like at Jeanne d'Arc beach, in Philippeville, when undertows pull at people's legs, suck them into the sea—"

"What're you talking about, Nanna?" Zizou scoffed. "I thought you went to a demonstration, not the seaside."

"That's what I'm trying to explain." I took a long breath to sort out my thoughts, to explain to my sister as much as to myself. "The demonstrators were like a calm, shining sea that suddenly turned treacherous. Like the sea, Zizou, people switched from peaceful and pleasant humans beings to vicious, mindless brutes just like"—I snapped my fingers—"that."

"So?"

"So, it felt like I lost my footing. Like the world turned upside down, never to be put right again. I was terrified." I took another long breath. "Thank God some people kept a cool head and saved the poor man."

"So," Zizou crossed her arms, "things turned out all right. Not all people are bullies."

"*Yaa*. But I'm thinking that, maybe, the brute in these people lives in me too. That, maybe, I could lose my head and hurt, maybe kill someone in blind anger."

Zizou shook her head. "You think too much, Nanna. You're going to get a headache."

The rest of the day went by with radio news of civilian anti-De Gaulle demonstrations in Constantine, Algiers, Oran, and numerous small towns. La Marseillaise and martial tunes filled the airwaves, but *Le Chant des Africains* filled my heart, made it beat with a pride that linked me in spirit to my fellow *Pieds-Noirs* and the hope that we would prevail and save our fathers' patrimony.

La Grande Zohra, though, shared none of my lofty expectations. In a radio and television address, he called on French military and civilians to oppose the putsch and declared a state of emergency in Algeria. A forty-eight hour curfew ensued.

Previous curfews had been manageably short. This one felt like total isolation from the rest of the world. As a police officer, Papa reported to headquarters. Not allowed outdoors, the boys became unbearable, with their running, screeching, and fighting. Mireille and Zizou helped Maman unravel old sweaters, wash and wind the wool into balls.

Unable to focus on so much as a book, I leaned on my balcony, choked with sadness at the sight of vacant streets—a frigid world devoid of living souls.

In the universal hush, eucalyptus leaves declined to exude their perfume into the still air. No dog barks echoed from farms beyond the fields. No laughter drifted from the compound across the street. The end of the world was at hand.

Broadcasters became more verbose as hours upon long hours crawled by.

Most conscripts fighting in Algeria hailed from France. Having no horse in the *Algérie Française*'s struggle, they heeded their General in Chief's call to resist the coup. One broadcast reported, "The President's successful appeal to the military not to join the insurrection is largely due to the use by troops of the newly invented transistor radio." Soon, the media reported that De Gaulle's successful call against the rebellion was dubbed, "*La Bataille des Transistors*."

Meanwhile, we huddled around our old radio as if competing to suck tiny sips of air from a fissure in the wall of a sealed cavern. In the end, one after another, the insurgent troops capitulated like dying comets falling out of the sky.

On April 25th, the radio announced, "In order to prevent the French atomic bomb from falling into the rebel generals' hands, Paris ordered the explosion of *Gerboise Verte* in the Sahara."

The next day, General Challe's surrender to French authorities stabbed the rebellion with the *coup de grâce*, bursting the last bubble of our hopes.

With his customary arrogance, *La Grande Zohra*'s smug voice declared, "*C'est la fin de l'Algérie de Papa.*"

"Daddy's Algeria," might be "over," as De Gaulle bragged, but I didn't understand why the *Pieds-Noirs* couldn't remain and help the new Algeria grow and prosper as they had the old one. This was our home. We had just as much claim to it as any of the previous conquerors who'd stayed put when the land had changed hands. And be they good times or bad times, Algeria remained *our* country.

Chapter Twenty-Seven

In the Quiet of Night

June, 1961

FOLLOWING THE PUTSCH DEBACLE, times went from bad to worse, without respite, like the ten plagues of Egypt.

One June evening, our parents were expected to arrive home late. Zizou and I were on edge, as the boys wouldn't quit horse-playing at the dinner table.

"Riri, stop teasing Yves," Zizou exploded. "And you, Yves, bring your chair and your plate over here."

Yves moved between Zizou and me, casting dark glances at his brother while dinner resumed in blessed silence. I was enjoying the quiet as well as my pork chop when a powerful blast shook the house. My mouth stopped in mid-chew. The boys jumped up with a yelp. Mireille clasped her hand to her heart and Zizou batted her eyelashes.

I swallowed my food as plaster dust flitted down from the ceiling.

The ceiling light bulb swung in a wide pendulum, causing shadows to grow and shrink as they rocked across the room.

Nauseated by the motion and unnerved by the boys' squeals, I slapped Yves and kicked Riri's leg into silence. *I need peace. Time to think.*

In the restored calm, the light gradually came to rest, anchoring the room's shadows, and I became aware of a ringing in my ears that filtered angry voices rising from the street.

I rounded the table and turned off the light. "Zizou, hide the kids under our parents' bed." I tiptoed to my bedroom window to peek into the street. The French doors' shattered glass crunched under my feet and scraped against the tile as I pushed them open against the wall. A piece of glass dislodged from the window frame and hit the back of my hand, leaving a gash that dripped blood onto the floor and broken glass. I compressed the wound with my other hand and peered between two slats of the closed shutters. I was watching a group of shrieking men run along the street, when Zizou's hand made me jump with fright. She held onto my shoulder and stood on tiptoe to survey the street. "It's Saïd's *hammam*," she murmured.

"Sounded like plastic," I whispered, grazing the lob of her ear with my lips.

Zizou kept her face glued to the shutters. "I bet the OAS got him."

Saiid had been the owner of the hole-in-the-wall grocery store two houses up, across the street. Through the years, my siblings and I had spent a fortune buying his fly-speckled *caca de pigeon*. We realized our munificent contributions didn't garner him the riches he needed to keep his store open when he converted the tiny establishment into a public steam bath.

"I don't recognize any of these screaming banshees," Zizou said. "Do you?"

I scrutinized the gesticulating, moonlit shapes. "I don't think they belong around here." I turned to my sister. "Zizou, go back to the kids. They must be scared."

"What about you?"

"I want to see if they are going to attack the house."

"Then what are we going to do?"

"I'll get Papa's Mauser."

"You don't even know how to use it," she scoffed. "Besides, Papa doesn't want us to touch his guns." She left in the dark, bumping into furniture as she groped her way to the back of the house.

I stood vigil as shouts of anger bounced into the night, hitting hard at the walls of the scattered houses, forcing their way through our shutters. In spite of the heat, I shivered, knowing that if the mob caught the OAS bombers, the butchery of a few nights back would follow.

* * *

ON THAT NIGHT, ALONG the road next to the vacant fields behind the compound across the street, terrorists had ambushed four European men traveling by car. The next day the paper reported that when the car's passengers opened the doors to escape on foot, the overhead light went on.

As I read the account, I pictured the men's silhouettes emerge against the light like bobbing ducks against the painted canvas of a shooting arcade.

The article reported that one man's mutilated body had been found later in a far field where he had been dragged. I didn't need to hear his screams of agony for them to echo inside my head and reverberate forever in the quiet of night.

* * *

TONIGHT MY BROTHERS, SISTERS, and I might be the ones screaming if the mob hunting for the bombers decided to extract another pound of flesh. For now, their attention was directed away from our house. I joined my brothers and sisters in the back bedroom, and in my anguish remembered God. I kneeled in the dark and prayed for our safety, begged for the lives of the OAS men—men I might not even know—pleaded that He'd give them asylum in the shadows of the moon. "*Seigneur*, make them safe. And, if you can't, *Seigneur*, please make them die quickly."

I prayed until my knees against the tile floor felt as numb as my tongue after a Novocain shot and my knotted hands as rigid as a hangman's noose.

I listened for the hunters' shrieks of triumph when they found their prey, but only heard calls ebbing and flowing as the search went on.

Then, the thought of my parents struck me like a thunderbolt. Of how they might become caught in a pack of raving men when they came home. The car would have to slow down then turn ninety degrees before stopping at our gate. Maman would get out to open it. That would be the moment they'd be the most vulnerable. My father wouldn't back away to flee without her. They'd be stuck with nowhere to run, no place to hide.

I opened the door of my parents' armoire, stepped onto the bottom shelf and reached on tiptoe for Papa's nine-millimeter. I knew its magazine was engaged, and though I'd never shot it, I had watched Pa target practice. Much later in life, I would wonder how it was that Pa had never instructed us on how to handle a gun, never taught us to shoot to save our own lives. But I knew I needed to chamber the first shell, keeping the muzzle pointed down. This done, not without a struggle, I sidestepped to the front door, back skimming the corridor's wall, as I'd seen Papa do.

I listened to the excited Arab words bounce back and forth. My heart bumped like a blind bird inside its cage while I toggled the switch to the *perron's* light. Back glued to the wall, I flicked the light on and off, signaling my parents something was wrong. STAY AWAY FROM THE HOUSE, the flicking light said. My right hand numbed from flipping the switch and my left arm was about to fall away from the weight of the gun, when the *paimpon paimpon* of ambulances and the screeching brakes of military trucks drowned out the chants of "Kill the *roumis*. Kill the Europeans."

I listened long after the pounding of soldiers' boots and orders to disperse had restored peace in the street.

I listened for claims that some stubborn hunter had rooted out the bombers, but the light breeze only carried the merciful song of crickets and gentle rustle of eucalyptus.

ꟑOT ONE OF US slept until after our parents came home and each had given his or her own version of the evening's events. I crossed myself with total fervor. *Thank you Lord, for keeping my parents safe and the bombers free.*

At lunch the next day, Papa looked up from the newspaper reporting the events of the previous night and said, "Men from l'OAS learned the *hammam* across the street was a meeting place for *le FLN* and left a plastic bomb in one of the stalls."

"I wondered why so many strangers used Saiid's *hammam*," Zizou mused.

"Did they catch the bombers, Papa?" I whispered.

"Looks like they got away."

I sighed, "Oh, good."

Yves looked at Papa, "Is this good?"

"What?"

"That they got away."

"Would you prefer they had been caught?"

"But they killed people," Mireille said.

Papa shrugged. "Either we kill the terrorists or they kill us. Which do you want?"

Riri stopped heel-kicking his chair. "So, when the FLN kills, it's bad, but when the OAS kills, it's good. *Oui,* Papa?"

Papa glanced at his brood, turned to Maman and raised his hands in a sign of helplessness. "What am I supposed to do with these bastards?"

Zizou winked at me and said, "You want the bottles, again, Pa?"

I kicked her under the table, Yves sucked on his lips, and Mireille glared. "This isn't funny, Zizou."

No, it wasn't funny. Not for anyone, as became evident several days later.

Sanctuary

SEVERAL DAYS AFTER THE bombing at Saiid's, Ali Ben Salah, one of the neighbors across the street, asked to see Papa.

They shook hands and Ali said, "Why did you not come out last night when we called for Elise?"

"We didn't hear anything." Papa's brow shot up. "What did you want?"

"French soldiers came into our homes. They searched the rooms, looking for terrorists. So we called for Elise to vouch for us. Tell them she has known us all her life. That we are peaceful people. And, since you are in the police, we needed you to speak on our behalf." Ali paused and looked into my father's eyes. "But you didn't come to our aid."

Papa shook his head with vehemence. "We didn't hear you, *mon frère*. Had we heard your calls, I swear on my children's heads we would've come."

Even though my father had called him, "my brother," a shadow of doubt crossed Ali's features before he said, "The families within our walls had a meeting. We are concerned that the soldiers will return one of these nights and we don't know what will happen then. So, we agreed to ask if you would grant us asylum at night until things calm down," he concluded, pointing at Tonton Gilles's unoccupied studio, his stare dark as a bottomless pit.

I wondered how he was aware that the studio was not in use. How much of our private lives did our Arab neighbors know while we knew so precious little of what happened behind their walls?

Ali laid his right hand on his heart as a sign of good faith. "Only for a couple of nights, *mon frère*."

Papa hooked his hands over his hips, his eyes staring at the ground at his feet. Then he bowed his head. "I tell you what, Ali, your women and children can move in the studio each evening until they feel safe to sleep in their homes. But I cannot allow the men in."

"Why not the men, *mon frère*?" Ali's dark eyes gleamed with veiled challenge. "Most of us have grown up with Elise. We've seen your children grow from the time they were born and you still don't trust us?"

"You know why not the men." Papa pulled his pack of Gauloises out of his breast pocket, offered Ali a cigarette, stuck one between his lips then struck a match and cupped his hands to light both. He inhaled deeply and exhaled slowly. "I'd hold my hand over hot coals as proof of my trust in you and the other men." Papa swept a hand in the direction of Ali's compound. "But I've seen many strange faces around here lately and there is no telling where they belong." Papa squinted through the smoke. "Can you?"

Ali extended his arms forward, palms up, and shrugged, while the smoke of his upside-down cigarette rose between his fingers. "*Laa*," he said, shaking his head.

"So, how am I to know they are not threatening you and forcing you to acknowledge them as part of your families so I'd give them a place to hide?"

Ali touched a hand to his heart again and inclined his head. "Allah bless you, *mon frère*. Tonight, our women and children will be under your protection."

Early that evening, many more women and children than I thought lived behind those walls across the street moved in with their bundles, sleeping rugs and mats. In the morning, they went home, only to come back the following evening.

After a few nights, the soldiers not having returned, our guests felt safe enough to carry their belongings home for good.

Later that day, Riri ran to Papa with the news that two men from across the street had walked through our gates and entered the vacated studio. My brother and I followed Papa there and found the men, Hajmed and Magid, leaving the studio carrying a trunk between them. Papa barred their way. "What are you doing here?" he challenged, hands on hips. "I thought I said, 'no men.'"

"*Bonjour*, Mr. Riri," said Magid. His smile revealed a row of betel-stained teeth under a thick moustache ending in groomed points. "When they moved out, the women left this behind for safekeeping," he added, pointing his chin at the trunk he and his friend carried.

"What's in there?" Papa's stern voice erased the smile on the men's face.

"Look, Mr. Riri," Hajmed said. "It's only our families' money and jewels."

"Open it." Papa's order clapped like a whip.

The men exchanged a brief glance and set the trunk down. They bent over and unhooked the leather strap securing the studded lid, which, once open, exposed jewelry, gold coins, and banknotes. "Show me the bottom," Papa said in a clipped voice.

Hajmed and Magid crouched down, moved the jewels and bundles of bills aside and glanced up at Papa. He gave a curt nod and told them they could close the lid. "How do you dare bring valuables in my house without letting me know about it?"

The men gave Pa a startled look and his voice, brittle as an icicle, went on, "What if one of you decided to keep the lot to himself and the rest of you accused me of stealing it?"

"Oh, but Monsieur Riri, we'd never think you'd do something like that. We trust you."

"Trust me. My ass."

"We'd never do that to you, Mr. Riri. We are very grateful for your help." Magid kissed the tips of his fingers to show his good faith.

Papa gave a reluctant nod, but I could tell he was as angry as I had ever seen him. *Why?*

We escorted the men and their trunk to the gate and walked up the stairs to the front door. "But why are you so angry with them, Pa?" I asked.

"For all I knew, the trunk could have contained weapons and ammunitions," he said. "Then I would've been an accessory to God knows what."

I nodded sadly, understanding that in these days of shifting allegiances, one might trust, but not blindly.

Chapter Twenty-Eight

Albert

August, 1961

IT WAS THE LAST week of summer vacation, three months after my seventeenth birthday. Maman had taken the bus to Constantine with Zizou and the kids to buy their school stuff. I was preparing the evening meal in idyllic silence and blissful solitude when the little black gate with the mailbox scraped across the walkway. I wiped my hands and went to the *perron* to check on the trespasser. A stranger looked up from fifteen steps below.

Gosh, he's gorgeous, I thought, in a half-swoon. The man's almond-shaped eyes and close-cropped beard framed classic features, and with his engaging smile, he was the spitting image of my conception of the Jaguar Knight in the Mayan story I just finished.

My imagination went on a rampage, writing a novel of its own. Looking forward to forfeiting his life, the vanquished Jaguar knight gazed up in awe at the high priestess—*moi*—gleaming in the resplendent sun. She stood at the sacrificial altar, ceremonial obsidian knife in hand, all set to carve the Hero's heart out ….

Yaa, sure. I slipped my hands into my apron pockets, took them out and, for lack of a better place, let them dangle at my sides. "*Bon— Bonjour*," I stammered like a stupid idiot.

"*Bonjour*, Mademoiselle. My name is Albert Lacroix. I recently arrived from France and am looking for lodgings. The school's bursar gave me this address. Is Monsieur Gilles Honninger here?"

"*Non*," I said, struggling to keep my voice steady. *Gosh, he wants to move in downstairs.* "But I can show you the room. I'll get the key." I pivoted on my feet—gracefully, I hoped—and sashayed into the house.

I peered into the bathroom mirror. *Lucky I washed my hair this morning.* I repositioned the tortoise combs that kept the curls off my face, slapped my cheeks, bit my lips to color them, and grabbed the key.

Past the front door, I traded my usual bounding down the stairs for a more regal bearing, wishing I wore pants—which I wasn't allowed to wear—or a long skirt—which I didn't own—to hide my chicken legs. *Thank heaven I just shaved them.*

I offered my hand. "*Comment allez-vous?* I'm Danielle, Monsieur Honninger's niece." Leading the way, I unlocked the door to the front apartment and pulled open the shutters to let daylight in. I stood in the middle of the efficiency studio and pointed. "*Voilà.* This is the bedroom-living room. The kitchenette is there. The bathroom, over there."

He appraised the surroundings and decided, "I'll take it."

I gazed into the most superb set of gray eyes. *Yesss!* "Did you say the school gave you our address?" I tried to sound detached, businesslike and sophisticated—all of which I hadn't the simplest inkling how to do.

"*Oui,* Mademoiselle. The school bursar did. I am doing my military service as a teacher."

OH BOY, PAPA'S GOING *to LOVE this.* His idea of a "Real Man" was one who fulfills his obligations to his country, especially his military service. A Real Man whose fortitude has been severely tested by crawling through mud and across beds of nettles—live munitions whistling by his ears along with the screams of barking sergeants and dying men. And, for good measure, if this "Man" had lived through innumerable battle field horrors, like my pa, so much the better. *Too bad. Teacher or not, Albert Lacroix won't make the cut.*

Once "Albert" had signed a contract and handed over his down payment, I gave him the key. He left saying, "Nice meeting you, Mademoiselle. I'll move in tomorrow."

The following day, Zizou and I peeked through the slats of our bedroom shutters, elbowing each other for a better view of Albert unloading his suitcases off a taxi.

"Didn't I tell you?"

Zizou shrugged, "*Boff.* Not *that* gorgeous."

I shoved her arm, "You say that because you are jealous. Remember, he's mine."

"He's too old. I prefer the guys in my group." Zizou turned her back on the shutters. "Come. Let's help him get settled."

"We can't do that."

"Why not?"

"I don't know. It's … not proper."

She shook her head and left. I remained behind, jealously watching her smile at Albert, shake his hand, and pick up a suitcase. *Now, why can't I do things like that?*

Papa Meets Albert

"SO, YOU'RE A TEACHER." Pa looked up from under the hood of his car as, the day after he moved in, Albert came out of his apartment.

Zizou and I stopped washing Papa's car for a moment and watched Albert carry a chair and books under the bower's shade outside his door. He set his books on the chair and walked over to Papa with his hand extended. "*Oui, monsieur.* I am Albert Lacroix."

Papa ignored the hand. "My daughter mentioned you are a teacher?"

Albert let his arm drop to his side. "Nice to meet you, monsieur. As a matter of fact, I am doing my military service as a teacher."

"Oh boy," I whispered to Zizou, "Here it comes."

"'Doing my military service as a teacher,'" Papa parroted. He tugged a rag out of his pants pocket and set his feet squarely apart. "Want to know what I think?"

Albert smiled with a nod of goodwill. A cherub's smile. A cherub whose wings would be pulled out one tender feather at a time. A cherub who'd be plucked, chewed, and spat out before he could say, "Mommy!"

"I'll tell you what I think." Papa wiped his hand with his greasy rag. "I think you came here as a teacher because you don't have the balls to put your life on the line to defend your country. That's what I think."

Albert's smile faded. "With all due respect, monsieur, Algeria is not my country. France is," he answered, reasonably.

"I see," Pa said, his anger rising. "The *Pieds-Noirs* were considered French enough to give their lives for France and free you and your families' asses from the krauts—twice—but we are not French enough for flat feet like you to help us keep what we earned during five generations of sweat and tears. Right?"

Albert blinked under the onslaught. "You have to understand, monsieur, this is not the same situation. Here, as colonists, you are exploiting the Arabs. They have a right to seek autonomy. Moreover, no one could alter the movement of independence that is sweeping the globe."

Zizou and I ducked out of sight behind the car, bug-eyed. We pressed our hands across our mouths to stifle giggles over the chewing Albert had coming.

"Ah. Now the truth's coming out," Pa triumphed. "Still wet behind the ears, but already espousing the communist propaganda that's rotting France's youth." Papa's stressed voice broke. He patted his breast pocket and extracted his pack of Gauloises. "Or is it that ...." He struck a match and lit a cigarette.

"*Yaa*," Zizou chuckled. "Not only isn't he fighting for his country, but he also turns out to be a rotten 'communist.'"

"You should calm down, *monsieur*." Albert extended a soothing hand toward Papa. "You don't know what you are saying."

"Calm down? Don't know what I am saying?" Papa sneered like a stalking hyena. "You are a young punk who's been lapping up the lies that a bunch of communists have drilled into the metropolitan minds. Now, you'll perpetuate the brainwashing and feed the same false information, disinformation, and lies to *our* children."

Eager to hear Albert's repost, Zizou and I lent ears big as gramophone speakers, but were disappointed when he simply said, "I'm sorry you feel this way, monsieur. Have a good day," and walked to his chair, carried it and the books into his apartment, and closed the door.

Rooftops

FROM THEN ON, ALBERT sightings were rare. Once school started, he seemed consumed by his work and whenever he and Papa crossed paths, they exchanged stiff nods like old men engaged in an ongoing quarrel.

Albert's silent greetings seemed to indicate he didn't hold Pa's verbal abuse against him. "I think it's because he wants Maman's cooking to keep coming his way," Zizou offered.

"Whatever the reason, I'm glad he's not mad at us," I said.

"You mean, not mad at *you*," Zizou corrected.

"What's wrong with that?"

My sister was right, I meant *me*. It would have been nice to form a relationship with someone from other climes. Someone who'd be a friend with no preconceived ideas of who I was or who I should be. Just a friend. And he was *so* gorgeous ....

School, house chores, and cold weather relegated neighborly interactions to the back burner. Life went on with the usual shots popping now and again, blasts going off here and there, the usual yield of spilled blood, and crops of dead bodies.

ONE EARLY WINTER DAY, sounds of machine guns and sporadic explosions flapped the air like eagles riding a storm of fireworks.

"*Mesdemoiselles*." The teacher's rod rapped her desk. "Fifteen minutes left."

The heads that had popped up at the first burst of gunshots returned to the English test before them.

I couldn't tear my eyes away from beyond our fourth-floor windows. European men I presumed to be OAS stood at the edge of rooftops across the street. I observed them with interest as they shouldered rifles aimed at apparently fast-moving targets and methodically pulled their triggers. I couldn't see their marks down below, but easily guessed they were FLN challenging this mostly European neighborhood. My cold fear of the *lycée* being overrun by terrorists lasted the flash of a gunshot as I took a deep breath and relaxed against my seat. *Thank you, God, for the OAS' vigilance and protection—*

Another rap of the teacher's ruler gave me a start, forcing me to refocus on the test.

By the time I turned in my paper, the shooting had stopped and the *paimpon paimpon* of ambulances and police sirens nearly drowned the ring of the electric bell calling the end of class.

Later that morning, the school's PA relayed the news that a twelve-hour curfew would be in effect starting at four o'clock this afternoon and that we'd be let out early.

MY FRIEND MONIQUE'S MOTHER arrived to pick her up on foot and invited me to go to their apartment, one block away and wait for my parents to pick me up.

After my phone call, Maman showed up from the cemetery's office in a taxi that drove us to the bus stop. We reached our house just as the siren signaled the start of curfew.

That evening, as Maman served Papa his *anisette*, she asked, "Do you know what the shooting was about?"

"The FLN rode trucks in an attempt to take over the Coudiat, but the OAS stopped them dead in their tracks." Papa added water to his *anisette*. "The police radio reported about thirteen dead and thirty-seven wounded. No details on who the casualties were."

I frowned. "*Dis-moi,* Papa, how can the FLN keep on doing things like attacking the Coudiat or killing those people on Algiers' beaches when they agreed to a truce during their negotiations with France?"

My father took a sip of his drink. "To convince the French negotiators that the FLN is a tough force to be reckoned with so they will agree to more concessions. That's all."

NEGOTIATING, WEIGHING WHAT WAS good and bad for our family became our focus two weeks later.

Lost

Papa CAME HOME, DISPIRITED, and dropped in a chair. Maman turned, holding the lid of her boiling pot. "What is wrong, *chéri*?"

Papa lit a cigarette and let it smolder between his fingers before taking a drag. He filled his mouth with smoke and blew thoughtful rings into the air. Watched them undulate and slowly unravel.

"What is wrong, Riri?" Ma's anxiety drew us in a tight ring around our father's chair.

"You want to know what's wrong? I'm going to tell you what's wrong," he said, his challenge the very image of the mythical Phoenix rising from its ashes.

He batted his mighty wings. "The fucking assholes at headquarters want to send me on special assignment in Tizi Ouzou."

"Tizi Ouzou?" Ma's eyes grew as big as the lid in her hand.

"Tizi Ouzou?" Zizou and I cried out.

"Where's *that*?" Yves asked.

"*En* Grande Kabylie," Papa said. "The north-central part of Algeria."

"But why?" Maman pressed. "That place is deadly."

"They say they need to replace their translator." Papa tamped his half-smoked cigarette in the ashtray. "I looked him up. The poor fucker got himself kidnapped by the *fellagha*."

"That's one good reason why you shouldn't go." Ma's already moist eyes lit up in alarm. "You have five children. They can't do this to us."

"Well, it's simple. I agree to go or I lose my job." He lit a new cigarette. "I'd receive hazardous duty pay." Maman didn't look impressed. He added, "We could use the extra income."

Maman went back to her boiling pot. "No matter how much they'd pay, it wouldn't be enough to make up for the loss of your life." She turned off the burner and banged the lid on the pot. "You're not going and that's that."

Whoa. I had never heard Ma be so assertive with our father. I was impressed.

"There isn't enough work at the cemetery. What would we live on?" Papa sounded more like someone plumbing the depths of a well rather than one looking for water.

"We'll manage. That's all." Maman crossed her arms. "I'll find a bookkeeping job somewhere and open the office at the cemetery only on Saturdays rather than the whole week."

"And during the summer," I offered, "I can keep the office open during the week."

Zizou, Mireille, and the boys cried out, "*Moi aussi, Moi aussi.*"

A smile flicked at the corners of Pa's mouth, the smile that betrayed his secret pleasure. "What will happen to our workers at the shop?"

"You'll have to let go of the younger ones," Ma suggested. "Keep Debbah and the older men like Moustache."

That sounded right to me. Papa needed Debbah as his right-hand man and Moustache had started working with Pépé Vincent as a young man. Also, during WWII, when I was a baby needing mineral supplements, Moustache had given his rations of chocolate to Pépé for me.

Mireille put her hand on Papa's shoulder. "You're not going away. Right, Papa?"

Zizou said, "We can do without the extra money, Pa. You can't go."

After each of us except the boys had offered our two bits, Papa spread his hands on top of the table and pushed himself off his chair. "All right, I'll hand in my resignation first thing tomorrow morning."

And Found

*M*AMAN FOUND PART-TIME BOOKKEEPING work in two small businesses downtown. I spent many summer afternoons at the cemetery office while Zizou took care of the kids and the house chores. Papa looked for new contracts in town and immediate surroundings and did maintenance jobs on existing monuments.

Weeks of starved cows followed the months of fat cows when Pa had drawn his police department salary until, one late-winter afternoon, my parents came home early from work. Papa had a spring in his step and Maman, a bloom on her cheeks.

Oh, Not again. I had seen these signs many times in the past—just before the advent of a new bundle of joy—with the distinction that my parents got the joy part and Zizou and I, the bundle. *Thanks, Pa. Thanks, Ma.*

"We have great news," Ma announced with a broad smile.

I snorted.

Zizou trumpeted, "We are getting a new baby."

"A new baby?" Yves didn't seem thrilled to lose his last-born status.

Mireille beamed, "What are we going to name her?"

I guessed she wished for a little sister to lord over just as Zizou and I lorded over her.

Riri didn't seem to like or dislike the idea.

Ma blushed.

Hands hooked on hips, Pa inclined his head sideways as if his left ear ached then turned to my mother. "How did you manage to produce such asshole kids?"

"Come, Riri, don't be crass."

Maman's mild reproach didn't faze him. "If they only learned to listen instead of wagging their tongues—"

She stopped him cold, "Your father found another job."

Five wagging tongues uttered, "A new job?" which, depending on who was doing the uttering, expressed curiosity concerning the new job or reeked of relief or disappointment that there would be no baby.

Maman forged on with undisguised pride. "He is going to be a teacher."

"A teacher?" Bulging eyes and sagging mouths greeted the news. "What kind of a teacher?" I asked.

Ma glanced at Pa, yielding him the floor. "They need a teacher at the vocational college in Constantine. I'll be teaching building construction."

I was happy my father had found a new steady income but, notwithstanding his colorful language, didn't believe he'd have the patience necessary to teach, or the credentials. "But, Pa, don't you need a teaching diploma?"

He shook his head. "My line of work more than qualifies me to instruct beginners," then added with a dismissive wave of the hand, "Besides, with people leaving right and left there is a shortage of educators."

Ma announced, "We have to celebrate."

A chorus of voices exulted, "*Yaa!* Let's celebrate."

She mused, "Let's see. We'll invite Yvette and Gilles." She briefly glanced my way. "And we'll ask Albert …." She crossed her arms and tapped her lower lip with her finger. "We'll have … *des têtes de moutons au four—*"

"*Têtes de moutons,* Ma?" We *loved* sheeps' heads. Split in halves. Roasted to golden brown and served with *pommes de terre au four* à la Elise. *Ooh-la-la.*

WE NEVER DRESSED UP when we were at home, even when we had guests. Pa frowned at the "Charleston" skirt Yvette had made for me for Easter— petrol blue and narrow with a wide pleated hem finished with a gros-grain flat bow—and at the light blue mohair top Ma had knitted to match the color of my eyes. It was a good thing she had made me wipe off the touches of lipstick, blush, and eyeliner I had put on. "Your father is going to explode if he sees you wearing makeup," she had said in a panic.

But she still arranged for Albert to sit next to me. Away from Pa who, once in a while, cast a probing glare in our direction, making sure our hands showed on each side of our plates. He didn't seem to remember from his supposedly wild youth that knees and feet are also made for touching.

As for the meal, it was a great success. Along with Maman's roasted potatoes, we had white bean salad smothered in olive oil and lemon juice with plenty of garlic and parsley. But the *têtes de moutons*—half a head each—was the prize dish.

Albert's face turned a waxy shade of pale as he stared at the half *tête* staring back at him from his plate. His breathing speeded up and he pressed his napkin to his lips. Maman frowned. "I'm sorry, Albert. I should have thought …. Would you like a piece of cold chicken with some mayonnaise, instead?"

Before Albert could respond, Papa intervened, his smile crafty. "What's the matter *Bebert*?" That was what he called him now, as if they had become best buddies. "Can't take our … 'ethnic' food?"

Tonton Gilles said, "Albert needs time to get used to our ways. Leave him alone."

Yvette shook her head at Papa. "They eat brains in France, don't they?" She smiled at Albert. "In black butter?"

Albert nodded, set his napkin down on his knees then addressed a jaundiced smiled to Ma. "*Non, merci, madame*, I love to try new dishes."

Well said, mon ami, I mentally applauded.

Papa raised the bottle of wine. "I see the man is beginning to grow balls, after all. Give him some more wine, Gilles."

Zizou winked at me.

I pinched a smile and picked up my knife and fork.

I liked to start with the brain. Dribble some lemon juice over its folds. Mash up a forkful in my mouth and let it coat my tongue like creamed butter—a luscious experience of fleeting duration, as sheep aren't known for their big brains.

Having finished his sheep's brain, Albert hovered over his plate, knife and fork in hand, unsure of how to proceed. I gave him a furtive nod and turned the head over. I forked out the oven-crisp cheek meat—really the only fleshy part of the head—from its hollow. Then, still chewing, scraped off the crackling skin covering the bone before attacking the lips that curled away from the blackened, long, narrow teeth.

When only the eye remained, I set my knife and fork down on my plate to signal Albert we were done. The eye was the only feature I made a point to not eat. Forked out of its socket, it looked like a spherical, small hard-boiled egg with the fogged black ring of the iris staring at you in congealed reproach ….
"*And the eye of Abel* …." I understood some relished popping the eyes in their mouths and crushing them like candy. I just couldn't.

Dessert was new to Albert, as he had never before eaten Arab pastries. Yvette had brought *makrouds* and *zlabeiyas*.

As a child, second only to Pépé Vincent, I had loved the sweet-honey *zlabeiyas* more than anything in the world, but as I grew older the *makrouds*, with their date paste sandwiched between two thick layers of semolina flavored with rose water and coated with honey, had become my favorite.

After dessert, the dishes done, the boys, Mireille, Zizou, and I played games of Lotto with Yvette and Albert, taking turns calling the numbers. I loved spending time with my uncle and aunt, but enjoyed my time with Yvette the most. We had lots of fun when she played games with us and even more when she taught Mireille, Zizou, and me new dances like the *cha cha cha*. To top it all off, she didn't take any bull from Papa and *that*, in my eyes, was her most admirable trait. But that day, as Albert sat beside me, his knee brushing mine, I focused more on his handsome face than on the game or Yvette, and my face heated up as her eyes shifted from Albert to me with a knowing smile.

CELEBRATIONS TOO SOON OVER, our lives took a different turn as Papa's job as a teacher called for him to stay home in the evenings and on the weekends to prepare lessons and grade papers.

Cinder Blocks

MA WAS DELIGHTED AT Pa's spending more time at home, but his novel presence put a damper on the boys' horsing around and curbed Zizou's escapades with her "girlfriend Viviane," as she called her boyfriend Alain. Mireille wallowed in the glory of Papa being a teacher and I, to my dismay, lost many opportunities to spend time with Albert.

Papa had even less time to manage his cemetery business than when he worked in the police force. Debbah filled in the gaps, carrying out Pa's directions and overseeing their implementation. This meant that he no longer could come to Sidi Mabrouk to produce the cinder blocks needed for the jobs.

"Do you want to help making *toubes*?"

"*Yaa! Oui*, Papa," Zizou and I said with one eager voice.

"I'll show you how."

"We know, Pa. We watch Debbah all the time."

Just the same, Papa demonstrated how to measure and mix the exact doses of sand, cement, and water to make cinder blocks. It was like mixing ingredients for a cake. A big cake for sure, but a cake just the same.

Zizou and I took turns combining the "ingredients" on top of a large metal sheet, using the heavy spade, its handle smoothed out by use and too big for our hands.

Mimicking Debbah, we spat in our hands and rubbed the moisturizing spittle into the skin of our palms. Then, using our right knees as levers, we folded the mixture of gravel and cement again and again until it was well blended—just like a cake—then we scooped the heavy mix into a bucket.

Zizou and I took turns mixing the concrete and pouring it from the bucket into the mold before turning on the switch. The vibrations tamped down the mix; then Mireille took hold of one set of handles at one end of the mold and Zizou or I, the handles at the other end to release the block. *Et voilà*. One *toube*. One.

Toube after *toube,* we produced the different types Debbah needed for the jobs at the cemetery. Each block part of the skeleton without which no monument could come to life. Without our *toubes*, there would be no monuments.

Each day, ignoring the blisters on my hands and the spreading bruise on my right knee from the spade's handle, I surveyed the ever-growing field of drying blocks. I could tell Zizou and Mireille shared the same sense of accomplishment and pride by the way they coolly dismissed their own blisters.

The boys insisted in sharing in the process and we had to shove and swat them away like horse flies. "If you stay out of the way, I'll let you water the *toubes*," I finally promised before spitting in my hands.

"When, Nanna?" asked Riri.

"When they've hardened."

"Now, Nanna?" Yves asked every half hour.

"Later."

"Now, Nanna?" until I turned on the tap and adjusted the flow of water. "*Attention.* It needs to be like a gentle shower and it's important you don't soak them. Just make them wet so they don't crumble. *D'accord?*"

"*Yaa,* Nanna, we know." They nodded gravely and studiously watered the blocks but soon grew bored with the task and Mireille took over.

When the blocks had cured, Debbah backed the truck into the yard and his team loaded *our* first batch. As the full truck drove away, I couldn't wait to go to the cemetery and soon watch *my* first monument rise out of the earth.

Chapter Twenty-Nine

La Valise ou le Cercueil

March 1962

*W*HILE WE RETURNED TO work, proud of our contribution to a building process, the *Accords d'Evian* conspired to bulldoze our lives. The FLN prodded the *Pieds-Noirs* to leave with a renewed campaign of violence and intimidation and a not so veiled threat of, "*La Valise ou Le Cercueil*," giving us the choice between the suitcase and the coffin.

Only then did I understand Pa's grand design behind his bringing home prospectuses on Corsica, Malta, Argentina, Australia, and other distant places. We read about these countries' history, geography, commerce and customs. We discussed whether we'd like it there, why and why not. I had thought it was my father's way of teaching us geography, but I saw, now, that he was preparing us in case we had to leave.

The process had titillated my imagination, stoked my curiosity for faraway places, causing me, once more, to regret not having been born a boy. A male free to pick up a bag and set out to discover a new world behind each horizon. To "see where it went," as Riri had said, long ago, when we thought he had been kidnapped.

But then, the thought of Albert living so close made me glad to be only a girl and, in spite of Papa's vigilance and warning to stay away from him, Albert and I became friends. Without realizing what was happening. A little at a time.

*W*HENEVER MY FATHER WASN'T home, Albert and I sat on the bottom steps of our stairway, talking about books and things. He not only seemed to enjoy my company, but also sought it out. His gentle attention and sense of humor, sophistication and good looks flattered my ego. Compared to him, I saw now, Angelo had been a mere boy.

Maman invited Albert to Sunday meals. She shrugged when Papa dusted up his earlier accusation of, "*Tu fais la Maquerelle à ta fille.*"

"*Non, chéri*, I am not being a madam again. Albert is a young man away from home. He has no friends here. It is only normal we invite him on Sundays."

"I'd like to read it," Albert said after I mentioned my Atlantis story.

Papa's rebuff of my first and only attempt at writing still stung. "I won't let you read it," I told Albert. "But I can tell you how the story goes."

As he listened, I had the urge to kiss the soft smile at the corner of his lips, but of course didn't dare.

"I like your descriptions of knights 'riding herds of spirited seahorses' and the 'silver clouds of baby sardines,' but the most beautiful image, in my view, is your likening of the glowing jellyfish to suspended moons," he observed.

My heart raced with pride. "You really think my story's beautiful?"

He took my hand and said, "You'll be a great writer some day," almost moving me to kiss the lids of his gorgeous eyes.

We also took advantage of Papa's absence to play gin rummy in Albert's room, being careful to leave his door and window open. These times with him were the most wonderful and exciting period of my life until, one fateful day, while we played *gin* on the eve of Easter Holidays, Papa's car unexpectedly drove up the street. My heart turned to ice. I dropped my cards and fled Albert's room in a panic, stepping over the threshold just as Papa opened the yard gate. Right under his nose.

I dashed to the stairs, took two steps at a time and, in the true tradition of our ancestors *les Gaulois*, waited for the sky to fall upon my head.

"*La trahison est entrée dans ma maison.*" Papa's dramatic statement was so extreme that, thinking he was joking, the assembled family laughed with relief. But he meant it. Treason had invaded his home.

For several days, my father studied me as if trying to decide whether or not I had committed an unspeakable offense. Then, one afternoon, he darted into my room like a hawk on a field mouse.

Sins of a Daughter

"Did you have sex with him?"

I knew well who 'him' was. "Who, Pa?"

"You know who. The flat foot. The communist. Did he dishonor you?"

"No, Papa. He didn't." *Hell, he didn't even try to kiss me.*

Pa went on as if he hadn't heard me. "I decided to have the doctor check you out."

I guessed what he meant but played stupid. "I'm not sick; I don't need to see a doctor."

"I want him to check whether you're still a virgin."

"I told you before, Albert never touched me. We are just friends."

"You think I'm a fucking ass?" His eyes flared like Roman candles. "'Just friends?' If he really didn't touch you he's an even bigger ass than I thought he was."

"*Non,* Pa, he's not an ass. He just doesn't have a filthy mind like yours."

My father raised his hand to hit me, but dropped it and turned to leave. "I'll have your mother make an appointment with Dr. Laurie."

"Papa!"

He faced me. Though seized by anger more powerful than any I'd known, I let my measured words fall one by one from my lips like ice cubes into an empty glass. "I cannot stop you from forcing me to be examined, Papa, but I swear …." I pointed a shaky finger at him. Tears of rage and frustration rolled down my cheeks. "I swear to you, Pa. On Pépé Vincent's grave. I swear that I'll run away and won't care what will happen to me."

Overcome by the effort to remain collected and not scream like a harpy, I gasped for air and enunciated each word, "The only way to stop me would be to beat me to a pulp or shoot me like a rabid dog." He chewed the inside of his cheek. His eyes wavered then he gave a determined nod. "We'll see who makes the rules in this house."

Wounded, enraged, and dearly needing to hurt him, I blurted De Gaulle's mordant words, "Daddy's Algeria is over." And, for good measure, I spat, "*Kaput. Fini.*" Wham! My head swung from left to right under the blow. My cheek stung with a thousand needles then turned boiling hot. Pride kept me from rubbing my face. I lifted my chin. *Bull's eye.* My shot had found its target. I glared at him with the same self-satisfied, mission-accomplished corner smile he had perfected.

He drew back his hand for another blow. Fearing nothing, save losing face, I stood my ground and smoothed my disheveled hair, again smiling his corner smile. Papa's arm dropped and his voice rattled as if out of breath, "You'll stay in your room until further notice," then he crossed the threshold and slammed the door behind him.

Clack—the key turned in the lock. "I'm leaving the key in the door." The wooden panels between us dulled his words, "Bitches in heat can always find ways to screw, even through key holes." His familiar jibe hit me even harder than the blow to my face, but plain, stubborn pride kept me from kicking and clawing at the door like a wild cat.

During the next few days, my anger festered into resentment. Sour resentment at not having been born a male.

As a boy, I'd have my father's respect, his support, and his trust. I'd travel from one country to another then another. As a girl, I could only dream.

I fantasized about building a giant kite—red. I'd ride the Sirocco across the sea, mount other currents and glide above the earth.

My red kite fantasy brought air into my lungs, cleared my head. I leaned over my balcony's railing and watched young Arab girls jump rope in the middle of the street. They sang ditties I didn't understand and laughed as one leapt to replace another in the arc of the whirling cord. Their carefree giggles and bouncing braids brought a smile to my dry lips. A smile that soon faded as I juxtaposed my future against theirs.

The moment they took their first breath, their fate was sealed. No matter how much their families loved them, their sacred, irreversible duty to their culture was unreserved compliance. They'd be veiled and confined at puberty. A marriage would be arranged, sometimes to older men. They'd be torn from their childhood homes and tossed into strange ones. Subjected to a mother-in-law or older wife and live their lives in unconditional submission to the family males. No appeal.

I was born lucky. Not a boy. But still lucky. I had a choice. I could choose to submit to my father's will or stand firm and demand his respect. *So, I'm confined to my room. How hard is this? After all, I get to enjoy time alone for a change and can afford to wallow in the conviction that I'm right and next time ….*

Next time, I'll make sure Papa will accuse me of something I really did. I'll show him. I gave a hard nod. *He'll see.*

WHILE FANTASIZING ABOUT GETTING payback on Pa, I thumbed through his Victor Hugo book collection, opting for *Ruy Blas.* I perused the story of a slave in Spain who's in love with the queen. Unable to appreciate Hugo's flowery style, I returned the book to its shelf and walked to my balcony to check on the racket rising from the road.

Arab boys were playing with a small square of cloth tied around a handful of sand. They bounced the pouch on the instep of one foot, hopping on the other to keep their balance. They counted the bounces in hypnotic sing songs, "*Ith-nain, thalatha, arba'a, khamsa, sitta, seba'a , thamaniya, tissa's, ash-ara*"— laughing, encouraging, and deriding one another. The lively challenges drew me in and I began counting in French, urging the players on, applauding as one bested another. Once they realized they had an impassioned spectator, the kids vied with added vigor, showing off, stealing quick glances at my balcony to make sure I watched, warming my heart with a sense of camaraderie, of connection to the human race.

ONE AFTERNOON, WHEN A hot wind swept the deserted road, I observed Albert retrieving a letter from the mailbox on the little black gate. On his way to his room, he glanced up at my balcony just as a gust of wind lifted the curtains, enfolding me. Albert winked at me. I brushed the curtain aside and curtsied, prompting a faint smile and a nod. *Gosh, he's beautiful and so sweet.*

That evening, Zizou handed me a small red box. "Albert asked me to give you this."

Heart thumping in my throat, I lifted the lid. It revealed a seahorse and a note, "Never stop dreaming."

Zizou asked, "What's the seahorse for?"

"Oh, nothing," I said with a silly grin.

A GRIN THAT LATER MORPHED from delighted to resentful as I watched Papa coax Albert to *La Guinguette* while I was still restricted to my room. They walked up the road like two old buddies—or was it my father's way of putting into practice one of his prized mottos, "Keep your friends close and your enemies even closer?"

I hoped Albert wouldn't fall into my father's net.

Non, he couldn't—when I had related my father's "Treason has invaded my home" comments to him, Albert had shaken his head in wonder. "A real character."

"Who do you mean?" I'd asked.

"Your father. I've never met anyone like him."

"Is this good or bad?"

"Both. He's very intelligent. He worries about the welfare of his workers. He cares a great deal about his family, yet his intense and extreme pronouncements make him sound cruel and, at times, foolish," Albert concluded, raising my chin with the tip of his fingers and brushing my cheek with a kiss.

No matter my father's reasons for courting Albert, I felt cheated. Cheated the way I had when my teacher read my Atlantis story to the class and "Froufrou" attempted to steal my thunder. That analogy moved me to close my hand and lift my index and small finger into a pair of horns.

In this case at least, the Arab custom to fend off the evil eye really worked. At the end of five days, Papa came in my room and announced, "Your mother and I believe nothing happened between you and Bebert." *Geese, what's a dove to do to prove her plumage's white?*

Pristine or not, I had spent most of the Easter Holidays locked up. At the news of my release, the rest of the family breathed a sigh of relief and, like an old dog settling down for the night, the house itself seemed to exhale.

But as usual, my father wouldn't let an old dog lie.

First Kiss

ON THE HEELS OF my release, my father called a meeting with Albert and me and without preamble said to Albert, "You'll have to marry *ma fille*."

Appalled, humiliated, I opened my mouth to protest, but the set of my father's mouth betrayed him—telling me his demand was a ruse to scare Albert away.

I turned to Albert, willing him to say no. "*D'accord*," he said with a hint of challenge.

Papa's lips thinned as if his best friend had spat in his soup. He turned to me, tilting his chin.

"*D'accord*," I said, calling his bluff.

And I was glad it was a bluff. I was sweet on Albert, but I didn't want to marry young, like my mother who had been sixteen years old against my eighteen. Have five kids. Count my pennies to the end of my days. I took a malevolent pleasure beating Papa at his own game. "Does this mean Albert and I are engaged, Pa?"

"Over my dead body," he spat, then left in a huff for *La Guinguette*.

I grinned at Albert. "You know that my father was trying to scare you—not into marrying me, but into staying away from me, right?"

Albert smiled. "I have been around him long enough. I knew what he was doing." He took my hand. "Did you mean it when you agreed to marry me?"

I liked the feel of my hand in his, but took it back. "I'm not ready to get married. I was only repaying him for playing mind games." I searched his face. "What about you. Did you mean it?"

"I played along to see how far he would go." Reaching out, he raised my chin and looked into my eyes. "No hurt feelings?"

"No hurt feelings," I said, meaning it. Still, I hoped he would take me in his arms and give me my first kiss.

THE EVENING BEFORE SCHOOL resumed, Zizou whispered, "Tonight, when Papa goes to *La Guinguette*, Albert will wait for you behind the house."

"Zizou," I whined, "You want me to get in trouble again?"

"Don't you want to speak to your *amoureux*?"

"*Oui, mais ....*" The objection died on my lips. Now was the time to give my father reasons to indict me. Time for payback.

"Just go. I'll keep watch."

My sister doing the *aoujak*, as the Arabs say, I went to meet Albert. I found him smoking under the twilight shade of the vine arbor. He gazed at the splashes of gold, purple, and orange streaking the sunset sky. "This is stunning," he said.

The dreamlike softness of his eyes made my heart quiver like harp strings. "The colors presaging Sirocco," I said, "the Sahara wind that carries sand to the Mediterranée and, at times, across it all the way to Spain."

He dropped his cigarette and crushed it with the tip of his shoe then turned and framed my face with his hands, studying it as if learning the paths to a newly discovered land. He took my hand and moved us to the stoop of Pépé Honninger's old tool shop.

We sat, facing each other. His soft gray eyes captured mine as he caressed my hair. My heart beat a slow tattoo under his gentle touch, then raced to a chaotic drumbeat as his warm hand slid down my cheek, along my neck, over the front of my blouse, and cupped my breast.

My gasp brought a slow smile to his lips and his thumb moved against my nipple. A tremor, at once painful and delicious, squeezed my lower belly and I moaned. He held my chin with his other hand and drew my face to his. My eyes closed at the immeasurable bliss of his lips prodding mine.

My skin crawled as if I were in the throes of high fever. My bones turned to jelly and I leaned into him in total abandon.

His moustache tickled the inside of my nose and a giggle bubbled up from deep inside my throat. A fleeting flashback to Zizou telling how yummy kisses were told me my reaction wasn't normal.

Dismissing the tickling hair in my nostril and the beard chafing my chin, I pressed my body against Albert's and threw my arms around his neck. Eyelids shut tight, I surrendered my mouth to his probing tongue. His saliva mingled with mine—exactly like in Ma's romance novels—but instead of hearing bells and fireworks, I felt as if a large, warm, wet worm was slithering inside my mouth. I gagged.

I shoved Albert away, shot to my feet and dashed around the side of the house, spitting with the same vigor I'd forced Zizou to spit after the toad squirted into her mouth.

I took the stairs two at a time, raced the length of the corridor to the bathroom and past Ma's bedroom, where she sat in bed, reading.

I flipped on the bathroom switch and slammed the door shut. Grabbing my toothbrush, I squeezed a big squiggle of toothpaste. I brushed my teeth, my tongue, and the lining of my cheeks so hard they burned as if I had chomped on a can full of *harissa*.

I peeked into the mirror and rubbed Nivea cream on my red chin and cheeks. Combed my hair. I opened the bathroom door, thinking my "payback" on Pa wasn't as gratifying as I had planned when I heard, "Come here, Nanna." Ma's stern voice worried me. I walked no farther than her open door.

"*Oui*, Ma?"

"What is going on?"

"Going on, Ma?"

"Why this sudden rush to the bathroom and running water?"

Oh, God, help me. "I ... I—"

Zizou strode pass the front door. "She ate something bad, Ma."

Our mother's eyes moved from Zizou to me and back to Zizou.

"I think I did too," Zizou complained, a hand on her stomach.

"I wonder why that is," Maman mused. "Get an artichoke from the garden, boil it for ten minutes, and drink the water," she said. "You'll feel better soon," she promised, and returned to her magazine.

In our room Zizou held her stomach, laughing like an idiot as I explained why I ran out on Albert. "Never met anyone like you," she cackled. "First Angelo, now Albert. What's wrong with you?" Her eyes popped open wide as a car's headlights. "Don't tell me you prefer girls?"

I felt miserable, inadequate, and angry at myself. A genuine misfit. But ... girls?

Naa. I'm sure I'd have liked Angelo's kisses—if it had happened. I knew I'd have liked them. *A lot.* I felt it in my bones. But he was gone and I would never know for sure.

Chapter Thirty

To Go or Not to Go

May, 1962

WHAT I KNEW FOR sure was that I'd be *very* embarrassed to face Albert after dumping him in the middle of a kiss. *Princesse de Glace strikes again.*

I eventually bumped into Albert two days later as he watched my father measure and cut plywood at his outdoor workbench. "Now that the *Accords d'Evian* have set the date of Algeria's independence," Papa was saying, "The *Pieds-Noirs* have two choices: '*La valise ou le cercueil.*' If we choose *la valise*, to go who knows where, we'll have to leave with only the clothes on our backs—"

Albert shook his head. "I don't think this will happen. *Les Accords* will see to the safeguard of your property rights."

"*Mon pauvre ami*," said Papa, with contempt. "How gullible you are." He lit a cigarette and continued. "How do you think France will manage to enforce the accords to the letter once Algeria is independent with extremists at its helm?"

Albert shrugged.

"De Gaulle has already given up the *Harkis*," Papa continued. "Not only has he ordered the army to disarm them but refuses them, as well as the over one million Muslims loyal to France, asylum in the *Métropole*."

Horrified by what I heard, I forgot my embarrassment vis-à-vis Albert. "But Pa, if these people aren't granted asylum in France, won't the FLN slaughter them?"

My father's silence pitched me into a well of anguish. While we, *Pieds-Noirs*, could claim our birthrights and set down our *valises* on France's shores, if we chose to, the Muslims who had cast their lot with mighty France would be left behind. For them, there was no choice. Only *le cercueil*. They would be massacred along with every single member of their families.

The betrayal of these people was an even greater infamy than that suffered by the *Pieds-Noirs*. An indelible stain on France's honor—*my* honor.

Anguished, needing the warmth of human touch, I sidled up to Albert. He furtively reached for my hand—letting me know, "No hard feelings."

"And don't even think the metropolitan French will welcome us with open arms—" Papa's quick side glance warned me to watch my moves. "They won't treat us as repatriates. They'll treat us as archaic exploiters who *'Ont fait suer le burnous.'*" He displayed the rough palms of his hands and his farmer's tan. "Are these the marks of a 'slave driver' or the marks of a man who works as hard as his Arab workers?"

"I know you are not one of the exploiters," Albert agreed.

Papa's voice held a sour note. "Tell me. How many 'exploiters' have you met since you've arrived?"

Albert remained silent and Papa filled the gap. "You've been here long enough, my friend, to know that the big farms, factories, and mines are owned by the *Grands Colons*—mostly metropolitan French—and that the majority of *Pieds-Noirs* are blue-collar workers, government employees, small farmers, and business owners—simple people who only wish to make a living in peace alongside their Christian, Jewish, and Arab neighbors."

Albert nodded in sober agreement. Papa pulled the carpenter pencil from behind his ear, measured a new sheet of plywood and drew a line between two dots. His cigarette quivered on his lower lip as he pursued his earlier thoughts. "If we choose to stay here, we'll be granted two options. One, become Algerian citizens, with the obligation to convert to Islam. Two, remain French nationals and lose all rights, including that of ownership ...." He set the smoldering cigarette on the side of the work bench. "That is, if we don't end up in a *cercueil* amid the general hysteria of the first days of self-rule."

"Then it's *la valise* for us. *Hein*, Pa?" I concluded, wondering how many thousands of others would make the same choice.

THE FOLLOWING MONDAY, AFTER lunch at the lycée's cafeteria, my friend Monique and I sat in a corner of the school yard. She had been unusually morose. Missing her pixie smile I asked, "What's wrong?"

"Oh, everything's wrong," she shrugged. "My father's family in France wants us to move in with them. They say it's getting even more dangerous here. They claim the earlier we go to France, the better chance my parents will have to find work before the rest of the *Pieds-Noirs* flood the job market."

I felt a little pinch at the very edge of my heart. "When will you go away?"

"Next week." She smiled that shy, broken-toothed smile that made her so special.

"Where in France?"

"In Nice, *sur la* Côte d'Azure."

I had only seen the French Riviera on postcards and in movies. *La Promenade des Anglais*, Nice's boardwalk, lined with the café terraces of luxurious hotels like the Negresco and rows of swaying palm trees—too posh for us to visit, let alone inhabit.

"Will you give me your address there before you leave, Monique?"

A few days later, we said tearful good-byes. Promised to write. And swore never to forget each other.

Soon after Monique's departure, people leaked out of the country a few at a time, like annoying drips from a faulty faucet. Drips grew into drops. Drops multiplied into an inexorable flow that also swept Susanne and her family away.

My friends gone, the *lycée* became a desert.

PEOPLE MOVED TO FRANCE, Corsica, Argentina, Australia …. Some took along their belongings. Others sold what they could, abandoning the rest. Locked up houses on our street and across town stood like sullen blind men with no place to go, yielding an emptiness eerie as a moonscape—too fantastic to grasp.

Meanwhile, Papa fashioned cut-up plywood into suitcases. That was no fantasy.

"Pa, why can't we buy some *real* suitcases?" Zizou griped.

"Because they're all gone."

"*Oui*, but *plywood*, Pa?"

"Trust me," he said, "I went through the campaigns of Italy, France, and Germany and saw many refugees. You'll do a lot of waiting around and will be happy to have these to sit on. Besides, unlike cardboard or leather, plywood is practically indestructible."

"But only two? How are we going to bring clothes for seven people in only two suitcases?" I cried out.

"We don't know what's going to happen there or where we'll end up. Two suitcases will be all we'll want to lug around."

Always meticulous, he took his time, whistled one of his tuneless tunes and broke out the old paint brushes and paint. "*Yellow*, Papa?" Zizou, Mireille, and I concurred—yellow was beyond the pale. Even for plywood suitcases.

"We'll be the joke of the other *Pieds-Noirs*," Zizou said.

"*And* of the *patos*," I added.

Our father didn't budge. "Yellow will make our suitcases easier to locate among thousands of others."

He attached a handle to a suitcase. "Now get off my ass. I've work to do."

He went on, building a small rusty-red square suitcase with a lock for the family papers, such as ownership of the house and *cimetière*, birth certificates, and school diplomas.

WE MARKED THE IMPENDING departure of Yvette, Gilles, and little Jean Pierre with a *couscous*. We played games of *loto*, gin rummy, and family. Then came time to say good-bye. Yvette gave Maman their temporary address in France. Maman wouldn't let go of her brother. "Make sure to let us know when your address changes. *D'accord?*"

Tonton Gilles held her hand. "Of course, when we move, we'll leave a forwarding address."

She wiped her tears. "You promise?"

He nodded and we kissed and hugged and said lots of *Aux revoirs* and *à bientôts,* with squeaky voices and phony smiles.

Les Carottes Sont Cuites

ONE JUNE AFTERNOON AFTER Yvette and Gilles left, Zizou and I took the bus to join the rest of the family at *La Boule Tricolore* and say farewell to more of my parents' friends about to leave.

Zizou and I climbed onboard the bus to Constantine and handed our fare to the *Vatman* sitting in the booth at the back of the bus. He wore a European suit and a Fez of red felt with long-fringed black tassels on top.

* * *

WHEN I WAS A kid during the days of electric tramways and the poles at the back of the tram unhooked from the overhead electric lines, the tram stopped cold. Face glued to the back window, I would watch with renewed curiosity as the *Vatman* stepped out, grabbed the tram's long, ungainly poles and, leaning back against their weight, maneuvered them with some difficulty to hook them back onto the electric lines. Then he climbed back onboard and the driver would restart us on our way.

* * *

GLAD TO BE OUT of the baking June sun, my sister and I collapsed on the last two empty seats, facing the *Vatman's* booth. Following the acquired reflex of checking my surroundings when in public places, I made a tally of the people and their bundles swaying in rhythm with the moving bus.

Women draped in Constantine's traditional black veils held down their white *hayeks* to keep their faces covered against the breeze blowing through the windows.

Men wore white flowing *gandourahs* and heavy turbans or embroidered skullcaps. Their immovable faces—varying from light shade, to coffee, to dark chocolate complexions—sported luxuriant moustaches, and their dark eyes were outlined with kohl.

A beardless man wearing a European suit over a collarless shirt clutched a straw basket that held a live chicken on his knees. The animal's head jerked this way and that way, aiming a sharp, accusing eye at the world.

An old barefaced woman with a small tattoo in the center of her forehead and a scarf over her hennaed hair sat next to two boys chewing roasted sunflower seeds. Across the aisle, a man with mint leaves stuck into his nostrils manipulated worry beads.

Of the entire bus, my sister and I were the only Europeans.

At the next stop, a woman swathed in black climbed in. Only her eyes and hands showed. Two bulky bags beneath her veil gave her the look of a bowling pin.

She scanned the length of the full bus and plunked herself in front of us, setting her bags atop our feet, and held onto an overhead handle. The bus lurched forward and she swayed, staring down her nose at us, demanding that we stand up with a firm tilt of her chin.

Zizou and I exchanged a to-hell-with-her look and didn't budge but for the down on my forearms that rose to attention.

Getting the message we would not concede our seats, the woman glared at the *Vatman* and gave a curt nod in our direction. Zizou and I swapped a blink. My guts tightened.

From inside his booth the man glowered at us. "*Cette dame* wants to sit. Get up."

I pursed my lips, shook my head and, hoping nobody would see it shake, pointed a finger at the two kids sitting on one side of the aisle, then at the young man with the mint in his nose on the other.

A few people cast dark looks our way. Others averted their eyes as if embarrassed by the *Vatman's* offensive tone. But for the humming engine, an ominous silence settled inside the bus. *A 'pregnant pause,' some would call it,* I reflected, but my tongue-in-cheek flippancy did little to relieve the tightening in my guts.

As the bus neared the next stop, Zizou whispered around the right corner of her mouth, "Should we get out?"

"They'll think we are scared," I whispered around the left corner of my mouth.

"Darn right we are." She flicked a glance at the *vatman*. "But I don't want him to know it."

We touched hands under the folds of our skirts.

I mouthed, "We stay."

At the stop, several seats emptied and the woman sat down. Her eyes spewed venom at us. "Ignore her," I suggested. "Let's talk about something."

The bus restarted with a grinding of the stick shift. The tail pipe spewed an oily cloud of smoke that streamed in through the cranked down windows.

My hands had stopped shaking, my guts, almost settled, when the *Vatman's* voice rose, loud and bitter, "It doesn't matter, anyway," he blustered. "For you, *les carottes sont cuites,*" and he kissed the tips of his fingers, thanking Allah, "*Hamdullah.*"

Everyone understood the expression, "The carrots are cooked," the die is cast, no turning back the clock. He meant to stress the point that my sister and I were on the losing side and better bow to the victors.

Although his comment was petulant and gratuitous, I understood the man's motives. I understood his need to have the last word, save face in front of the other Arabs. I understood that, during these times of transition and turmoil, everyone was weary of retributions from anybody and everybody. Everyone dreaded the vengeful finger-pointing for considered slights. The bone-picking, getting-even, that would be meted out after Independence Day. The same retribution, revenge, payback, that had systematically occurred among the Arab population along the years, the *Harkis* being the latest targets.

I looked into the eyes of this man who had made change for our bus tickets from the time we were babes in our mother's arms, through our growing years, and all the way to this moment, but found no recollection, on his part, of shared cordial experiences. Only the reflection of a consuming, unadulterated personal hatred I didn't understand—hatred that seemed to seep from deep inside his soul, like pus from a pressed boil. An enmity that vaporized the regard and trust I had felt for him up to this moment.

I lost all sense of self-preservation. "You are absolutely correct, monsieur, 'Les carottes sont cuites.'" Then, using the imagery that is part of the Muslim speech, I went on, angry, scared, and breathless, "But while we are eating them warm—" Loud and clear, my voice filled the bus. "You, *monsieur*, will eat them cold."

Speechless, the man jerked his head the other way. Dismissing us. The tassel's silken strands of his fez swayed wildly, a couple clinging to the red felt like squirming worms.

Head high, I scanned the other passengers' faces. A few, including the woman who had challenged us, cast scathing looks at Zizou and me. Most looked down at their bundles or glanced out the windows as if the exchange had not taken place.

For the rest of the way, the *Vatman* and I made it a point to ignore each other.

When we reached our stop, Zizou and I bounded off the bus steps like two mountain goats leaping over a gaping abyss.

"Yaa, Nanna," Zizou said. "*Tu as vraiment poussé la Mémé dans les orties, cette fois et sans culotte, en plus.*"

"*Aïe aïe aïe!*" I laughed at the popular *Pieds-noir* saying, the image of pushing grandma in a bed of nettles without her underwear—looking for trouble.

But Zizou was right. As the adage went, I pushed the altercation with the *Vatman* a bit too far for our safety, but darn, it had felt good.

Well aware of how close we had come to being in real trouble, we ran, giggling like *la Folle de Chaillot,* Giraudoux's madwoman who wanted to put the world to rights, all the way to *La Boule Tricolore.*

SEVERAL DAYS AFTER *LES carottes* episode, Maman and I stood in line outside the Air France travel agency, in Constantine, to buy our plane tickets out of Algeria. Out of this land we didn't wish to leave for one we didn't wish to go to.

France made no provisions for the *Pieds-Noirs'* exodus from Algeria and we had to arrange for our own way out. Some sailed, others flew. The long wait under the hard sun was made even longer by the jeers and taunts of young Arab men.

Ma agreed with the queuing women, grateful their men had not come along. "You are right, *mesdames,*" she said, "My husband would not take these provocations quietly."

I nodded. Papa would have responded to the heckling with his fists and gotten us in lots of trouble. Might have missed the plane. Even disappeared forever.

A woman with hennaed hair said, "So would my husband. That's why I told him his time would be better spent closing down our business."

Another woman nodded. "I totally agree with you, *mesdames,* women are better at taking insults."

"We are used to keeping our mouths shut and our egos in our pocket," said a portly woman with a sad face.

"And stuffing our handkerchief on top of it to make sure it stays there," concluded another, fanning herself with a folded newspaper.

Several hours of shuffling in the sun, drawing fortitude from the other women in line, allowed us to secure seven inflated-price seats to Marseille-Marignan for the *caravelle* leaving on the twenty-fourth of June.

Chapter Thirty-One

WITH ONE WEEK LEFT to decide what to pack, we each built ever-shrinking piles of personal effects—judicious nitpicking that had to fit inside the two *yellow* suitcases along with everyone else's judicious nitpickings.

Last Sweep

June 23, 1962

IN SPITE OF THE previous month's spring cleaning, Ma decided we must give our home the proverbial *"coup de balai"*—the sweeping one gives to a house, which also referred to the resolution of pending matters before starting anew.

We moaned and groaned but picked up brooms and rags.

"But Ma," Zizou argued, "We already cleaned the house. Why do it again, when we are not going to live here anymore?"

"*Oui*," Yves said, "why should we clean for the guys who are going to steal our house from us?"

"We don't want strangers to see our dirt."

I almost laughed at my mother's absurd assertion, but her dignified stance sealed my lips.

She stabbed a stubborn finger into the air. "Remember, 'Cleanliness is Next to Godliness.'"

"*Yaa*, Ma," Mireille said, then asked, "Is it like when you want us to wash between our toes and behind our ears and wear clean underwear, just in case we get into an accident?"

"*Oui, ma fille*. Something like that."

Zizou's eyes and mine examined an old water stain on the ceiling.

At first, I resented the redundant work, but as I went through the house with a mop and dust rag, the full impact of our looming loss hit me square in the belly. I knew every corner of this house as intimately as the lines in the palms of my hands—each nook and cranny, each mark on the furniture, each water stain on the ceiling plaster, blemish on the wallpaper.

Each blotch, scratch, crack, a testimony to my personal and family saga. Happy. Sorrowful. Funny. Tragic. Each intricately woven into the essence of our home.

Each bestowing on it a unique soul—an essence never to be found in any other home. Any other family.

The enormity of our loss lent a boost to my cleaning zeal. *Oui*, my beloved house, we'll leave you looking finer than ever.

While polishing the never-used china at the bottom of the china cabinet, I found my green tin box. I sat, legs stretched along the cold tiles, set my rag aside and lifted the box's lid, uncovering nearly forgotten bits and pieces. *L'Oeil de Malika*, buttons with jet-black or diamond-like stones, butterfly wings, and my *Atlantis Sous Les Flots* story

I rose to my feet and fetched Albert's seahorse, added it to the box, snapped the lid shut, and set the box on top of my pile when my father's voice boomed in my mind's ear as if from above, "On-ly-the-es-sen-tials."

I didn't think he would deem my box essential, except that leaving it behind would convert my own treasure into someone else's trash. I couldn't bear to let strangers' hands rummage through my box, discarding its content like rubbish with the exception, perhaps, of the unique buttons.

I drifted about the house in a futile search for a hiding place when, Eureka!

I strode downstairs to the backyard and snuck into Papa's workroom, wrapped my green box in oilcloth and took the bundle to the back garden. I dug a hole among the laurel's roots where I knew the Barbary Corsairs' treasure trove rested. I carefully laid the box into the earth and covered it with the loose soil. But as I tamped it down, I had a change of heart. I unearthed the box and retrieved the seahorse, slipped it inside my pocket then returned the box to the *laurier's* care and scattered bits and pieces of garden refuse to cloak the disturbed earth.

I turned my back on the buried milestones of my youth, and wrapping my hand around the seahorse inside my pocket, wandered about the garden, gathering as I went a last harvest of memories.

I stroked the smooth bark of the pear and fig trees, breathed in the familiar fragrances of lemon verbena, rosemary, and lavender. Heard the lost echoes of our fleeting childhood—the laughter, songs, and cries of hurt glancing off each and every corner of our yard.

Glancing off the mulberry tree and grape harbor where, in summer months, the wasps and bees flickered in dry sunbeams.

Off the neighbor's mud shack where, winter and summer, the Arab boys droned verses of the Qur'an.

Off the now deserted poultry yard and the bamboo grove still teeming with tadpoles and, no doubt, a slithering snake or two.

I didn't know whether to laugh full throated in celebration of joys past or sob desperately in anticipation of our looming loss. Instead, I wiped a lone tear and smiled.

Memories. One treasure no one could ever steal away from me.

Twilight in Sidi Mabrouk

STILL UNDER THE SPELL of past visions, I tied a silk cord around the seahorse's neck and slipped it around my neck. Then I walked to Albert's door and knocked.

"*Bonjour*," he said, opening his door wide with a warm smile. "I was about to look for you to say *au revoir*."

"I came to say *au revoir* too." I pulled at the rope around my neck. "I don't know if I'll ever see you again, but this," I stepped closer and showed him the seahorse, "*this* will remind me of you. Always."

His eyes shone and he searched his pocket with a mischievous smile. "I've something else for you to remember me by." He handed me a folded piece of red cloth woven with gold threads.

"What is it?"

"Open it."

I opened the small bundle one red fold at the time, holding my breath, willing the moment to last forever.

The ring sparkled in the mid-afternoon sun, setting my face on fire.

"Put it on," Albert urged.

The thin gold coin wrapped around the top part of my finger and around the whole of my heart. I looked into my friend's eyes through brimming tears. He reached out and pulled me close. "When we see each other again, and if that's what you want, we'll get engaged to be married."

I didn't know whether I loved him, but knew I needed the comfort of his arms around me. I whispered against his shoulder, "When will I see you again?"

He pointed at the suitcases lined up in his entry hall. "A taxi's taking me downtown. I'll be staying at a hotel until the day after tomorrow when my plane leaves. But I will be back for the next school season." He pulled a piece of paper from his breast pocket. "Here is my address in France. Send me yours when you're settled somewhere."

He brushed my lips with a soft kiss and held me at arm's length. "Take good care of yourself, I'll be thinking of you."

I reluctantly walked away, stroking the sparkling ring with a finger then turned. "Thank you," I said softly and ran up the stairs.

By late afternoon, we had finished cleaning the house like deck hands battening down the hatches before a storm. The packing finished and nothing else to do until dinner; I stepped onto my balcony and beheld a familiar scene, a scene many centuries older than me.

It was the time of day, just before dusk, when no sound made by man or beast can be heard.

Arab boys clad in short, stained tunics beating their skinny sun-roasted calves passed by, bare feet raising puffs of dust. They wielded long, inoffensive sticks of whittled twigs on the flanks of a herd of cows that needed no prodding. Bearing their curved, pointed horns like royal crowns, the beasts trod the centuries-old dirt path, moving homeward at a sedate pace.

Their long-lashed, soft eyes had reflected my sphere-shaped image with unchanging indifference whenever I'd stood close to the side fence.

Tonight, they still switched their tails from side to side, swatting at the pestering flies from their mud-caked haunches and swollen udders. From my perch at the balcony, I caught a whiff of the bitter aroma of crushed grass they left in their wake, the sweet, rich scent of milk seeping from their dirt-stained teats, and the pungent tang of freshly dropped dung patties.

They forged onward, backs swaying in purposeful bovine tradition, and soon disappeared behind the rosemary hedge lining the side road.

Across the street, coiffed in heavy turbans and embroidered skullcaps, my neighbors crouched, backs propped against the adobe wall of their enclave. Forearms nonchalantly leaning on bent knees, hands hanging in repose, they looked like immoveable outcrops standing vigil over fertile valleys.

Their skin, crisscrossed with deep ruts, bore the look of brown parchment, and their unreadable expressions spoke of wisdom untouched by the inexorable march of time.

On occasion, a slow smile uncovered a row of betel nut-stained teeth and creased the skin around their eyes with good-humored crags. Causing me to smile back. These simple men wore their white summer robes draped around their bodies with the panache of kings bearing jeweled mantles of rare silk.

Their tranquil, inscrutable features spoke of centuries of dogged acceptance and of undemanding lives spent in hard physical labor under a merciless sun.

As they recovered from the broiling toil of the day, they waited for the cannon to sound the end of daily fast in this month of Ramadan and the beginning of the feast their women prepared on the other side of the adobe walls.

Smoke rose in lazy blue ribbons in the tranquil air, carrying the acrid smell of cooking fires, then dissolved into wisps that melted in the growing shadows of far purple mountains and paling pinks of the twilight sky. Tomorrow, no sirocco would carry sand from the Sahara. Tomorrow, a plane would carry us away from paradise.

As if mourning for our loss, the air was filled with a universal silence. Even the raucous cicadas ceased their unnerving and never-ending concert. In communion with all living things, they convalesced from the desiccating heat of the day.

The unwavering faith that the familiar scene before me would go on long after we were gone filled me with gratitude that good things do survive.

A mood of spiritual union with all things brought a balm to my soul as, in the distance, one dog answered the desultory barking of another. Thus, from farm to farm, their echoing voices partook of an ancient knowledge of peace, now forgotten by man, as it traveled in a soothing, reverberating tongue, telling of serene villages and sanctuary.

Serenity shrouded, at this moment, with the sadness of *aux revoirs*.

DINNER UNFURLED LIKE A post-funeral meal, punctuated by sounds of silverware against china. The dishes done, we bathed and readied the clothes we'd wear for our passage into exile. We went to bed with distracted, whispered kisses, *"Bonne nuit, Maman …. Bonne nuit, Papa …. Bonne nuit, les enfants."*

I FELL ASLEEP WITH THE heaviness of a timbered oak and woke up at dawn in the hush of a household lost to slumber. I lay on my side of the bed, filled with unease, trying to make sense of the dream I had just shaken off—a dream in color.

Primary Colors

IN THIS DREAM, I stood unmoving but could still see every detail of the three-hundred-and-sixty degree panorama surrounding me. It felt as if a mesmerizing painting had caught my spirit, sunk it into the weave of its canvas till it meshed with the colors, and turned me into an unsubstantial element of the scene.

I was royal blue sea with no shimmering zones of lighter blues and greens, no swells and no foam-hemmed waves stretching over sand. Only an inert royal blue plane.

I was cloudless pastel sky with no fading intensity as it met the sea in a hard, uncurved horizon.

There was no sail, gull, or rustling surf. No breeze, humming motor, or playful bathers. No beach. No tree. No tuft of grass. Only the royal blue, lifeless water scoring the base of an orange-sienna cliff that soared out of sight.

High above water, a path no wider than a one-man tent with no beginning and no end trailed the infinite length of the rock.

The open flaps of a sand-colored tent framed its blank inner darkness.

I was absence of movement, sound, and living things. Absence of heat, cold, wet, dry, love, hate. Absence of hope and despair.

I was unfathomable silence lost in a petrified abyss of primary colors ....

Farewell

June 24, 1962

IN SPITE OF ITS wealth of colors, the dream's desolation and lack of pulse perplexed and distressed me, in perfect keeping with the blur of morning ablutions and tasteless breakfast.

Compliant lonely ants, we went about our tasks until the time came to dress. I untied the strips of rags that curled my hair during the night and slipped into my new, straw-colored silk blouse. I tucked it into the belt of the A-line skirt of burnt sienna I had cut and sewn from a remnant of shantung silk, just for this trip. As a fashion statement, I slipped a narrow tie of the same material as the skirt under the shirt's open collar and hung the seahorse coupled with Albert's ring around my neck inside the shirt.

My curls and outfit were meant to demonstrate to anyone watching at port of arrival in France that, however loathed and looked down upon, *Pieds-Noirs* did have a sense of style.

That morning, no sense of style or pride animated me. The colored dream weighing me down, I went through the motions and helped my unusually subdued brothers get dressed.

Before heading for the airport, Zizou and I walked about the house, securing shutters and windows, but Papa said no. "We'll leave the house wide open."

Our eyebrows shot up. "All the windows?"

"All the windows." He sauntered down the stairs with the precious rust-colored suitcase. "And the door."

"And the gate?"

"Wide open."

No doubt meaning to spare our pride, not one neighbor turned up in the deserted road to observe our retreat.

A teacher colleague of Papa's who'd leave in a few days drove Maman, the boys, and the yellow suitcases in our father's car. A taxi drove Papa, his small suitcase, my two sisters, and me.

The taxi sputtered then started behind Pa's car through the gates and down the road.

Mid-slope, I couldn't resist looking back. I turned and watched, dead-hearted, as my house shrunk into the distance, her shutters and windows thrown open wide. Her front door gaped in an "Oh" of dismay. Her gates stretched like arms that seemed to say, "We'll wait for your return."

Only the little black wrought-iron gate with the mailbox remained shut in a solemn promise to keep trespassers at bay. Pa had never gotten around to fixing its hinges, and its bottom still scraped against the concrete beneath.

I frowned, sad at not feeling the pain of loss, but as the car rounded the bend, the sight of the old oak on the outer corner of our yard hit me like a fist on the side of the head with the raw awareness of things cut in mid-bloom. Tonight, Pa wouldn't be taking potshots into the tree, and the perennial owl dwelling among its limbs would, once again, get the last hoot.

The road's curve erased the house and I faced forward, taking in the familiar scenery as it sped by. Hoarding the colorful images I had taken so long for granted. Fastening them to a corner of my memory the same way one pins the brilliant wings of butterflies.

As brief as a daydream and as endless as a nightmare, the nine-kilometer ride to the airport came to an end, and we joined the hundreds of shuffling others.

The sensory blur that had shrouded my day became even hazier.

My brain snapped shots of inconsequential details—a couple holding hands, an old man's careful steps, a suckling newborn, children chasing each other in a game of catch ....

In a daze, I lost all sense of time as family groups gathered on the hot tarmac—piles of sand waiting for Sirocco to scatter them across the globe.

Photo by W.A. Dahl

FROM A FAMILY OF fourth generation French settlers in Algeria, **Danielle A. Dahl** was born and raised in Constantine, where she came of age during the Algerian War of Independence. A week before Algeria celebrated self-rule and just before Danielle turned eighteen, she and her family fled their home and life as they knew it. Destitute and facing a bleak future, they took refuge in France. Eight years later, hoping the soil of *L'Amérique* would be better suited to a happy life than that of France, she moved to the United States. There she studied commercial art at the Art Institute of Boston and worked in Filene's art department.

Later on, she moved to Washington, D.C., where she met her future husband, Walter. The couple lived in Washington, D.C., Pennsylvania, and Illinois before retiring to South Carolina, where Danielle wrote her memoir, *Sirocco*.

Aside from writing and reading, Danielle likes to paint, take pictures, bowl, and hike.

Danielle is a member of the South Carolina Writers Workshop, Sisters in Crime, the National Association of Memoir Writers, and the Seneca Writers Critique Group. She won second place in the 2011 Carrie McCray Memorial Literary Awards for nonfiction and was semi-finalist in the 2011 William

Faulkner Wisdom Competition for a novel-in-progress as well as for a short story. Lastly, two of her creative nonfiction stories appeared in the 2011 and 2012 *Petigru Review Literary Journal.*

At present Danielle is writing the first draft of *Mistral*, the sequel to *Sirocco*, which depicts the struggle that she, her family, and over a million and a half others like them faced after they fled Algeria and searched for new places to call home in France and across the globe.

You can find Danielle on the Web at www.dadahl.com.

Made in the USA
Charleston, SC
10 April 2014